# Hitmen for Hire

*To B, H and N – people of the upperworld*
*In memory of Stephen Ellis, 1953–2015*

# Hitmen for Hire

Exposing South Africa's Underworld

Mark Shaw

Jonathan Ball Publishers

Johannesburg & Cape Town

Published in South Africa in 2017 by
JONATHAN BALL PUBLISHERS
A division of Media24 (Pty) Ltd
PO Box 33977
Jeppestown
2043

ISBN 978-1-86842-711-6
EBOOK ISBN 978-1-86842-712-3

Twitter: www.twitter.com/JonathanBallPub
Facebook: www.facebook.com/JonathanBallPublishers
Blog: http://jonathanball.bookslive.co.za/

Cover by publicide
Design and typesetting by Triple M Design, Johannesburg
Printed and bound by CTP Printers, Cape Town
Set in 11pt/17pt Minion Pro

# Contents

'If it makes you feel any better, this isn't murder. It's not even killing. It's assassination … Here's the shopping list. Go and bag some … That's all it is. Nothing to feel sorry about. Nothing to cry about.'

– Viet Thanh Nguyen, *The Sympathizer*, London: Corsair, 2015, p. 257.


'The use of violence is always concealed by lies, and the lies are maintained by violence.'

– Jana Arsovska, *Decoding Albanian Organized Crime*, Oakland: University of California Press, 2015, p. xi.

# Prologue:
# Killing Laylah

'It was killing me,' she said. 'The fact that I was just a tool – a tool for men. I wanted to make my own way. Hold my own life. So I became a shooter. Not, like, all at one go, but after a while.'

Perhaps we have become too conditioned by James Bond movies. The assassin par excellence of popular culture, whether working for criminals or the government, has a certain cachet in our imagination. The tuxedo, or at least the smart shirt, well-groomed looks and self-confident personality have come to form a certain image in our minds.

But the young scowling woman sitting in front of me in the Nando's certainly did not look the part. She looked damaged, in fact, in the way so many people who pass you in the street do. A look of exhaustion, dark rings under her eyes – and a sense she doubted that I was who I said I was.

The chicken franchise was in that gritty buffer zone of bustling post-industrial Cape Town between the city and the Cape Flats. It is where parts of the new Cape Town are being born, but where some of its harder bits refuse to die. 'Edgy,' as someone once described it to me, although that does not quite capture the place. The sense of twilight menace about the place, often drawn upon in crime novels about the city, was suddenly broken by an old lady carrying a baby on her back past the window of the take-away.

I am being deliberately vague about the location because the arrangement for the interview with 'Laylah' (not her real name) had included, unnecessarily in my view, an agreement that the location was to be a secret, and I want to stay true to that. Suffice to say it is a part of the city recognisable to anyone who has driven along the arterial roads that connect the fragmented geography of apartheid. It is one of the places where a cosmopolitan place like Cape Town comes together geographically, but also quite literally. Outside the windows of the chicken restaurant, taxis drew in and out, offloading their passengers, cars snaked past, and people walked briskly by carrying their bags and bundles.

The meeting was part of a two-year quest I had begun at the University of Cape Town to explore organised crime in South Africa. It was a tough assignment: what was organised crime in the South African context? That's what I was researching. Interview after interview, and a parallel research project on measuring violence in the country, had brought some focus. What, I increasingly wanted to know, drove the organised market for violence in South Africa? This market for violence, and its connections with other criminal markets, seemed to be having a series of consequences for all South Africans. And it had not been explored. That meant I needed to find out more about it by searching for the hitmen of the criminal underworld. Or, in this case, a hitwoman.

Like all such interviews, the introductions had been arranged through a string of intermediaries. Yes, so and so did that sort of thing, but they were hard to reach. I will come back to you, I would be told. Silence for weeks. I – or a go-between – would end up driving to people's houses, asking, 'Would they speak?' Not about incidents – about killing people, as such – more about their lives. 'But their lives are fucked,' said one intermediary. 'What's of interest there?' It's for research, I would explain, in what seemed to be a slightly self-important tone, given the litany of 'fucked-up' lives in front of us. 'Come back again – let me see what we can do,' I'd be told. Backwards and forwards like this until this Nando's meeting was set up – and several others. Tales of murder, mixed with chicken and washed down with a Coke.

The Nando's was quiet, the smell of grilled chicken hitting you like a wave on entering. She was already there. Some restless-looking gang types were sitting a few tables away. Her minders? Hard to tell. Would she talk? Not quickly, it seemed. The best way in, I thought ... talk about growing up. It sounds neutral enough, although in such a context it is far from it. In this city, saying where you grew up may be as good as saying which gang you work with. But there seemed no obvious alternative; she did not look like one for small talk with strangers.

'So ... er ... where did you grow up?'

'Hanover Park,' she answers. You could picture those tenement blocks, row after row, outside staircases, washing draped between the buildings. Such buildings always reminded me of my school classrooms, as if apartheid-era architects had a failure of imagination and designed all buildings the same – square, blockish and with brown window frames. The smell of dagga in the air. People crammed in – a contradictory place: a sense of community but one pervaded by fear.

But, in the end, Laylah didn't say too much about growing up. What she did say, though, almost immediately, was that she had been raped. More than once, in fact. That was how it was for a girl in the gang, she said. It was as simple as that: when I had asked her about growing up, she had told me where and then added that she had been raped.

But there was an important link between the rapes and what she had become. 'It made me angry. *Fok*, it really peed me off!' And, as if to emphasise this last point, she indicated the pistol strapped to her ankle. (Now that is a bit more James Bond-like – but it seemed almost incongruous: a piece of heavy, cold metal strapped to her slight, bony female body. Not that the circumstances made the gun any less deadly.) The boys in the corner shifted around, adjusting their leather jackets, stroking their hair. Laylah ignored them.

'You see,' she said, 'the thing about girls is that gangs and taxi people sometimes use them because they are not like what you would expect.'

Too true. Laylah didn't look like a killer. In fact she said she was not one at the beginning. She said she was a 'lure'. 'A what?' I ask. Well, you know, those fishing things. Shiny, dangly, vulnerable. Makes the prey come. 'I acted as a lure. That was the first time. I got him to come.' She smiled grimly. 'Not to *come*. Although I would have done that too. I got him to come to an area where my gang could kill him. They did it. That was my job.'

It was a story that I had heard before. Another woman, in tears, had explained to me a few weeks earlier – on a bench, next to a jungle gym in a dusty Cape Flats park – that her job had been to ring the bell or wait at the gate. A woman standing there: gang members think with their dicks, and if you think with your dick, you are liable to be shot in the head.

Laylah shifts on the bench. She is dressed in a pair of tight jeans. She is wearing a baseball jacket and a scarf on her head. And an unlikely piece of steel strapped to her ankle. Would it have made her walk lopsidedly? I wondered. In the end, I did not find out. She remained seated until I left – prim, perched on the bench. Perhaps 'petite' would be one way she could be described, although it's not a word that seems to fit her perfectly. But it's enough to convey that she is not masculine and muscular. Yet she is not exactly feeble and feminine either.

She got raped by a gang boss too. 'He was an ugly bastard,' she said, like she might have if we had been making a movie. 'He was drunk, pawing at me ...' She stopped. 'Anyway, that's what happened.' Even in its truncated form, the story of the rape was shocking. What is even more shocking is that it is a standard feature of every gang woman's story. Told in countless interviews.

Even in just those few words, I could tell it sounded cruel – and it left her angry. There were other cases, too, but she had been drugged up. Then she hitched up with a gang member, 'a real killer', as she described him. 'He shot a lot of people,' she said chillingly, her lips spelling out the words slowly for emphasis, so that I would understand that he was not your run-of-the-mill criminal. He left his guns with her. That was a sign of trust, I suppose – to leave the hardware with the girlfriend. The trust seemed to be a one-way deal, though: the killer, it turned out, was having an affair with another girl. Laylah's response: to shoot the other girl. '*Fok*, she deserved it … carrying on like that! Everyone knew.' Not shot dead, you understand. She was not good enough for that yet. She shot her in the arm. She said this so matter-of-factly that it took my breath away. She did not rage at her lover, the killer. Instead, she shot the killer's side entertainment. In the arm.

'The arm?'

'Yes, she put her arms up and the gun went off.' Nothing came of it. At the hospital nobody asked any questions and, after all, who would have gone to the cops for that? Not the killer's bit on the side – she was too much part of the pack.

'He's dead now,' she said.

'Sorry … who is dead?' The killer. He was shot by another gang. They pumped him full of bullets, shot him in the face. Hard to explain the motive, but it seems he had changed gangs or allegiance within the gang. Difficult to tell, for sure. I had heard about something similar before in Manenberg, a gang-afflicted hellhole notorious for a recent spate of gang turf wars. Shooting gangsters in the face is done as a way of denying those who change allegiance a final identity. You lose your face, the ultimate mark of dishonour. One literally carried to the grave.

Laylah did not want to say too much more about it. What was clear, though, is that his killing devastated her, perhaps accentuated by the fact that it seemed to have been delivered as a mark of disfavour, the killing of an outcast. That seemed to harden further her already hard exterior. Before dying, the killer had given her life – they had had a child together. She had loved the man. And he had provided for her – provided in the way a mid-level gang boss does: there was food, drugs of course, and fast cars. And there was status. She was held with a certain respect because of who she was with. She had cool clothes. People knew who she was connected to and that she was not to be messed with. But now the killer was gone – and she was on her own. Vulnerable.

In his absence and without his support, Laylah considered the options and moved from being the lure to acting as the fisher woman. Poor metaphor, this. She struggled to explain: 'I moved from attracting them, drawing them in to be killed, well, to doing the killing. You won't believe me, but that is how it is. You know, I got a rush from shooting that girl in the arm. It was *fokking* easy. Bang! Blood. She went down. I can't tell you more. It just that that's where I found myself: I was well looked after and then I looked after myself.'

I am interpreting here. Putting a gloss on it. I didn't take notes. I doubt she would have spoken if I was jotting down her words on an exam pad. But that is basically what she said.

The Nando's was getting busier now. We got some food. 'I needed resources,' she said, a chicken wing between her front teeth. 'Like nobody really understands. I hate when you people' – she waved the remnants of the chicken wing in my general direction – 'say you must break out of the gang. Break out! I was totally trapped from school. I can't break out. It was the opposite – I needed to break *in*. Earn respect. I never finished school. They needed me. Not as a lure, something else. My first one was linked to some taxi argument. The gang boss got money from the taxi guys. A troublesome guy had to be handled. I went with another guy. Girl, boy – looks less suspicious that way. We shot the guy. I don't remember much. Just the thrill afterwards. … Later I went to prison.'

# Preface

The issue of murder in South Africa had fascinated me since I returned to the country to take up a post at the University of Cape Town. I had left South Africa 15 years previously for a job at the innocuous-sounding United Nations Office on Drugs and Crime. There, as a senior advisor, and later as a partner in a consulting firm, I had traversed the world, conducting assessments and dishing out advice on justice reform and countering organised crime – even if the solutions I proffered seemed like technical tinkering given the scale of the challenge. There was no corner of the globe, including some of the most fragile and conflict-ridden states, that I had not visited. It was a dream job: one moment I was in the dusty streets of some godforsaken Somali pirate town, the next reporting back in Vienna or New York.

But, like all expatriates, my heart had been at home. South Africa's crime problems were not new to me: I had earlier worked as a researcher and then as a government official in the quaintly titled National Secretariat for Safety and Security. But things had changed. South Africa's level of violence, while still way too high, had declined during the time I had been away at the UN. Then, a year before I returned in 2012, the homicide rate edged up again. And in Cape Town it skyrocketed to double the national average. I was eager to find out what lay behind this.

Analysts and academics have long asked some searching questions about why South Africans died so violently and so often. The debate has bounced back and forth between a series of causal factors: inequality, alcohol, guns, a general culture of violence. To make our own contribution to that discussion, a UCT colleague, Anine Kriegler, and I had trolled through the murder data since 1910 to determine long-term homicide trends in the country. At the same time, I scrutinised the news reports with their daily staple of bloody bodies and the standard refrain from the police that 'the case is under investigation – no arrests have been made'.

What seemed surprising in these reports is how often, and it seemed to me increasingly so, cases occurred under circumstances that suggested there was a direct instrumentality – a clear purpose – in the killing or attempted killing, murders where people were killed in their driveways or taken away and shot in the back of the head. Police officers at the scenes would intone that these were 'hits', although generally the motive remained unclear. I would urge you to do the same: read the local newspaper and see how often murders are reported in this way. As this book was being completed, for example, a prominent criminal defence lawyer, Noorudien Hassan, was shot in Cape Town in what was clearly a hit, followed a few days later by a hotel manager who worked for one of the city's most notorious underworld figures. In Johannesburg, an individual with known links to cigarette smuggling, Raymond 'Razor' Barras, met his end in a suburban driveway in Kensington. A few days later, Sibusiso Sithole, the municipal manager of Richmond in KwaZulu-Natal, known for his opposition to corruption, was executed while walking in the town. The bodies keep stacking up.

It troubled me greatly. Should we not understand this phenomenon better, I asked myself. And, after over a decade of asking questions of law-enforcement officials in dingy offices, and civil-society people and journalists in places where the presence of mafia-style forms of control oozed from the walls of empty buildings, I found that South Africa bore some striking parallels with countries associated with mafia organisations. These types of targeted killings smacked of mafia-style violence, murders carried out to achieve some purpose in the illicit economy (and sometimes the licit one).

My first bosses at the UN, Jan van Dijk and Samuel Gonzalez Ruiz (the latter a former deputy attorney-general of Mexico, whose focus was organised crime), had long maintained that such killings were a useful measure of the strength of mafia-type organisations. But surely these incidents of bloodied bodies killed with a single shot to the head happened in places like Italy or Mexico, and not Cape Town, my new home? South Africa's violence was supposed to be more 'social', a product of people's circumstances. At least that is what the Minister of Police, Nkosinathi Nhleko, in the 2016 release of the crime statistics had claimed. The police, he argued, could do little about this form of killing. Some criminologists agreed. Violence was bad, but at least South Africa was spared the worse forms of organised crime: the underworld at war with itself. But something in the violent ecosystem in which I now lived seemed to suggest otherwise. Were we looking correctly at the problem of violent death in our society?

As the killings continued to mount up and gang violence in Cape Town soared from 2013 to new peaks, a fellow researcher, Kim Thomas, and I, designed a data-collection project on criminal assassinations with the aim of building a better picture of the phenomenon. Then we began to review the press for cases of targeted killing from as far back as we could.

At the Centre of Criminology at UCT we built a database of every hit or attempted hit over a 17-year period. We followed the broad methodology adopted in similar studies on contract killings, mainly from the UK, and adapted these to the information sources we had available. Of course, a British study on reported hits has far fewer cases to go through, and there is much more likely to be a media story published there if a drug dealer in a small town cops it outside his nightclub than if a local-government official dies mysteriously in KwaZulu-Natal.

South Africa does have some interesting research resources, however. We drew on a comprehensive electronic database, SABINET, which hosts print media records of local, regional and national news. And we supplemented that data with searches of electronic news sources. We searched under four categories: 'contract killing'; 'political assassination'; 'hitman'; and 'taxi killing'.[1] These search terms alone generated 14 000 media articles. That is a very large pile of paper. These stories were each reviewed to identify cases where the circumstances and the commentary provided by the police, court proceedings, the community or families involved suggested that the victim had been the subject of a hit, or attempted hit. Cases were then sorted by date.

The main point of all of this is that we tried hard to make sure our findings were as accurate as they could be. We eliminated cases that were likely to have been hits but where there was insufficient evidence to categorically confirm that. As I will emphasise, it is difficult to draw any trend data from these results – but the fact remains that there are a remarkable number of reported hits in South Africa. And many others, it seems, don't make it into the newspapers – not even the local press.

Three criteria needed to be met for a case to be recorded in our database as a hit – in other words, where there was enough information to determine that the murder was an assassination-like killing that had been well planned and where somebody had been paid to do it. The first is that the police, or the criminal-justice agencies or the families of the deceased had declared the murder to be a hit. Secondly, the circumstances must have been such that it was clear from the facts of the case that a hit had taken place – for example, that one person had been clearly targeted. Thirdly, if there was evidence that the circumstances surrounding the murder involved a burglary or robbery we generally excluded it from our database. We also recorded attempted hits that had failed. These were often the saddest of all, because other people, sometimes children, were killed by mistake.

The results of this research informed this book. The findings were stark: we recorded 1 146 incidents of hits in the UCT database over the 17-year research period from 2000 to 2016. That's a lot of cases – and clearly enough to determine at least a set of initial conclusions around the linkages between targeted killings and criminal markets. We also found there was a dramatic increase in cases in 2016.

We sorted all the cases into four broad categories of hits: those associated with the minibus taxi industry; political assassinations; contract killings related to organised crime (or the grey or illicit markets they were present in); and those related to personal or family matters. Of these, 484 could be linked to the taxi industry; 248 were politically related; 261 were linked to organised crime; and 153 arose out of domestic wrangles (e.g. marital or family disputes). However, many of these broad categories overlap. They are analysed in more detail in Chapter 1, and updates of the data can be found at https://assassinationwitness.org.za.

In the vast majority of cases, we recorded the names of the victims, but this was not always possible, most commonly in the cases of targeted assassination of less prominent people.

In a surprising number of cases, mainly those related to personal disputes, the contractor approached a hitman who was either an undercover police officer or who reported the matter to the police.

Given the sheer scale of the problem that the accumulated data pointed to, the phenomenon of targeted killing seemed worth studying more closely. It was certainly not something that had been looked at before in

South Africa, largely because there had previously been no relevant data – only the much awaited annual release of the country's murder rate. And, truth be told, that data irritated the life out of me. The media wanted a neat sound bite about whether things were getting better or worse. However, not all murders are the same. So, disaggregating the numbers and linking them with a phenomenon that I had been working on for almost my whole career – organised crime and its illicit networks – seemed to offer an opportunity for deepening the policy debate. I believed these new research findings would help make sense of things and understand killing for what it often seemed to be: an instrumental tool for achieving influence – either politically or economically. That is more meaningful than just a generalised annual statistic, a number of dead bodies published in a news report, argued over, and forgotten about until the next year.

Laylah seemed to represent something bigger at work. Speaking to Laylah, it was apparent to me that a set of economic, political and structural conditions had bred a market for killers, and nurtured the killers themselves. People were being paid, just like those who work in the formal economy, to do a job. And there were lots of such people in South Africa – perhaps more than in other countries. The transactions and exchanges made within this economy of violence had been key to shaping a series of criminal markets. The use of commercialised violence, or the threat of it, had become a currency in its own right. It was even beginning to define South Africa's fragile democratic order. Addressing this violence means defending democracy. That is the motivation for writing this book.

Understanding this market for violence meant that I needed to reach into the underworld to explore it. But would the underworld be prepared to talk to me? People who work in the criminal world are not normally disposed to opening up about their work with outsiders – the risk can be very high for them. If they are discovered by the law it may mean the end of a profitable career, or angering an associate with indiscretions may cost a life.

But, like people everywhere, those who populate the underworld also have stories to tell, and some do want to tell them. To make contact with the right people who could give me information, I led a small team of researchers who identified people in the underworld who would explain things to us. Over a period of two years we conducted over 100 interviews. Without those team members and those interviews, this book would not have been possible.

South Africa has seen a recent flurry of good books by journalists on underworld activities, much of the material spurred by the assassination of Brett Kebble, a well-known businessman with strong political connections.[2]

Nevertheless, research on organised crime and the underworld, particularly in South Africa, is underdeveloped. All over the world, though, given the prominent place that organised-crime figures have assumed in many societies, journalists and researchers have been trying to understand the nature of the beast: a number of recent books that provide ethnographic case studies of organised crime in several developing countries must now be regarded as the models for others to follow.[3] In each case, the researchers spent considerable time talking with people active in, or close to, the underworld, drawing the links to historical developments. They found that the nature of organised crime is never separate from the context within which it is shaped, and which, in turn, it shapes. The same applies for South Africa.

Writings on the underworld in South Africa have only covered some parts of the criminal ecosystem, most recently the network that developed around the Czech gangster Radovan Krejcir. Yet the underworld has many parts, and the purpose of this book – to follow its title – is to expose a wider cross section of that ecosystem. As will be shown, if targeted hits are a measure of organised-criminal activity, then the media has focused on a remarkably narrow slice of the underworld.

Information on the underworld needs to be collected in various ways. But, given that the nature of the underworld is hard to discern from public sources alone, the main way of getting an idea of what is going on is to speak to the people who operate in it. Here, the researcher has an advantage over the police officer or private investigator. Research is less threatening to most people, particularly if they feel it will serve as a conduit for their own story. But gangsters, like ordinary people, are likely to talk up their side of the story and their own role in it. That means an added responsibility for the researcher: stories need to be verified, multiple interviews conducted and their results compared. One needs to continually assess whether the truth is being told.

While conducting research for this book, it became clear that some in the underworld were ready to share their experiences.[4] Which of these were prepared to speak to me, and where and how they agreed to be interviewed often provided as much insight as what they actually said. These interviews serve as a reminder of the degree to which people engaged in the criminal economy are integrated into the upperworld.

Arranging the interviews was seldom ever just a question of a single phone call. It meant using intermediaries – people who have knowledge of the underworld or connections there. Our intermediaries were police officers, businessmen, lawyers, community leaders, or religious or social figures. The question is not just to find anybody with knowledge of the underworld, but people who are considered well placed to explain it and who would be willing to talk. After the intermediary had sounded out the prospective interviewee, contact was made and a meeting arranged. In many cases, it was only by the second or third meeting that enough confidence had been built to enable a meaningful discussion to ensue. The preferred venues was distinctly 'upperworldy' – the shopping mall coffee shop or, as in the case of Laylah, a take-away joint. Few interviews for this book took place in dodgy nightclubs or dark street corners late at night.

No one in this business wants to talk in a place where everyone knows them.

Those most prepared to talk openly were often characters who have distanced themselves from organised crime, although the phrase 'I am no longer involved', repeated often enough, suggests that in fact they might still be. As I have already suggested, conducting underworld interviews from an outsider's perspective relies on the ability to sort bluster from truth, to compare notes across different discussions, and to not necessarily accept every statement at face value. Yet people who work or have worked in the underworld should not always be assumed to be untruthful, and many recounted their stories in an even-handed and remarkably analytical manner. They would not have talked had their identities been revealed, and I have respected that throughout this book.[5]

The genesis of this book goes back some time, to the playing fields of my high school on the eastern side of Johannesburg. It was there that I first encountered some of the men whom you will meet in Chapter 4. Those were the hedonistic days of the mid-1980s as South Africa's night-time economy was beginning to grow and the late-apartheid order fought to retain its power. Those men were boys then, but they were aggressive, sometimes hard for the teachers to control. I kept my distance, but, as it is said, fear breeds fascination – it was from them that I was conscious of the development of what later came to be called the 'bouncer mafia'. It is a fascination that I have retained throughout a career that has focused on analysing and responding to crime, most particularly its organised variety. So it would be appropriate to thank them from the outset: if I had grown up somewhere else, perhaps my interest in the underworld would not have developed.

This in many ways then is the book that I always wanted to write but never felt ready to, and in some ways still don't. As a young security analyst in the post-apartheid government, I found it difficult to understand the development of organised crime in the late 1980s and early 1990s, and, as I suggest later in the book, it was easy to rely on generalities, including what rapidly became the standard one: that transitional societies carried within them a series of factors that gave rise to criminal forms of governance.

In the euphoria of the first years of South Africa's democracy and the reconstitution of the police force, the possibility of reducing violence beckoned. To have suggested back then that violence would have become highly commercialised – that there would develop a market for hired assassins – would have been greeted with derision. In retrospect, perhaps we should have been less surprised. The makings of commercialised violence were already present in South Africa at that time – most significantly in the taxi industry and, increasingly, in the country's illicit-drug markets, but also elsewhere in the emerging post-apartheid criminal economy and its links with the networks that had engaged in the near civil war of the late-1980s and early 1990s.

Understanding these connections, and tracing the evolution of organised crime in South Africa and its link to commercial assassination is the purpose of the book. Its most basic assumption is that killing people in ways that can be linked to illicit markets, and what is widely called the underworld, is something that may help us to understand our society better. Put differently, if assassination is a kind of indicator of the development of the underworld and the strength of organised crime, what does this say more broadly about South Africa and its violent social and political economy?

The first two chapters of the book consider the results of our database of over 1 000 assassinations, introducing the reader to the hitmen who made this happen and the hits culture in which they operate. It then examines (Chapters 3 to 5) three criminal markets that have served both as sources of violence and as the breeding ground for assassination: the taxi industry, the extortion or protection economy and the country's drugs market, with its particularly violent manifestation in the Western Cape. The book then explores (in Chapters 6 to 8) the symbiosis between organised crime and the police, external foreign criminal groups, and politics in South Africa's evolving democracy – all in the light of the evolving market for killing.

I conclude by looking at what must be done to weaken the link between the social and political economy of the country and the commercialisation of assassination.

# Introduction:
# Removing obstacles

'Outside of popular culture there are no highly skilled hitmen,' a prominent analyst of organised crime, Mark Galeotti, was quoted as saying in *The New York Times* recently.[1] He was talking about Russian organised crime, but his assertion seems to fit the case of Laylah and others in South Africa.

It was, ironically, Laylah's vulnerability that had made her so dangerous and unpredictable. She caused damage but she was also fundamentally damaged herself. Why was I surprised at this? Had I been expecting something else? Someone more sinister, perhaps: smartly dressed, fit and clear-eyed, like you would imagine one of the female guards, the appropriately named Revolutionary Nuns or Amazons of former Libyan president Gaddafi.

But Galeotti's overall point was that stereotypical conceptions of Hollywood-style hitmen were overwrought. And it seems to me in fact that we have bred a level of 'professional' killers in South Africa. That professionalism may not suit the requirements of a Hollywood producer, but it works just fine in the environment in which we live. Murder has purpose and a group of people are paid to do it. Killing for hire therefore shapes South Africa's fragile political economy. Laylah was her own sort of Revolutionary Nun.

Before proceeding, it is probably worth defining what we are talking about here. There is a fair amount written on the contract-killing business (elsewhere, though not in South Africa), so certain details seem pertinent. I define 'hits' in the South African context as the targeting of specific individuals for murder, generally by contracting a third party. These hits are generally undertaken for economic, political or personal gain, or sometimes a combination of all three. 'Contracting' in this case usually means the transfer of financial resources in exchange for murder, although in some cases other forms of remuneration (for example a job, sexual favours, high status in a criminal gang) may be provided in exchange.[2]

As this definition suggests, and consistent with the literature on assassinations, targeted murder is carried out with the specific objective of changing a particular context or environment to the perpetrator's advantage, by eliminating an obstacle.[3] Payment for killing in this context provides a useful distance between the person who benefits and the killer or killers themselves.[4] Hits, then, have a particular utility – an issue that is examined in this book in the various markets or environments where they occur.

The data we uncovered in these environments (as explained in the Preface) seems to suggest a trend: the mafia-like commercialisation of violence. But, from what I knew from my travels to examine mafia markets elsewhere, mafia-style violence develops within the markets themselves: it is a form of regulation for sale because state systems of ordering are not available – you could call it a market within a market, but a crucial one to determining the shape of illicit activities.

Recent studies in places with far lower levels of murder than South Africa also suggest that while criminologists had largely assumed that most murders occurred where victims and perpetrators knew each other, the notion of the independent contractor as murderer was not well understood or well studied, and likely to be far more prevalent than had been previously assumed.[5] One expert had even used the neat term 'criminal undertaker' to describe players in the underworld who assume this role in the context of messy and overlapping criminal markets.[6]

A point often mentioned in studies on organised crime is that violence flares up in criminal markets when there is a fight for control and it becomes highly targeted, when one criminal group prevails. In that reading, spurts of violence appear to be a battle for control of the illicit economy (and sometimes parts of the licit one too). When powerful organised-crime groups win, then mafia rules apply. But those markets have suffered from bouts of violence as unstable criminal coalitions fell apart and then reformed. Targeted assassinations, underworld-style hits and associated instrumental violence must, then, to some degree be a feature of evolving characteristics of organised crime in a country.

But how to test that hypothesis? Does South Africa display the same characteristics, albeit in a different context, as those of, say, Mexico or Central America, with their high levels of criminal-style assassinations? In those places, targeted violence has been driven by specific circumstances linked to the drugs market, and killings were often highly symbolic, encompassing brutal levels of violence and the prominent display of bodies (or parts of them) to send out a powerful message. The approach I thought best for South Africa was to look at certain criminal markets and see which ones generated the most violence. Perhaps the answer lay there.

And what was the purpose of the violence in these illicit economies? Was it a fight for control? A struggle for market share by competing criminal actors? The South African illicit economy – its underworld – seemed to have changed dramatically since the beginning of democracy. Several colleagues, and some of my own earlier work, had noted these changes, but the linkage between the development of organised crime and violence was underdeveloped. The link was made, but it was more assumed than well understood. And it begged another troubling question: what if South Africa's 'upperworld' of business, politics and society were increasingly drawing on the underworld to use violence in an instrumental way to achieve certain objectives? Hitmen are used by a remarkably wide segment of society. There were certainly parallels elsewhere. It was a chilling thought because it suggested that the table had been turned: the underworld was perhaps driving the daily interactions of the upperworld.

For example, in one remarkable incident in 2013, the boyfriend of former South African communications minister Dina Pule (she having been recently accused of fraud) was alleged to have tried to contact a potential hitman to eliminate the chairperson of the Parliamentary Ethics Committee and the Registrar of Members' Interests. Additional security was provided to those threatened. The police subsequently reported that the person tasked to recruit the hitman, and who had gone to the press with the story, proved to be an uncooperative witness.[7] What does this incident say about South Africa and its bumpy trajectory as a democracy, and about its evolving underbelly? That assassination – for the purpose of obstacle removal or spreading fear – is discussed around the dinner table more commonly than you might think.

Contrasting the lower reaches of society with the supposedly licit world above makes us think about what the underworld actually is. It is a term often used in the press – 'he is regarded as a member of Johannesburg's underworld' – with the assumption that we know intuitively what it refers to. And perhaps we do. For those of us who live in the upperworld, the underworld is a cautionary tale of bad guys and bogeymen. It is a zone where laws are broken, where people are brutally hurt and promising futures come to nefarious ends. It is the place into which the dregs of society fall and which we avoid at all costs, insulating ourselves behind

4

barbed fences and institutions of security to the best of our ability.

But, surely, if we take a closer look, the distance between the upper-world and underworld is not so great. Perhaps this is why we take such care to ensure it remains an abstract concept. And, just as crime novels are often said to pass social commentary on society, the story of the under-world shines a light upwards to reveal important and often unattractive truths about the upperworld.

And we too often take our cue about the underworld from people who most visibly symbolise it. Lolly Jackson is a good example, with his images in the media and beautiful girls and shiny suits. But that gives an imbal-anced picture and does not represent other underworld players. We are too ready to define the underworld by its most glamorous occupants. That's only part of the story. To take one example of the faceless, invisible side of organised crime, I once met with a former drug trafficker in his office in Johannesburg. The office was in a factory, where he was the super-visor. With the noise of the busy warehouse in the background, and as he twisted a paperclip into different shapes, the interviewee spoke soberly about the challenges of running a criminal business in the late 1980s and early 1990s. He described how the source of his drugs was the police drugs unit, who had seized the contraband, or in some cases, apparently, imported it themselves. His role was to sell the merchandise. He described in detail the two protection networks that he had run, one within the police and the other among a group of city bouncers, real practitioners of violence, who protected the floor space in clubs where he sold the drugs. This was a normal way of doing business, he explained. When his police contact appeared likely to be exposed, he skipped town and went overseas. He made his money, he said, and keeps away from the drug industry now.

What seems remarkable from many of the interviews I conducted for this book is how key individuals in the underworld are aware of one another and are often in contact. The underworld in South African terms is as it is elsewhere: a network of individuals with some parts that interlock with each other; people are aware of the actions of the other constituent parts, often exchanging services. And, like everything else in South Africa, the organisation of the underworld is defined by race.

Within these networks, some key figures stand out as bridges between the underworld and the upperworld. The murdered Cyril Beeka, a well-known Cape Town gangster and violent entrepreneur, once performed such a role, as did the flamboyant Radovan Krejcir, the now jailed Czech mobster notorious for leaving a trail of dead bodies in his wake in Johannesburg. People such as Beeka and Krejcir are nodes in the underworld, but this also makes them targets if they threaten the interests of other powerful figures. In that sense, the underworld is a perennially unstable place. Beeka was killed in an assassination, and there have been attempts on Krejcir's life.

Powerful figures in the underworld sleep with loaded guns on hand for good reason – and this is not just a glib turn of phrase. Positioning is everything and is often closely linked to the ability to practise violence, not necessarily directly, but through economic transactions with those who have developed the skills for doing so. And violence procured from the underworld has the ability to shape the upperworld.

Fundamentally, are not the underworld and the upperworld more intimately connected than we might wish to assume? The underworld is a political, economic and social creation that is defined through its formal exclusion from legitimacy – and in that sense it is a by-product of the upperworld, a product of the laws and institutions designed to regulate social, political and economic life, and set standards for behaviour. The underworld is what we choose to exclude from 'legitimate' society and the people who operate in it exploit the gaps in those laws for their own purposes and to meet the demand created in the upperworld.

The most obvious case perhaps is drug trafficking. Some drugs have been declared illegal, but people still need and want them. The underworld ensures that those drugs are delivered to meet that need. Is violence not the same? If there is demand and supply, then there is a market for violence. And, is not the clearest expression of that market the commercialisation of assassination itself?

Could such a market for violence then be governed by a similar set of economic rules? When acts are criminal but the demand is high, so is the profit margin. To exploit that requires organisation and other crimes like corruption, such as paying off police officers to keep them on one's side, which facilitates and protects illicit transactions. The market for violence, then, is an important part of maintaining what we might call organised crime, and those who sell and buy violence – we might call them violent entrepreneurs – are essential to maintaining organised crime.

What can be said about the broader ecosystem of violence in South Africa in which targeted assassination takes place, and what, in such a context, is the utility of hits?

South African society is characterised by multiple forms of violence, often intersecting with and reinforcing one another. The nature of this violence has evolved historically from conflict primarily related to confrontation with the apartheid state – although this too masked a wider array of political and economic conflicts – to one around accessing resources within the democratic order. In South Africa these broad historical shifts have aligned with a growing emphasis on personal interests over ideological or political ones, symbolised by growing corruption and patrimonial politics.[8] As Karl von Holdt has argued, such types of violence are often seen as symptomatic of the failure of democracy, but '[r]ather than democracy and violence [being] mutually exclusive, democracy may configure power relations in a way that violent practices are integral to them'. Von Holdt aptly terms this system 'violent democracy'.[9]

The hits culture is an important part of this system, arguably standing at the apex of expressions of criminal governance. Hits represent the commercialisation of targeted violence to achieve political, economic and/or personal gain. They are possible because of a series of 'nurseries of violence' that provide resources in the form of people and expertise that can be hired to carry them out, including from within the state's security institutions. Nurseries are a place where things are shaped and nurtured – for good and bad – so to identify the sources of hitmen in this way has important implications for our understanding of the evolution of the underworld and the place of violence within it.

The market for targeted violence is part of two main trends. The first is the commercialisation of violence itself. The second is that commissioning hits marks a shift from the more overt use of violence to achieve particular ends to more discreet violence. With the latter, the objectives and perpetrators are concealed. Political, economic and criminal actors appear increasingly less likely to engage in open violence and more likely to resort to hidden violence to achieve their objectives (a theme I return to later). Such targeted violence in a democracy aims to mask its perpetrators and attains symbolic value as a result and, as we have seen, this blurs the boundaries between political, economic and criminal interests, whereby targeted violence comes to resemble accepted behaviour.

By and large, it would seem that commissioning a hit is not expensive and subcontracting violence is a relatively easy process. The going rate is something in the order of R10 000 to R15 000, although this fee increases at the more sophisticated end of the spectrum, with over R100 000 being recorded as having being paid in several cases. Court records are a good place to confirm these figures. In comparison, for example, with the profits to be made in the taxi business, or the potential gains to be had from winning tenders or through political appointments, hits are highly cost-effective. One reason for the low price tag is that there appears to be an oversupply of hitmen available in the market.[10] Hits are also fairly easy to arrange. They are a feature, at least in part, of the availability of violence for hire in a context where the norms of ordinary social and economic interaction have come under considerable stress or change.[11]

The critical importance of subcontracting violence is that it generally introduces a high level of uncertainty as to the identity of the perpetrators who order the kill. There is enormous symbolic value in this. Hits and assassinations literally come out of the blue, they can affect anyone and, at least to most outsiders, why the person has been killed remains unclear. The burden of proof is also challenging.

Subcontracting targeted killing as a way of exerting influence in the absence of systems of effective state governance provides a means to disconnect those who order the murder from the actual act of murder. As one analysis notes, 'just as there are animals that let other animals do their killing for them – vultures and hyenas', by employing a 'trusted proxy when one's available' means that if the plot is uncovered there will be someone to sacrifice.[12]

But who are the subcontractors? From media coverage of court proceedings, court documents and the interviews we conducted, it seems that hitmen, and more generally the capacity for underworld-sourced violence, are generally drawn from a limited number of distinct environments. We found that they are largely recruited from the enormous violent capacity within the taxi industry; from the bouncer or debt-collection business, which has its origins in the night-time protection economy; from the system of increasingly well-armed gangs in the Western Cape; and, as illustrated by a case involving a police captain allegedly acting as an assassin, from within state-security institutions.

These nurseries, or pools,[13] of violence are perhaps unsurprising in the South African context. They are the core recruiting grounds for killers. Their easy availability, and the connections between these nurseries of violence and certain established economic and political actors, goes some way to explaining the growing use of assassination as an instrument for other ends.

There is a strong relationship between nurseries of violence and politics, which suggests a mutuality in their services. Criminal networks rely on political protection to maintain their operations, so it is in their direct interests to support candidates for political office who are likely to be supportive. And, as a landmark study of organised crime and politics elsewhere notes, politicians, 'even the most upright, have a lively sense of the active part played in politics and elections by underworld characters'.[14] That role includes the use of violence when politicians and criminal bosses both benefit from its application. We can see quite clearly the debilitating result when that link becomes strong. South Africans often consider the overlap between crime and politics as something exceptional to the country. Unfortunately, it is not.

In all places where violence has currency, its occurrence can often have deeply symbolic value. That may be the case, for example, where public violence involves lots of people (violent protests, for example). However, assassinations can also be choreographed to make a point. 'Violence,' as Diego Gambetta notes, 'can serve a quintessential communicative purpose.'[15] In this sense, hits do not have to be regular, but they must be regular enough for the perpetrators to remind the economic and political system what they are capable of. This is why murder hit lists are used in the underworld: one or two killings have a multiplier effect, generating fear. Killing a particular person for a purpose is often about sending a message. And, even if that was not the intention, it may be the result. It is for this reason that the circulation of hit lists is a chilling development in our politics.

It should be recognised that resorting to assassination is not a new phenomenon in recent South African history. The Truth and Reconciliation Commission and media accounts have long ago exposed the role of apartheid-era 'hit squads', which targeted political activists, the most notorious being led by Eugene de Kock.[16] South African intelligence and special-force units also carried out targeted killings in neighbouring states and further afield.[17] And, for its part, the ANC engaged in targeted assassinations of 'problematic' members of the organisation and others, most notably municipal councillors and other 'sell-outs'.[18] High levels of violence, particularly on the Witwatersrand and in KwaZulu-Natal from the mid-1980s to just after 1994 often involved the targeting of individuals.[19] Assassinations have shaped the course of South African history on several occasions, the killing of Prime Minister Hendrik Verwoerd in September 1966 in Parliament and the gunning down of Chris Hani in April 1993 being just two examples. In that sense, assassination constitutes a form of learned behaviour, translating from one form of governance to the next.[20] The future of South African murder has been conditioned by the past.

But, while assassinations may not be new in South Africa, the degree to which they are now used is indicative of mafia-like violence: namely the use of targeted killing, or the threat thereof, to obtain political or economic gain. As Jan van Dijk has noted in a comparative study of indicators for organised crime, 'instrumental violence', such as targeted assassinations, can serve as a proxy for the extent of organised crime.[21] The use of targeted violence to influence economic and political outcomes is a core mafia activity.[22]

'Mafia' is a term that is not used as often as it should be to describe events in South Africa (we will return to this later in the book). It is a focus that is missing from most discussions of assassination in the country. Yet my interviews with hitmen suggest an awareness of the symbolic, mafia-type nature of assassination, namely that killing does not have to be regular, but only a threatened possibility, reinforced by actual cases that are surrounded by suspicion but impossible to resolve.[23] This type of violence, a recent study of violence survivors in KwaZulu-Natal concludes, leads to fear, greater risk aversion and 'a dampening influence on political participation'.[24] These are features of what is generally termed 'organised crime'.

But organised crime evolves. The actors change as economic patterns and those who control them shift – sometimes because of violence. These are the kinds of forces that have led to the likes of Laylah. She was a typical product of a market for violence entangled with other illicit markets – being paid to defend and alter it as others saw fit. She was the tool of the illicit trade but also a shaper of it. The likes of Laylah had been studied elsewhere in the world, but the foundations of analytical work on the underworld everywhere are shaky. It requires looking into places that are by their nature hidden from public view. It is hard to get people like Laylah to talk. But doing so provides a window into the underworld, changing our perceptions of the idea that violence is merely an accumulation of random acts that are reported in the form of a murder rate every year. A significant proportion of those murders may be much more instrumental, governed by a set of commercial transactions and shaped by violent entrepreneurs and the needs of criminal markets. If that is the case, we can do something about it.

# 1

## Junior 13:
## A grey ghost brings death

The well-dressed man in his mid-40s had just drawn up in a Toyota Hilux in front of a popular butchery and restaurant in Mamelodi West, near Pretoria. It was a mild Sunday evening in early November 2015, the heat of summer still a few weeks away. People were out on the streets enjoying the last fading hours of the weekend. In the bakkie were three other men. They were talking – most probably about business deals that needed doing and opportunities for the future. The smartly dressed man had considerable investments in the township, including the profitable butchery/restaurant. His Audi RS7 was parked nearby – a symbol of his success.

Accounts of his death differ, but they go something like this. It was dark, about nine o'clock. He had entered the butchery but was then called outside and got back into the Hilux. At that point, a sleek, grey Golf 6 drew up. That part of Mamelodi is a bustling place, even on a Sunday night, and the grey Golf would have attracted no attention. 'It was like a grey ghost,' a man who had been at the butchery that night told me as I wolfed down the outlet's delicious boerewors. The more I spoke to people about the murder, the more the word 'ghost' resonated: the life of the man who was about to die seemed an enigma, just like the many conflicting details of his death.

The men in the Toyota watched as customers selected their cuts of meat and took them to the cook, who manned the braai opposite the seating area. They continued talking; there seemed nothing immediately untoward about the new arrivals in the VW. But then, the doors of the grey ghost opened slowly and two men stepped out wearing balaclavas. They were armed. Professional hitmen. At that point the four men in the bakkie must have sensed trouble – balaclava-wearing men with guns at night can mean only one thing to those practised in the art of violence.

The men from the grey ghost moved swiftly to the parked car, guns clearly visible; one had a pistol, the other a semi-automatic. They looked briefly through the car windows in search of their target. Once they established he was there, they emptied their guns into the car in his general direction. As the shooting diminished, a door opened and two men bailed from the Hilux and ran away as fast as they could down the street. The remaining two occupants of the car were not so lucky. They were slumped forward in their seats.

The execution complete, the masked gunmen quickly got back into the ghost and the car drove off, its tail lights disappearing around the corner.

In the bakkie – having just breathed his last – was one of the most celebrated gangsters in South Africa. His name was Monare Ignatius Selokwane, or 'Junior 13' to those who knew him. His name was not on the lips of the public as a widely known gangster, like Cyril Beeka or Radovan Krejcir, but it should have been. Junior 13 was one of the most daring and prominent organised-criminal figures South Africa has ever seen. He was responsible for a spate of bank robberies in the first decade of the 2000s, which may have netted him as much as R50 million, half of it from one bank in Nelspruit.

Junior 13 was, by South African standards, a sophisticated thief, described by one journalist as the South African equivalent of Ocean's Eleven. The bank heists that he was suspected of pulling off relied on detailed preparation and complex operations. The bank blueprints were obtained or bought from employees, and he entered the facilities through the air-conditioning ducts or by tunnelling into the buildings. A trained technician was recruited to bypass the alarm system. Outside, corrupted police and traffic officers (who had been recruited as members of his gang) would be deployed to block or divert traffic and delay the arrival of genuine officers of the law.

In addition to the meticulous preparation for each bank heist, say those close to him, Junior 13's success in the underworld seemed to rely on two other factors. First, he made sure to replace his team members, so that few people knew all the details of his plans. Secondly, he made a specific point of recruiting police officers into his operational network.

Interviews suggested he was also involved in hijacking trucks, targeting in particular those carrying shipments of cigarettes.

But Junior 13 was never convicted of any crime, although he did appear in court for murder. He seemed to have avoided being convicted by making sure that case dockets 'disappeared'. In August 2003, police officers investigating organised crime and the Asset Forfeiture Unit attached his assets, including a mansion he owned in Kyalami. He hardly batted an eyelid: Selokwane is said to have stood at the door of his rapidly emptying house asking the officers if they wanted tea. After a court application in November 2003, Junior 13's assets were returned to him. He seemed untouchable.

There are mixed views about Selokwane in Mamelodi. Depending on whom you speak to there, he was either widely respected – a pillar of the community – or widely feared, willing and able to kill anyone who stood in his way. One young man recently released from custody spoke of how

Junior 13 had become a role model and father figure to him. A woman who owns a small business in the area described him as 'a father of his community', somebody with the interests of ordinary people at heart. He was, she said, an inspiration. Selokwane is even said to have handed out grocery hampers to people in the township. His mother told me he phoned her every day at five o'clock in the morning to check she and the family were well. He spoke little about business, she said.

When questioned about his shadier past, most people claim such stories are baseless. Yet there is undoubtedly another, darker side to his reputation. Junior 13 was feared, and widely known as a gangster who would not hesitate to use a gun – or a hired one – if he needed to. He owned several businesses in the township, including a fleet of taxis. I phoned some well-connected contacts of mine in Mamelodi to check things out and then paid them a visit. They told me that when they spoke with people away from the public eye, a consensus became evident: Junior 13 was not a man to be crossed.

A resident of Mamelodi described Selokwane's relationship with the people and place where he had grown up: 'Although Junior was seen as a Robin Hood figure who helped out in the community, that does not mean that he was not feared ... He was known to be ruthless, a criminal mastermind.' His career had also had its ups and downs. Selokwane's roots may have been in Mamelodi, but phases spent in and out of the township marked a measure of his accumulated wealth and success. After he spent a spell in prison on charges that were later dropped, it appears that his ex-wife acquired much of his wealth. Moving back to Mamelodi on his release and starting again, he was on the up and up. At the time of his death, he was planning on moving to a palatial home he was constructing in a nearby suburb.

On the day that Junior 13 died, photographs of his shattered head, taken in the mortuary on a cellphone, made the rounds on social media. Some people must have been quietly celebrating.

Junior 13's alleged involvement in violence had affected local politics in Tshwane. According to police, Selokwane had been arrested in 2002 for the murder of a mayoral committee member who had been killed in what looked like an attempted hijacking. There were whisperings that the murder was connected with the award of tenders for the allocation of taxi routes – but nobody is sure. Either way, the case seemed to fall apart and Junior 13 walked free. But there was little doubt in the minds of locals: Selokwane would use violence when he needed something, or to get someone out of his way.

Although there is little doubt among his family and people in the community that a group of hitmen were hired to kill Junior 13, the police investigation into the murder appears to have stalled. There are two theories explaining the motive: the first is that Junior 13 was killed in an underworld dispute about a business arrangement that had gone bad – in other words, someone resented Selokwane's success. The second is that his murder was linked to a broader dispute in the taxi industry, given that he had ties to the Mamelodi Taxi Association. It is not inconceivable that the two theories are linked.

But, either way, Junior 13's run of business, and crime, was over.[1] Much of what is known about the man may have died with him.

## Hits culture in a violent place

What is known is that Junior 13's murder was not the first in Mamelodi West. It had, in fact, been preceded in previous weeks by three other hits that bore remarkable similarities. One was the killing of Oscar 'Patch' Letsoalo. Patch owned several clubs on the township's busy Tsamaya Road. Some eight weeks before Junior 13 was murdered, Oscar Patch was alighting from his Porsche outside one of his clubs. A VW Polo with three men in it drew up next to him. One man quickly got out and fired three shots at Oscar Patch, who fell onto the tarmac. At this point another man leapt out of the Polo with a semi-automatic firearm and shot Oscar Patch seven times as he writhed on the ground, finishing the job.[2]

The killing of Oscar Patch came only a few days after the gunning down of two of his colleagues in the Mamelodi Taxi Association. The previous week Oscar Patch's friend and the taxi association secretary, Buang Maubane, had been shot and killed. Before that, Lucky Mahlangu, the taxi association chairman, had been assassinated.[3] It seems hard to disentangle this cluster of killings. Junior 13 was by far the most prominent figure, but the others were in their own right all business and community members who were held in some respect.

Incidents such as this set of shootings seldom attract much attention in a country with high levels of violence. The phrases 'shot execution style', 'killed in a suspected hit' or 'assassinated' have appeared so often in the South African media over the years that most people now just ignore them, assuming it is an underworld phenomenon, or attributable to the growth of violent crime. Yet those descriptive phrases are important indicators of something far more serious and pernicious – the commercialisation of violence sourced from the underworld.

The nature of violence in South Africa is widely commented upon, but not well understood. For one, both foreign and local commentary that suggests that the country is now significantly more violent than it was in 1994 at the dawn of democracy does not reflect the reality: the statistics actually show a slow decline in the number of homicides since then.[4] But the last several years have seen worrying increases again. What has escaped analysis altogether is the significant number of killings that are the result of hits paid for by someone else. Junior 13, Oscar Patch and the other men who died in Mamelodi West are just a small representative sample of what appears to be a growing national trend of 'solving problems' by paying to have people killed who might stand in your way.[5]

Determining the extent of the hits culture in South Africa is challenging. National homicide data provided by the police provides little indication of the reasons why people have been killed. There are some cases that suggest there hits were involved, but the samples are too small to draw meaningful conclusions. And, as with most murders in South Africa, even clear cases of assassinations might not be described as such. The shooting of a well-known gangster, Junior 13, for example, attracted almost no media attention. His death may have reverberated through Mamelodi West, but it got only limited press coverage. The death of Oscar Patch and the earlier hits linked to him received no coverage at all. Perhaps these kinds of murders have just become an accepted way of life.

The lack of attention paid to what are termed 'hits' in South Africa's daily parlance is a surprising oversight given the regularity with which such incidents occur, and the degree to which they are connected with political actors (more of which later in the book).

To give an idea of the extent of the hits culture, in 2016 the media reported that the South African Local Government Association stated that 450 local officials had been assassinated since 2000.[6] More recently, and in a dramatic announcement, the high-profile former Public Protector, Thuli Madonsela, was reported to be the target of a threatened hit, with a prominent gang boss from the Western Cape having been allegedly hired to do the job.[7] And in the run-up to the local-government elections in August 2016, the death toll mounted as local politicians jockeyed for position on party lists, most particularly within the ANC in KwaZulu-Natal.[8] Most of these people were killed in circumstances that suggested hits on their lives had been commissioned.[9]

The data on hits or suspected hits that my colleagues and I compiled and analysed suggest that their proportion is likely to be upwards of 0.5 per cent of all murders committed in South Africa, and probably far greater.[10] That figure is roughly equivalent to the total homicide rate in many other countries – and larger than the number of people recorded by the police as being killed for xenophobic motives in South Africa.[11] It is a significant number – and the hits culture is growing. The large number of murders in South Africa – there were 18 673 in the year to March 2016, with our database showing some 111 hits for 2016[12] – effectively means, however, that it is easy to mask cases of hits.[13]

This high incidence of assassinations committed in South Africa raises several important questions. Is there a changing trajectory to their occurrence? Can hitmen be identified as a distinct group of people with similar histories? Is a particular set of conditions evolving that ensures that hits are an increasingly common part of the South African political economy? Why are people, both in the underworld and outside of it, increasingly likely to pay other people to kill for them? And who are this shadowy group of mercenary killers?

It is very likely that 1 100-plus hits we identified in our database from 2000 to 2016 is an under-count, as the database was compiled from only those cases that were reported in the media and that were identified as either being hits or displaying characteristics common to hits. But it is a good place to start.

Drawing on this pool of publicly accessible information fills an important gap in what we know about murder in South Africa. There has been no consistent collection of data on the topic and no analysis has sought to disaggregate targeted murder in the context of shifts in the country's politics, economic relations and criminal underworld.[14] Such work therefore has wider implications than just for South Africa, as the intersection between such targeted violence and business and politics is a feature of several other transitional and developing countries.[15]

However, the greatest challenge to measuring an illicit social phenomenon such as contract killing is the obvious one that such activities are concealed given the consequences of their discovery. Criminology is in that sense a bit like archaeology: you need to draw a series of conclusions from data that is hard to get at. It's buried away, and some of it raises lots of ethical questions. Interviews with hitmen run all sorts of difficulties that make university ethics committees break out in a cold sweat.

There are significant methodological obstacles to collecting data and studying the phenomenon.[16] Nevertheless, as in the collection of information in any research field, the available data casts a useful light onto a wider problem, even if it is unable to reveal the full extent or nature of the phenomenon.[17] And there is considerable experience of collecting such data in South Africa.[18]

The challenge of accessing data is exemplified by the cases of Junior 13 and Oscar Patch. Although the community may have spoken openly about the deaths, the authorities did not publicly announce that they had been killed in a hit. Patch may have owned a fancy car – a potent symbol of wealth and success – but his killing was not deemed significant enough for a newspaper to cover it, even though he was gunned down in a public place, and his body was readily discovered. (One retired hitman told an intermediary that I use that burying the body and hence keeping the facts obscured for a while was a good way to reduce the coverage. 'Disappeared' is not quite the same as being gunned down in broad daylight.)

Where violent death is commonplace, as is the case in South Africa, only so many examples are recorded in the public domain. However, where they have been recorded, our research found that the circumstances under which hits took place were remarkably consistent. Victims were often shot while travelling in cars, or while arriving at or leaving their homes; attacked in isolated places; or shot by assailants who had entered their homes, mainly at night. The latter seems to be a standard modus operandi. Interviews with hitmen suggest that killing people on their doorstep is regarded as 'good practice'. Apart from the fact that there is a reasonable likelihood that the victim will turn up at some point, when a person is about to enter the safety of his home, is fumbling with the keys or looking forward to supper with the family, his defences tend to be down.[19]

As mentioned in the Preface, we sorted all the hit cases that we analysed into four main categories: those associated with the taxi industry, politically connected assassinations, hits broadly related to the world of organised crime and those linked to personal or family motives.

Of the 1 146 cases that were recorded, just over 40 per cent, we found, are in some way related to the minibus taxi industry. Cases that could be classified as politically motivated constitute about a quarter and a similar proportion are linked to organised crime. Hits associated with personal motives, such as family or marital disputes, represent about 13 per cent, the smallest recorded number, although these often receive disproportionate coverage in the media (*see Figure 1 in the appendix*).

It should be emphasised that these categories and numbers provide only a broad distinction between the different types, as we found that political, economic, criminal and often personal motives tended to merge with one another. And, in a broader sense, every incident on the database constitutes some form of organised crime. Therefore, definitively categorising those cases is sometimes difficult. For example, if a taxi boss or business owner who is also a political office holder is assassinated, is this a political, taxi-industry or economic act?[20]

The case of Junior 13 illustrates this blurring well: it is unclear whether he was killed because of his taxi connections, his role in the criminal world, or competition arising from his legitimate business affiliations. Nevertheless, even if such distinctions need to be treated with caution, they do provide at least some indication of the motives behind most hits.

The difficulties with defining these categories soon became apparent, but one distinction that was analytically useful was separating out targeted killings related to the taxi industry. The overall trend represented by the data shows a series of spikes, or increases in hits associated with the taxi industry (*see Figure 2 in the appendix*). In contrast to these dramatic fluctuations, all other categories remain at a remarkably consistent level over time, with approximately 40 reported cases a year, or three to four cases a month, being reported.

Two points should be made in respect of the overall trend. First, there is a marked increase in the number of hits in 2016. That is partly the result of violent political competition associated with the local-government elections that year. But this alone does not explain the trend. There were significant increases in hits associated with the taxi industry and an upswing in killings related to organised crime (*see Figure 2*). This increase is probably higher than our recorded data suggests given that our experience of collating the numbers indicates that in many cases the fact that a hit occurred often only emerges later during court proceedings. The recorded figure for 2016 may therefore still increase.

Secondly, given that the data is a reflection only of hits reported in the media, it must be interpreted very cautiously as a trend over time. Although there was extensive media coverage of politically linked assassinations in relation to the August 2016 local-government elections, which put the issue in the spotlight, the evidence suggests that the phenomenon of contract killing is a much more long-standing one.

One additional point in relation to taxi-related hits is also worth mentioning. The various spikes in taxi-industry hits might appear to indicate that these corresponded with a series of 'taxi wars' that broke out in those peak years. However, in a review of the data for the six years in which taxi-related hits peaked, the highest volume of hits being recorded in 2016 (*see Figure 2*) shows a more complex reality, namely that these incidents are geographically widespread. The taxi hits occurred in almost every province in the country, indicating this as a more dispersed and systemic issue, rather than one of localised turf wars. In 2016, a year in which we recorded some 56 taxi-related hits, incidents were reported across KwaZulu-Natal, in various towns in Gauteng, as well as in the Eastern Cape and Mpumalanga.

This, of course, is just data. It is worth remembering that there are real people behind all of these numbers. To illustrate how these hits actually affect people, and society in general, the following are some real-life case studies of assassinations (or attempted assassinations), across the four categories into which the incidents were sorted. These are only a selection of the cases we have on record, and all are drawn from just a six-month period – January to June 2016. But their complexity and the degree to which they involve a wide range of actors – police, political and other state officials, members of the judiciary, businessmen and ordinary community folk – mean that they are a good reflection of the kinds of cases we have in the database. Their geographic dispersion highlights just how widespread and serious South Africa's hits culture has become. And the ubiquitous hit lists bearing the names of people to be targeted – which often make exciting stories for the press – make their presence felt, raising levels of fear and intimidation.

Cases of hits that we placed within the political category targeted individuals who held political or administrative offices, almost always in local government. The motives were in most cases economic, often linked to disputes over accessing local-government tenders. There are also several cases of municipal officials who were killed after they acted as whistle-blowers.[21] The number of hits targeting political office holders or municipal civil servants grew over the 17-year period we analysed and this trend continued through 2016.

Take a recent case reported in Mpumalanga. On 25 March 2016, Moreko Mahlobogoana, an employee of the Dr JS Moroka Municipality, was killed. He was shot in the head, execution-style, and his body was found in a graveyard with his car abandoned nearby. A police spokesman suggested that the killing had something to do with 'issues in the municipality, internally and externally'. In the words of the provincial secretary, Bonakele Majuba, 'The way Moreko was killed is a clear assassination. In municipalities in Mpumalanga, people are being killed and no one gets arrested.'[22] The case was reported in only one national newspaper; we could find no local reports.

In another case, in April 2016, Jeffrey Mpulo, number nine on what has been described as the Msunduzi hit list (named after the eponymous municipality in KwaZulu-Natal), was attacked but survived. The list was leaked through social media and names several targeted people who are regarded to be opposed to corruption. The list contained 15 names, including municipal officials, political office bearers, Umkhonto we Sizwe (MK) military veterans, traffic officers, union leaders, Correctional Services employees and VIP protection officers. Mpulo was reported to have been behind a series of marches by Msunduzi municipal workers who were opposed to the suspension of a municipal manager. Mpulo had hired a security guard after the person at number eight on the same hit list, Pumla Joe Dlamini, the acting manager of public safety in the Msunduzi Traffic Department, had been gunned down at his office in a hit.[23]

In March 2016 it emerged that a hit list with 21 names on it was circulating at the Glebelands hostel in Umlazi, south of Durban. These people had been identified for 'elimination'. Glebelands is a large complex housing some 20 000 people. It has a notorious history of politically related conflict and violence.

Between April 2014 and May 2016, no fewer than 62 people were killed at the hostel. Referring to the hit list, a police spokesperson said that it was 'not clear if the motive [was] Glebelands [i.e. internal] conflict-related, taxi-related or another criminal act'.[24] Administered by the municipality, the hostel has experienced a great deal of conflict, including lack of transparency in the use of funds and their diversion to certain beneficiaries, and an extortion racket around bed allocation run by thugs. Dissatisfied with the councillor representing the hostel, several residents brought a vote of no-confidence against him. Some of these men, a number of whose names were also on the hit list, were subsequently killed.[25]

In the category of cases that fall under 'organised crime', hits are generally used as a type of instrumental violence targeted at achieving illicit economic outcomes.[26] Curiously, we found that several assassinations over a number of years have taken place in the bread industry and more recently in relation to the 'sale' of teaching posts.[27]

The same six-month period, January to June 2016, saw a prominent and particularly sad case of business, political and criminal interests coalescing with the assassination of Sikhosiphi 'Bazooka' Rhadebe. An environmental and community activist in the Eastern Cape, Rhadebe had vigorously opposed the opening up of community land to mining exploitation. The community was deeply divided over the issue and as a result Rhadebe's life was constantly in danger. A colleague said that because Rhadebe was a taxi owner and entrepreneur, 'he was accustomed to the threat of violence' and 'knew how to protect his family'. Just before his death, Rhadebe had said: 'The only way to kill a struggle is to kill its leaders.' He advised his colleagues not to sleep in one place. Rhadebe, said a colleague, would not have recognised his killers. 'They must have been hired hitmen … we want to know who paid them,' he said.[28]

There have been numerous cases of hits involving high-level criminal figures related to disputes, most commonly around drugs. For example, a series of hits were allegedly paid for by the high-profile underworld figure Radovan Krejcir (of whom more later). In a worrying number of cases, magistrates involved in the trials were killed in targeted hits, as well as numerous witnesses, including several who were, ironically, in witness-protection programmes.

For example, in early 2016 Krejcir drew up a hit list. The Czech mobster allegedly hired a middleman to seek out a hitman – one, presumably, who could not be linked back to him. It was alleged that Krejcir wanted several people killed, including private forensic investigator Paul O'Sullivan (named on the hit list), who was vigorously assisting investigations into Krejcir's criminal activities and his link to the state. The plot was foiled, but not before it became clear what the price being offered for each of the hits was: R250 000 per guaranteed kill. Given the hefty fee on offer for the hits and the publicity around the hit list, the conjecture is that this plot seems to have been put together by the appropriately named William 'King of Bling' Mbatha, an underworld figure who conducted armed robberies while dressed as a policeman, and who is currently imprisoned with Krejcir.[29] Previously, allegations had emerged during his trial that Krejcir had also sought out a hitman from Eastern Europe to kill the presiding judge.[30]

In a case with a bizarre twist, a businessman who sought to hire a hitman was also foiled in the attempt. A certain Dain Neveling allegedly wished to take out a hit on his business partner, who he believed was withholding financial information from him in their debt collection company. He is said to have pestered two intermediaries to find a hitman. In the end, however, the police staged the hit and then arrested the suspect after he had paid R10 000 for the job.[31]

The cluster of assassinations in the personal category includes cases related to love triangles, attempts to obtain insurance payments and instances of children arranging for their parents to be killed. In a surprising number of cases, family killing shaded into other categories where business (including the taxi business) and family disputes overlapped. The first six months of 2016 were no exception to this trend.

In one case, a KwaZulu-Natal teacher allegedly hired a hitman to murder her sibling over their late father's will. In a gruesome tale befitting any respectable crime novel, the hitman then proceeded to extort both parties. After accepting an agreement for R20 000 for the completed job, he approached the victim and suggested that he would not kill her in exchange for R10 000. The understandably nervous woman duly handed over the money. And then, in a bidding war with deadly consequences, the original contractor of the hitman then promised to up her payment by an extra R10 000 'and more, once the job was done'. The hitman then lured the unsuspecting victim by telling her he had killed her sister, the original contractor, and that they needed a sangoma – a traditional healer or diviner – to cleanse the victim's spirit. The victim was then abducted from her home, killed and decapitated.[32]

In another, a man hired a hitman to murder his 'intolerable' father who apparently made him work without pay, would not allow him to live with his wife and was hard on his sister. The hitman was paid R30 000 for the job.[33]

Finally, the same period saw numerous examples of taxi-related assassinations. In Johannesburg in April 2016, for example, a taxi boss was killed – apparently in a dispute over the control of taxi routes to a major new mall development in Midrand.[34] A few days later, Warrant Officer Andries 'Boy' Zungu, also a taxi boss, was assassinated in Umbumbulu on the KwaZulu-Natal south coast. Said one of Zungu's drivers:

> It's a pity we can't celebrate openly because we may face a similar fate, but it is good riddance. He would charge us R1 000 for overloading – and this was R1 000 for every extra passenger. He was also a loan shark, who would lend you money if you wanted a new taxi, but did not think twice about repossessing your taxi if you failed to repay the loan.[35]

In Johannesburg, and again in a case that illustrates the grey area between categories, an ANC ward councillor who was involved in resolving disputes between rival taxi drivers was targeted. Mbuyiseni Dokolwane was murdered after arriving home. A man waiting for him in a parked car shot him four times.[36]

In Tembisa, a township east of Johannesburg, a taxi boss, Dumisani Mlambo, was assassinated in a manner strikingly similar to the way Junior 13 was killed. When Mlambo drew up at a set of traffic lights, an old Toyota Corolla pulled up alongside and its two occupants began firing at Mlambo. Then one man calmly emerged from the car, walked up to Mlambo and shot him 15 times through the windscreen at point blank range.[37]

In another taxi-industry incident, a police officer, Captain Skhumbuzo Khumalo, was charged with a series of crimes related to his alleged role as the leader of a group of hitmen in the taxi industry. Khumalo had been involved in a struggle between two competing taxi associations over a route between Newcastle and Gauteng. He took leave from his job at the Brixton Police Station in Johannesburg and was contracted by a group of taxi bosses to eliminate competitors. Prosecutors say that the taxi bosses rewarded the police officer by giving him a stake in their taxi fleet. Khumalo was also accused of stealing guns from his workplace and supplying them to the taxi industry. As Khumalo appeared in court to face charges, Mduduzi Twale, one of the key witnesses in the case against him, was ambushed and assassinated by an unknown assailant.[38]

In the South African context, as these examples all show, hits are a mechanism by which to regulate certain intersecting political, economic and criminal interests. The difficulty of disentangling their motives, and the strong evidence of a crossover between the political, economic and criminal, are a reminder of the overlapping nature of these interests in South Africa's violent democracy.

The culture of hits in South Africa often relates to this regulation of often illicit activities. Junior 13 was gunned down in an underworld dispute that – although it remains murky – bears all the hallmarks of a form of regulation. Perhaps he had not delivered on a promise, or had killed once too often, or had simply become too big for his boots, threatening the criminal operations of a younger, emerging set of crooks.

In illicit commercial transactions for protection, such as in the case of extortion, the threat of violence is almost always unspoken, but by definition it is the key incentive for the transaction to take place: if payment is not forthcoming, targeted violence will result.[39] Such a position applies more widely to violence in all markets. Although the results of assassinations do not always meet the original objectives of the perpetrators, we must distinguish between the (sometimes failed) political, economic or personal aim, and the damage (beginning with the loss of life) caused by its implementation.

Quite apart from the loss of life, it does not take much imagination to deduce the other forms of damage that such violence incurs in the political, economic and social spheres. If, for example, political decisions and policy are determined by the threat of violence, then politics is ultimately shaped by hidden criminal forces. Or if municipal officials who prepare tender documents fear for their lives, contracted work may be much more expensive than required, as it gets allocated to unscrupulous parties who have no intention of fulfilling the terms of the contract. Although the focus of this book is less on contract killing for personal reasons, such cases in South Africa have generated widespread negative news coverage that far outweigh their proportion of the total number of hits.[40]

As the case studies of assassinations in this chapter suggest, organised crime entails incorporating violence into transactions – the *sine qua non* of mafia-like activities. This has hugely debilitating effects, undercutting development, distorting democratic practice, reducing transparency and accountability (particularly when whistle-blowers or the press are killed or threatened) and increasing personal fear. Where there is a crossover between the involvement of state and criminal actors in perpetrating such violence, or cooperating in ways that facilitate violent outcomes, the position is particularly serious, blurring the distinction between the licit and the illicit and reducing levels of trust, and replacing them with violence, or the threat of violence.

One of the most worrying aspects of the hits culture is its potential to permeate up through the system. In South Africa hits are, for the moment, largely confined to certain criminalised markets and certain parts of the upperworld – including, sadly, local and provincial politics. But we should not express surprise when they affect national politics too. It is perhaps only a question of time.

# 2

## It's just a job:
## The hitman's work

'**R**unning a business like this is not easy,' said Simon (not his real name). 'You need to make sure the work comes in and that people pay you.'

In studying the phenomenon of hits, it seemed hard to avoid the need to speak to the people at the heart of the system – the hitmen themselves. So, using several intermediaries to make contacts, I had set out to see if people in the hit industry would talk to me about their work. People like Simon.

In Johannesburg and Durban, I relied on a trusted intermediary who had opened doors to the underworld for me before. She really is someone you can call up and ask if she would arrange a meeting with a hitman. For her, this seems like an everyday request. 'I'll see what I can do,' she said. 'What's your deadline?' It's movable, I explained, thinking anxiously of the pained expression on my publisher's face last time we met. She and her colleagues didn't want their names in the book, but suffice to say their Rolodex had a number entries under 'I' – for '*izinkabi*', the colloquial name for hitmen in Zulu.

In Cape Town my introductions to hitmen came through links to the world of gangs and taxis that I had developed in my earlier work. Without the credibility that my intermediaries had with the Cape Town gangs, there would have been little chance of being able to conduct the discussions. The intermediaries have excellent links to, and enjoy high levels of trust among, several gang bosses. After a while, doors were opened enabling a series of interviews to be conducted. The interviewees participated voluntarily. We began by explaining the purpose of the interview and the study. We asked each interviewee about their experiences, and then we spoke about their engagement with the gangs. The names of the hitmen whom we interviewed are not known to me or my intermediaries, and, beyond offering the odd chicken meal and Coke, I did not pay the interviewees.

To demonstrate the complexities of speaking to *izinkabi*, let me give you the story of my meeting with Simon, described as a prominent killer for the taxi industry in Gauteng. Commercial hitmen for hire have conflicting objectives: on the one hand, they want to be available for work; on the other, the nature of their job means that they would prefer to stay underground. Hence the need to use a trusted intermediary. (Curiously, in many respects this process exactly mirrors the way murderers hire their hitmen. If you read the accounts of those who stand accused of hiring someone to kill someone else, this is invariably the story they tell. Intermediaries lead them to people who are, or who pose as, professional hitmen.)

Getting to Simon had been a tough assignment. I had nagged my contact for weeks to find out whether their contact had a contact who could get me in front of someone like Simon. Eventually things began to fall into place. Simon had agreed to talk, but with certain conditions. Basically, he would not discuss individual cases and he insisted I should do nothing to identify where he could be found. There could be no filming or recording of the interview – I would need to be searched first to prevent that. Fair enough, I thought, if that's what it took. To keep it vague, Simon is based in a large hostel complex in a township in the greater Johannesburg area. It's a bustling place, with people coming and going. The meeting was to be carefully choreographed. We made a phone call near the entrance and then we waited.

After some time, two men emerged and signalled to my intermediary and me. One was old and scrawny, the other squat and powerfully built. After brief introductions I was banished to my car while a discussion ensued about the boundaries for the interview. Then a younger man appeared from behind a nearby pavement restaurant where scores of chickens were sizzling over a braai. I was summoned back. We had bought one of the chickens, and, standing in a group, we shared the bird, breaking the meat off with our hands and dipping it in sauce. Not a word was spoken.

With a wave of his hand, the newly arrived young man summoned me to follow him. He must have been observing the proceedings from afar because he walked knowingly towards my car as I followed. We climbed in and he directed me to drive through the neighbourhood, as he kept a careful eye on the wing mirror to see whether we were being followed. Eventually he settled on a place for the discussion to take place – an empty piece of land near a railway line. Thus, with the sound of crowded passenger trains thundering past, we began to explore Simon's life and what his job meant to him.

The market in which *izinkabi* operate is competitive, he explained, and one of the more common and irksome requests from clients is for professional hitmen, like Simon, to prove they have actually completed the work. Finished the job, literally. I had also had this from others.

The problem is, many customers have been defrauded. In several cases, hitmen would tell their prey to disappear – threatening that otherwise they would have to kill them. The hitmen then claimed to their clients that the targets were dead, and they would claim their fee. So, it's now become fairly standard practice for customers to send an emissary to make sure that the job has been done as per the order.

Simon said he would prefer that there were no witnesses; he does not like people hanging around his workplace. But that's the system: a witness has to be there to confirm that the deed has been done. That's how it works. This is business, after all.

Simon did not want to be described, but let's just say he wouldn't stand out in a crowd. He is probably in about his late 30s, and looks young and fit. He wore expensive running shoes without socks, chinos, and a well-cut shirt that matched his shoes. He squatted down under a tree, rocking back and forth on his haunches as I tried to get him to talk.

Slowly, Simon opened up, but in a guarded sort of way. He originates from KwaZulu-Natal. From a tough town, by the sound of things. 'You grow up with a lot of killing there.' It's where he first learnt his craft and became connected to people with interests in the taxi industry. It's not something that he was keen to discuss, though. The talk was laboured, each point being extracted detail by painful detail. But, as with many conversations about business, talking money is a useful way to get things started.

'Pricing a hit is a measure – like water in a cup,' said Simon. It really depends on who is to be killed. I am summarising here, but there are two basic criteria: status and difficulty. The two are interlinked. Higher status means that you might get the police after you more intensively than normal – political pressure, that sort of thing. Or, worse – far worse, it seems – you get the hitmen from some other 'warlord' on your tail. 'Sometimes there are hitmen who watch hitmen,' explained Simon. 'It can get complex.' Those with the real money are prepared to pay to make sure that the killing is as far removed as possible from them. In this game, hitmen both target the victim and are targeted themselves.

The difficulty index of a hit is a measure of how much protection surrounds the target. The presence of bodyguards obviously increases the stakes. In the taxi business today, some bosses virtually deploy private armies to protect them. The more bodyguards, the more important the person. Hence the higher the value of the kill contract.

Payment is strictly in cash and negotiated in advance. Small jobs are cheap: anything from R5 000 upwards. 'Big targets', like a taxi boss, are likely to be expensive. 'A taxi owner is about R20 000. A real taxi boss or a high-profile person is something like R150 000 or more.' For big hits, there is often an initial discussion and some planning. The difficulty will be talked about for a bit. Information on the person's movements is presented. That sort of detail is usually conveyed by the person ordering up the hit. They may have been observing the target, or may know him. In most cases, a person who has collected these details will also act as the witness to make sure the job is done properly.

Simon implied that a lot of innuendo is used when talking about a hit – no names, just a reference to 'removing' someone. This roundabout way of talking is not out of fear of surveillance or police informers, but, said Simon, because it is just easier to discuss someone else's death like that. Hitmen are human too. It's unseemly to talk about killing too directly. How does he salve his conscience? With alcohol, for a start: whisky is his favourite. He needs to do this, he said, in the same way that people with different jobs do other things to get their mind off work. It's just that, he emphasised: a job.

And, as with all jobs worth the pay, reputation is the key to his business. Reputation is a measure of how many successful hits you have done, and their level of difficulty. Being known to have taken out three taxi heavies gives a hitman a highly marketable reputation. 'Your cellphone rings', is how business-conscious Simon describes it. But this is a fragile business, he emphasised. 'Hitmen don't live long. They know too much and they are in danger when doing the job. But the money is good and I now can't do anything else.'

In the end, it all seems to be about money. 'Hitmen have been known to kill the very people they are supposed to be protecting,' he said. 'I wouldn't do that. But it happens.' Hits are simply a matter of negotiation, and payment, Simon emphasised. Hitmen who have learnt the trade in the taxi business are those who tend to do most of the work outside of it. That's a common story and says a lot about how mafia violence with origins in the taxi industry has had wider implications for South African society.

Just before we part, as he is about to make his way back up the road, I ask Simon if he has any regrets. 'Not many. It's really just a job.'

But then his face darkens and he adds: 'The way to survive in this business is to make sure there are no witnesses, apart from the man guaranteeing that the work is done. If it comes down to it, a good hitman must kill more than the target. He must kill anyone who gets in the way too.'

## The hitmen hierarchy: The professionals and the not-so-professionals

Hitmen at the top of their game, like Simon, trade for profit. Most, as Simon mentioned, seem to have a link to the taxi industry (more of which in Chapter 3).

Either way, those operating at the high end of the market do not come cheap and the price is a reflection of their experience. As mentioned, in Simon's case, the fee for a hit can be as much as the price tag of a new car, or the equivalent to a year's wages for many working in the licit economy. What is clear is that there is a limited number of such men and they are widely sought after. And, given the number of killings they perform, they must be on speed dial.

A Cape taxi boss gave me an example of an incident when hitmen were called in. Passengers travelling in taxis from Delft were being mugged by several well-known gangsters. 'We summoned the hard men, and told them to solve the problem. The gangsters disappeared one by one,' he said, snapping his fingers to indicate gun shots. 'You see, when it comes to disrupting business, to wait for the police is a waste of time. We turn to the professionals.' He said this without the slightest hint of irony.[1]

As Simon indicated, hitmen develop a reputation. In Cape Town's black townships and informal settlements, several names are repeatedly mentioned. The sinisterly named 'twins' are said to operate from Lower Crossroads, as are 'Boko Haram', a pair of young men with a bloody reputation. An individual called Sepho is said to have a good reputation in Khayelitsha. The Umtata boys, hailing from the town of the same name, are called when tough jobs need doing. 'Those at the top of the pyramid won't do just any job,' said a hitman who claims to be retired, 'but they will find you people who can do the job'.[2]

Contrast this higher level of professionalism with the case of the hitmen allegedly hired to kill a young woman, Jayde Panayiotou, in Port Elizabeth. Her brutal murder and the details that unfolded afterwards in court have gripped the South African public. Bundled into the boot of a car on 21 April 2015, Panayiotou was killed execution-style, with three bullets. The state has alleged that her husband, Christopher Panayiotou, paid one of the bouncers at a nightclub he owned, Luthando Siyoni, to recruit hitmen to carry out her kidnapping and murder.

Siyoni said in his testimony that he spent some time looking for a hitman, eventually approaching one Sizwezakhe 'Sizwe' Vumazonke through Facebook, of all places. Sizwe mysteriously died in hospital, some say by poisoning, as the trial proceeded. Hitmen, even not very good ones, are expendable.

The weakness in the plan, Sizwe might have argued, was that the middleman, Siyoni, got weak-kneed, or rather his girlfriend did – a woman with the unlikely name of Babalwa Breakfast. Sizwe, who was out on bail following an armed-robbery charge, had been recruited to do the job, but he subcontracted the work to others. It all turned into a dog's breakfast when Ms Breakfast spilt the coffee beans and the band of subcontractor hitmen were arrested.

I suspect a professional like Simon would have shaken his head in despair at such a botched execution. He had suggested to me that some in the profession lack discipline. Middlemen are often the weakest link, he said – not up to doing the job themselves, but keen to get their hands on the biggest cut of the money. The inept group who allegedly killed Jayde left a trail of clues behind them. Although at least one of the group had killed before, the details of this case suggest low levels of experience and organisation. The payment was allegedly made at a branch of Kentucky Fried Chicken. And the motley crew celebrated at a similar chicken joint after completing the job.

If one compares the work of the confident, experienced Simon with the bungled performance of the alleged murderers of Jayde Panayiotou, it becomes evident that there is a wide spectrum of expertise in this market. Indeed, the international literature on contract killing identifies a three-level hierarchy of contract killers: highly sophisticated professional hitmen whose murders are seldom solved; middle-level killing, often conducted by proficient killers, generally drawn from criminal gangs or performed by bouncers and debt collectors; and low-level, once-off killings, contracted out to other people who have little experience of murder, but something to gain by carrying it out.[3] Siyoni and Sizwe fit into this third category.

There may well be some blurring between these three levels of professionalism and some graduation, as expertise is acquired as one moves from one level to the next.[4] The degree of skill and professionalism makes the hits business resemble many others: like the guy you are looking to hire to tile your bathroom, there may be a lot of cowboys out there in the market who talk up their skills and down their price.

These levels of professionalism among contract hitmen is a phenomenon that has been identified internationally in the literature on this subject. And this hierarchy generally holds true for South Africa too. However, the term 'professional' should not be overestimated: somebody with just a few kills under his belt might describe himself as competent – like the guy who tells you which other bathrooms in your neighbourhood he has tiled, to secure some business.

At the top end, in the world of organised crime and in the case of some high-level political assassinations, professional assassins appear to be used. These are hitmen who leave little evidence and in most cases have not been brought to trial. For example, several killings related to the Chinese triads in South Africa appear to have left no trace, and in the notorious murder cases of Yuri the Russian and Cyril Beeka, both underworld figures, professional hitmen were reportedly employed.[5] (We explore these cases in more detail later.) At the other end of the scale, hits conducted for personal reasons tend to display the lowest level of professionalism in their execution. Often in these cases inexperienced hitmen are hired to do the deed for the first time. Hence the likes of Sizwe.

Hits in the taxi industry have generally been conducted by people with a moderate level of experience or training who could be labelled as part-time hitmen but who have a degree of professionalism. Simon fits the bill here, although he is at the top end of this group. These hitmen often have a military or security background. They may be individuals with experience in township militia formations, such as the so-called self-defence or self-protection units that emerged during the conflicts of the late 1980s and early 1990s.[6] They have also been involved in political hits.

But, as the market has expanded, a new generation of hitmen are emerging, partly because they undercut the price. This new category of hired assassins are less experienced and more in need of work than their older, more experienced counterparts. They are often in their mid-20s and many have migrated from rural KwaZulu-Natal, finding accommodation at men's hostels in and around Johannesburg. 'These young men,' a former senior security official, who has studied killings in the taxi industry, said, 'don't necessarily have a history of involvement in hits but are known to be violent.' Their inexperience, she concluded, makes them loyal to individual bosses who pay them – at least until they acquire some experience, 'graduate' and 'go out more on their own'.[7]

However, such broad typologies, or measures of professionalism to designate where hitmen fit into a hierarchy of competence, belie the complex reality of contract killing. This is not a static market, but one that is constantly evolving. It's also important to challenge the global academic literature on the subject, which is largely written by people in developed countries who have not spoken to any hitmen. For example, Mexican journalists have provided a much better picture – and one that is more akin to the South African context.

Interviews with professional hitmen that colleagues and I conducted in KwaZulu-Natal and Cape Town suggest that their existence is a precarious one and that categorising them as professionals – understood as the ability to kill without leaving any trace and thus any chance of being caught – fails to take into account the vulnerability of even practised contract killers. The evidence suggests that far from being highly professional individual operators, contract killers are reliant on the broader network of taxi associations or gangs for their protection, while at the same time being threatened by them. In short, the biggest danger for hitmen may be those they work for – not the police or those they kill.

This sense of dependency became immediately clear when setting up the interviews. Although hitmen said they would speak to us only if they received 'clearance' from their taxi or gang bosses, in the interviews they often styled themselves as 'independent'. This seeming contradiction would attest to the reality that contract killers are very much a product of the environment from where they emerge. Self-styled independent hitmen, particularly if they are at the high end of their trade, may be less independent than they appear.

## Oxen and ants

Although hitmen can be sourced almost everywhere in South Africa, the most common recruitment markets are the KwaZulu-Natal and Eastern Cape taxi associations, whose tentacles extend to Johannesburg and Cape Town, and the gangs of the Western Cape. In both environments, hitmen are generally engaged in killing within one particular criminal market, be it the taxi industry or the drug turf battles associated with the gangs. That's where they earn their spurs. But, once they have acquired some experience they may also be recruited for outside work.

Taxi hitmen tend to be associated with KwaZulu-Natal, and the name derives from a Zulu expression, *'ukuthenka izinkabi'* – literally, to use oxen to plough the land. But the original Zulu phrase has a layer of meaning not apparent in the literal translation. The underlying sense is that just as a powerful ox ploughs its way doggedly through obstacles in the fields, so do their namesakes in the human world, *izinkabi* – people who are hired to eliminate 'obstacles' that thwart the aspirations of their handlers or to exact revenge.

In isiXhosa, hitmen are known as ants, or *imbovane*. The name is apt. 'They are everywhere and nowhere,' a taxi boss told me. 'You hire them at night and then they fly.'[8]

In the Cape Town underworld, the term used for a hired killer is 'hammerman' – a description with a double meaning: on the one hand, as a noun, it denotes the hammer of a gun, and on the other, as a verb, it graphically describes the act of killing or attacking someone. I find this use of terminology like '*izinkabi*' and 'hammerman' intriguing – in neither case is the word 'killer' used. The label provides a degree of sanitation; and it can almost be said with a sense of pride.

Many *izinkabi* we spoke to said they have been operating within the taxi industry for a number of years and ply their skills across the industry, around the country, often hiring themselves out to the highest bidder. Most experienced *izinkabi* originate from mainly rural KwaZulu-Natal. They often lead a solitary existence, and may well not get married, given the nature of their lifestyle. Hostels provide a conveniently discreet operating base.

Describing these *izinkabi*, one taxi owner we interviewed stated: 'These guys are heartless and have no mercy whatsoever. They often carry out these tasks any time of the day. When it's done in broad daylight, it shows courage and brings fear to other owners. It tells them not to mess with whoever organised the killing.'[9]

A taxi driver from Umlazi, when asked about *izinkabi*, replied: 'These guys feel nothing when they kill. They have no conscience.'[10]

These words illustrate just how much fear hitmen instil. Generating this level of fear through violence, or the threat of violence, is a system of criminal governance. If you are a taxi or gang boss, contracting out the killing to defined groups of people is a way to regulate violence and control it, while keeping your distance: targets are selected, unwritten contracts entered into and people 'removed'. But criminal governance is a messy business: by sustaining a group of killers who work above all for money, the bosses have created a monster that may turn against them. Bosses may contract but they also become contracts, being killed by the very people whom they have previously employed.

In the gang environment of the Western Cape, assassinations are a key strategy employed by the gang bosses to enforce their will, expand their reach and manage their business.[11] Having hitmen on hand to do the job is therefore essential. Looking briefly at the criminal career of just one hitman illustrates how assassins are introduced and socialised into the system of violence – and reveals the personal costs that they bear as a result. Take the case of a practised hitman (whom I will refer to as Ben). Ben is in his early 40s and has a son, who is currently serving a prison sentence. It is difficult now for Ben to visit areas of Cape Town where he is known, as he fears he will be recognised by other gangs and by members of vigilante group People Against Gangsterism and Drugs (PAGAD). This organisation is no stranger to assassination itself, having picked off a score of gang leaders in the late 1990s.

Ben grew up in the gangs and served a 15-year sentence for violent crime. It was in prison that he began a career as a killer. Prison gangs in South Africa have a complex mythology and provide powerful systems of ordering in the country's jails. The three most important are the 26s, 27s and 28s. Given its numerical basis, the system is often referred to as the Number (this is described in greater detail in Chapter 5). Based on sets of rules and processes, the Number can order the killing of other prisoners or warders. Ben was asked to do just that – and he performed well. With a reputation for being quietly competent in his trade, he was recruited by a set of gang leaders on his release from prison. His handlers needed him as the fight over drug turf in the city intensified. But the scale of the work over the past few years has left its mark on Ben. He said he has been busy – too busy. While outwardly calm and contained, he is at times jumpy and nervous, fearful he will be exposed. His conscience clearly weighs heavily on him. Ben is the closest I have come to a contrite hitman.

Like Ben, all our interviewees confirmed the notion that gang-related violence on the Cape Flats is closely related to the control of drug markets.

As a senior gang leader put it: 'Most of the killings happen because of drugs or power. Drugs, and selling drugs, is the most important thing for the gangs. Wars and deaths come because of it.'[12]

Corroborating this, another gang boss spoke about how he had been targeted in an assassination attempt. He was in no doubt about the motive: 'This was because of drugs and them wanting to take over my business.'[13]

Violence is also engineered for purposes outside the drug economy, however. Property auctions, for example, are sometimes said to be manipulated by gang bosses, and violence is a tool to distract attention from them. It's like lighting a fire in one place, a gangster explained to me, so that people are distracted from the damage you are causing elsewhere. A gang shooting attracts the attention of the community and sometimes the media, drawing it away from some other activity going on there. In the case of property auctions, fewer people attend when there is a shooting in the area, making them easier to be fixed.

Hitmen who operate for the Cape gangs have a key function in the local political economy of violence. For the gangs, the targeted kill is primarily deployed in two interrelated criminal markets, both closely aligned to gang turf. The first involves targeting other gangsters to ensure control of drug-distribution markets. The second is violence deployed in the extortion market. Both are carefully calibrated.

To be effective, to send the right messages, and to leave as little evidence as possible, killing in this context requires specialised skills, perhaps less to do with the actual act of killing, although this is of course a factor, than the requirement to keep one's mouth shut. A key requirement for a hitman is not to speak – ever. (Hence our need to use intermediaries to secure interviews and the difficulty of teasing out the nature of the job.)

To achieve the perfect and untraceable hit, a degree of specialisation is required. Although anyone can be persuaded to kill, the results may be damaging to those who ordered up the hit. This was perfectly illustrated to me in a discussion with a gang boss, who emphasised that drug addicts could be persuaded to kill people in exchange for drugs. This might be an inexpensive solution, but bears a serious risk for the bosses: 'This may come back to you, as these people do not think straight and the police will get you because they will squeal,' he said.[14] Hence the need for a relatively small number of professionals without whom the gang bosses would not be able to regulate and control criminal markets. The hitman is now an essential tool for the ambitious gang boss.

If hitmen are seen as simple tools to achieve criminal governance for gang bosses, this says little about the costs of being employed in such a function. While the gang boss may order up a killing, and send someone to check that it is done to specification, in the actual moment of the kill itself, there is only the hitman and his or her prey. In that encounter between the killer and the soon-to-be-killed, as other studies have concluded, our interviews showed that hitmen achieve a form of what has been described as 'psychological reframing' of their victims.[15] This may be a fine term for the academic seminar room, but, to give one practical example, one interviewee made the point of saying that he never looks into his victims' eyes, and that if he did he would be unable to continue.[16] Recall also how Simon in his interview with me suggested that it was better not to use names, as that helped depersonalise individuals – they are targets rather than human beings, in his mind.

An important defence mechanism, interviewees said – again this was corroborated by Simon – is to define what they do as a 'job'. The argument here is that the act of killing is often a way to 'normalise' reality or, psychologically speaking, to return things to what they should be – to 'correct' them. For example, recounting how people were killed in prison, one interviewee, who had begun the conversation saying that he abhorred sexual relations between men in prison (ironically, he had been imprisoned for a sexual offence), concluded: '[People were] killed to correct things. It is wrong how these 26s are sexing everyone. That is not the Number. It makes me sick.'[17]

In the complex environment of the Cape Town gangs, assassinations are also a means of 'correcting' things – setting things right, restoring the balance. One hitman alluded to how the system worked in prison, describing a murder for which he later was convicted. He was asked to assassinate another gang member in line with the policy of *gahzie optel*, meaning, literally, to pick up blood. This can be hard to grasp, but, basically, it is a form of revenge killing where the accepted norms of gang organisation have been broken. It is not dissimilar to the mafia conception of a 'made man' or 'man of honour', someone, who because they have been through a rite of passage to join a criminal group, cannot be killed without an elaborate process. In the case of *gahzie optel*, a senior gang elder cannot be killed without permission from those in the senior gang echelons. If this occurs, then 'blood has fallen on the floor' and must be retrieved by a revenge killing, which achieves balance, or a settling of scores (the Afrikaans is *maak die nommer rond* ('to round the number')). For various reasons related to the recruitment of prisoners to the Numbers gangs, there is considerable contestation over how these rules should be applied. Either way, targeted killing is seen as a way of maintaining a form of internal balance in the gangs, and of protecting senior gang leaders. This shows how the code of prison gangs is now used outside of prison in wider gang conflicts on the streets.

The view of killing as a form of 'corrective medicine', or cleansing, was evident in several of the interviews. One female interviewee recounted how she had served a prison sentence for the murder of her boyfriend, whom she had killed, she said, in self-defence. Because she was a drug addict, and drugs were being sold from her home, the prosecutor had taken a hard line against her and she was given a ten-year sentence. That sentence defined her, cutting off her options, such as formal employment

47

on her release, and compelled her to be beholden to the gang for whom she had worked in prison. Her account contains the implicit suggestion that she is putting things right, balancing off what society has done to her – a personal form of 'rounding the number'.[18]

Earlier, we saw how a group of less experienced hitmen prepared to work for lower fees were beginning to enter the contract-killing market. Unskilled and often uneducated, many of these young men struggle to make a living and are open to opportunities, particularly if there is the potential to earn unheard-of levels of income and acquire a degree of status in the process. Those with the necessary social or clan links and a reputation for aggression, bravery and loyalty are drawn into the business of contract killing, often paid on a retainer for providing 'security work' for taxi bosses. But entering this enforcement system requires a degree of socialisation. Like corporations, the taxi industry therefore has a system of induction or onboarding, akin to the team-building exercises employees may experience in the formal economy, such as competitive games with one's colleagues played during the office retreat.

Estimating the numbers of young men who are contracted as muscle to work for the taxi industry is difficult, but even if a few associations retain only a small number, the total is likely to be in the order of several thousand. Like their brothers recruited as the killers for the Cape gangs, this new generation of inductees are tested for loyalty and competence.

A former taxi boss told me that these younger recruits are initially hired in surveillance exercises. Information is key in this industry. 'You need to know what drivers are doing, and where things are getting out of hand, or can be exploited,' he said.[19] The young men are 'put into the field' on reconnaissance missions, often in hired cars, watching and reporting back on activities. Unlike the older, more experienced generation, who may be called to carry out hits, the younger set are said to be hired as thugs when taxi association bosses raid a rank, relieving drivers and owners of cash.

They also perform the witness function that Simon dislikes – it's a good way to learn the ropes of the business.

As they gain experience, they might be deployed at hotspots to provide additional security or to intimidate competitors, often in conjunction with the regular commercial security companies that are hired by the taxi associations. Having passed through an initial phase of proving their worth in these more basic tasks, and having shown their loyalty, they are then promoted and assigned to carry out hits. This career progression echoes in some ways personnel development in the formal economy.

On the other hand, while it is present, we should also not overstate the formal recruitment procedure for hammermen in the Cape. There, the system does indeed rely on identifying someone with the necessary characteristics and skills, including proficiency in the use of firearms. It is in the interests of the gang to identify successive generations of hitmen, but equally, much depends on individual circumstance and the willingness of the person concerned to gain a reputation as being a reliable killer. It is not possible to be an unwilling hitman – even if regrets may later creep in. As I illustrated with the case of Ben, hitmen are identified and approached, usually by gang bosses, receive some instruction, and then earn their stripes by carrying out a number of 'jobs' (akin to a probation period in the workplace).

One of the interviewees indicated that when he was released from prison for a sentence he was serving, someone suggested to him that this was a 'line of work' that 'maybe he would be good at'.[20] In several discussions it became apparent that hammermen were often recruited or identified while in prison. One proudly explained: 'They knew of the work that I did in prison, so they asked me to continue. The money is good. I use a knife.' Another interviewee said: 'So this guy was good at killing inside prison; now we let him kill for us on the outside.'[21]

In one Cape gang that we know of, there is a 'gatekeeping' process,

whereby the prospective hammerman 'applicant' has to undergo a gruel-
ling recruitment exercise. He is left at a particular point on the outskirts of
the city and has to negotiate his way through the territory of five opposing
gangs, armed with a handgun and eight bullets.

Other initiation rituals entail what was described as 'killing a mark',
in other words taking out a hit on someone. One of the interviewees
explained that a first-time hammerman applicant may be tasked with killing a rival gang member in his own backyard.[22] These processes suggest
a degree of professional skills acquisition and a recruitment process that
attempts to identify the best applicants and weed out hopefuls who may
not have the personal attributes to perform the function.

An interviewee suggested that there is often some degree of training in
the use of weapons, apparently given by former military personnel from
the defence forces and MK.

Another way of recruiting potential hitman is to use the technique of
talent spotting. In this process, ambitious young men, seen to have the
right balance of skills, work their way up the ranks. But it is not without
its challenges:

> A rising star [who] wants to work his way up the ranks of the gang
> must kill someone. He may be asked to kill someone from a rival
> gang. Many times this *kak* is about drugs. Make no mistake, we make
> it hard for him. He maybe has to go into a gang area where they know
> that [he] is associated to us. So these fuckers want to kill him badly.[23]

Making one's way up through the pecking order and becoming a hammerman appears to be a contradictory process: on the one hand, you
develop support within the gang, and earn the favour of the leader; on
the other, you begin to separate yourself from the main workings of the
gang, partly because you are now an outsider, a threat both externally and

internally. Therefore, a hammerman is part of the gang and yet simultaneously peripheral to its operation, while at the same time being close to the
gang boss, who 'whispers in his ear' when work is required.[24]

This apparent conflict is important to understanding how hammermen
themselves view the world. While in some cases they get caught up in the
material excesses – flashy cars, easy money and access to drugs – that the
position seems to offer, the more experienced, wary and successful individuals recognise that this is a fool's route. One interviewee said that his
work is like 'coming out of the shadow for a short while and going back
in there again quickly, without anyone knowing'. A hammerman who is
too conspicuous and vocal is a contradiction in terms, and ultimately a
threat to the well-being of the gang leader. That is a dangerous position to
find oneself in. Said one hitman: 'Low-level idiots brag about these things
when they are drunk to intimidate [people], but they have no discipline
and that is why they are caught.'[25]

Discussions with hitmen revealed that 'watching one's back' and
maintaining a strong sense of autonomy are of particular importance
in the fragile world of those who kill for the gangs or taxi men. When
questioned on the requirements for success in this job, our interviewees
pointed to the importance of individualistic self-reliance, as opposed to
the forms of group support that the gang offers. One hitman, for example, stated: 'You must have no fear. You must have the proper training
and self-discipline. In fact you must project the right mindset – and
prison, in some ways, can give you that platform.'[26] These qualities are
acquired if you grow up on the street and it may often mean that you are
a more of a loner, he said. The task of a hitman is, in the final analysis,
highly individualistic. This is evident in the importance of individual
reputation as a defining factor for acquiring work and obtaining a
degree of self-worth, ironic as that may be under the circumstances. The
role requires characteristics of self-sufficiency and confidence that are

not necessarily required in the groupthink mentality that characterises most gang interactions.

By contrast, the gang bosses paint a rather different picture, emphasising how the gang, as a collective entity, provides the essential elements for the hammerman to succeed. These contrasting perspectives are significant in this environment: gang leaders are eager to claim allegiance, whereas hitmen are wont to emphasise independence.

This reliance on gang support is in contrast to the inherently independent nature of the position – a conflict that highlights the inside–outside nature of the hammerman's place. He is of value to the gang only as long as he does not cross certain boundaries. Implicit in this is the fact that hammermen can only advance so far: they are well paid to maintain loyalty, but do not constitute the core of the gang. The hammerman is therefore ultimately expendable.

Unsurprisingly, being a hammerman comes with significant emotional and psychological costs. As the case of Ben suggested, hammermen are surprisingly aware of the damage that the job does to them. It is not something that can be easily articulated, but they are not all bravado and boasting, as may be suspected. They are in some ways remarkably reflective. They are well aware of the fragility of their own position. Ben, for example, spoke about accepting death when it comes. The need for psychological sanity has led him to decline several hits, he said, saying that a 'just cause' must now accompany his choices.

That 'just cause', in his view, aligns closely with the Number-gang mythology, that of rounding the number, or making something right. He focused in our discussion on the 'discipline' that he needs for his life, and that he 'makes his bed that way every morning' – implying that he meditates on life and death.[27]

If such forms of self-doubt do arise, it seems, however, that getting out of this business is not that easy. Making an exit is a process in itself fraught with danger. And stepping down, it turned out, surprisingly, was even a sensitive topic for discussion. One interviewee suggested that an assassin who had proved his worth would be permitted to go to the *weivelde* (pastures), meaning that they can take a break from their work. However, this must be preceded by some show of loyalty. Ironically, a spiritual break, by embracing God, may also provide an acceptable exit strategy. How the legitimacy of such a request is determined is hard to discern from the discussions, but the process seems to rely on displays of loyalty and an indication that absolute discretion will be maintained post-exit.

If a hammerman is found to be dishonourable, perhaps being seen to look for an easy way out, then he will become a *skietbaan* (literally, a target in a shooting range, a sitting duck). The gangs will look to assassinate the assassin if they sense that the request to step down, to abstain from killing, is not legitimate. At least one of the informants suggested that it is for these reasons much easier to exit 'this game' outside prison, where levels of surveillance are lower. In prison, you are owned by the gang and there is no chance of shedding your gang identity. It was said that sufficient money is needed for a hitman to 'disappear'. But, as one hitman told us, 'if they want to find you, if they want you dead, they will find you – even if you change your fucking face'.[28]

The socialisation of a hammerman, as we saw earlier, implies displaying some degree of loyalty to the organisation, but also means that he or she often falls outside its formal structures. Cape gang bosses maintain that their hammermen are gang-aligned or, as a gang boss put it, 'gang loyal' and that they cannot be outsourced to other gangs. If a hammerman does work for a rival gang, however, a gang boss explained, he puts himself in a very precarious position: 'He may not have a home to come back to and we may feel the need to kill him for working with the Nongies [other Number gangs].'[29]

And in a similar way in the taxi business, the sense that these hired guns are likely to be responsive to the highest bidder makes some taxi bosses nervous. 'They shoot for me today; tomorrow they shoot me' is how a former taxi boss described the dichotomy.[30] The issue of loyalty is important because hitmen know a lot: they know who is targeted, and often by whom.

In the taxi industry, this prevailing insecurity is one of the reasons for opening up opportunities for the emerging cohort of younger killers for hire, driven in part by the desire of some taxi supremos to eliminate *izink-abi*. In some cases, an observer of the industry explained, this is because taxi bosses have been prepared to kill even their own family members and business acquaintances in their insatiable drive for power. The men who did the work are now the threat: not only are they hireable by the competition, but they know, quite literally, where the skeletons lie. They know the key secrets of the gang bosses – they know who has been killed, although not necessarily why. The mere fact that they know who the target was and who ordered the hit means that they now constitute a threat. As a consequence, taxi operators are increasingly hiring a new generation of hitmen.[31]

There are some parallels here with the gangster hitmen of the Cape Flats. Among them, too, loyalty is prized above all else. Loyalty is also essential for personal security. To betray the gang or the organisation, by doing work for someone else, for example, would mean almost certain death. As a former security official observed: 'For the new generation, it is a life that entraps them. Since they increasingly "know too much", leaving the fold or showing any signs of ambivalence or disloyalty could well prove fatal for them.'[32]

In a weird kind of reverse logic, recruitment strategies, preparation and the lifestyle breed a divided loyalty among hitmen from the beginning. Hammermen are 'trained to integrate with wider "respectable" society,' a well-known gang boss explained. 'They must be well dressed, well-spoken and be able to blend in.' He reflected ruefully on what he regarded to be a distorting culture of materialism he had witnessed that causes some to bite the hand that feeds them:

> I have seen many of my brothers changed. They feel the rush of fast cars, money and women, and they immediately know that it is different than life in the ghetto. So, now they want that life … and they will be willing to kill their brother to have that life. I brought one up through the ranks into this lifestyle and soon thereafter he turned on me and tried to have me killed, so that he could run things. Now I scan everyone for a long time before they come up to a higher level. Greed is a killer.[33]

Any suggestion of disloyalty turns the assassin into the target. Hammermen, because they in effect constitute the violent tool that maintains the system, are liable to be suspected of disloyalty if they too easily assume the trappings of gang wealth and power. I also ascertained that hammermen who break the code of loyalty may be given up to the police by their bosses – if they choose not to have them killed.

Unsurprisingly, then, the Cape gangland interviewees implied that, for hammermen, greed generally comes before a fall. A well-known gang boss spoke animatedly on the topic of the rise and fall of the contract killer:

> These fuckers sometimes get hooked onto fame and that's how they fall. The life up there is great 'cos we come from shit. You get to *jol* with the bosses of big companies … [But] these guys lose their code. They are out of discipline 'cos they [go and] tell these white guys [about their work] … You can't trust anyone but yourself. You don't tell anyone about your business. My guys know how to be quiet 'cos we train them that way … you are asking to die if you speak of our business.[34]

For the gang boss, as for the taxi baron, the main fear therefore seems to be that the hitman's loyalty will evaporate and their hitman will turn on them. In the words of the gang boss: 'You have to watch them 'cos they can come for you someday. You must keep yourself close to these people and watch their psychology. They don't give a fuck who they kill.'[35]

My assumption hitherto had been that hitmen were generally 'free-lancers' – self-employed agents advertising their wares, free to trade their service independently in the underworld. But there is another nuance to this story. Contract assassins are also very much dependent on securing work by developing professional relationships with certain criminal bosses. In that sense, freelancing really means working with a well-circumscribed client base. But, outside of that base, given the competition prevalent in the underworld, hitmen can and do enter into other contracts.

For this reason, the notion of nurseries of violence, which we saw in the Introduction, is of central importance in the discussion of hitmen, as these nurseries or pools provide a source for recruiting and a resource for projecting violence into society. That makes the evolution of organised crime and its forms of violent regulation critical to understanding how violence is shaped in the underworld, but also by implication in the upperworld too. Doing hits in the upperworld may, ironically, carry fewer risks than below – primarily because you don't offend any other powerful criminal players.

And what about the police? you may legitimately ask. How do they mesh in with this environment of violent regulation? Underworld bosses in South Africa have a critical role to play in terms of their relations with the state, and the police in particular.

Working successfully as a hitman requires certain personal character-istics, such as self-discipline, as we have seen, and an ability to control fear. But having a wider network of protection, particularly from the police, is also helpful. Criminal bosses are in a position to assert a real influence over the police. The reason for this is simple: they have the most money. However, determining the exact nature of the underworld's connections with the state is one of the hardest parts of this puzzle to solve.

In Cape Town in particular the superstructure of support provided by the gangs, including their ability to disrupt police investigations, seems to be essential to the long-term survival of hammermen. An essential function performed by the gang bosses, and one that assists the work of the hammerman, was described as 'maintaining relations' with the police. As the gang boss explained: 'We get guns from them [the police] and we pay them to lose evidence. If another gang really wants our drug business, then they will pay those *fokken* cops more money to make cases stick.'[36]

What was perhaps most striking from the interviews, however, was how certain police officers themselves are practised in the art of targeted killing – sometimes killing directly but more often by not stepping in to prevent gang conflict or assassination, either to protect informant networks or particular gangs and their bosses. Although this has now become a more commercialised arrangement, it is consistent with the historical context of police involvement in violence during the liberation struggle in South Africa, when the police force would deploy gangsters to target the state's political opponents.[37] These relations are now, however, much more complex to understand, driven by local relations between gangs and the police.

How this scenario is unfolding in South Africa is remarkably similar to the role played by police in contexts in Latin America, where deals are struck between organised crime and law enforcement. There the police may kill for organised-crime networks, and organised crime may kill for the police.[38] A chilling version of this phenomenon is also evident in South Africa, where prison inmates, it has been said, have been released to conduct assassinations, and when behind bars again they benefit from greater privileges. Basically, they are rewarded by the state for doing the state's dirty work.[39]

These mutual exchanges, which, given the difficulties involved, remain largely unexplored by researchers, illustrate the macabre symbiotic relationship (a theme we will look at in more detail later) between the gangs and the state – the police primarily, but also the prison authorities. On the one hand, a relationship is maintained whereby the gangs pay a form of protection fee to corrupt police officers. On the other, the police must crack down on the gangs at some point, precisely because, in this complicated relationship, police action, when it occurs, demonstrates to gangs the importance of buying protection from the police – in effect, it shows what the police are capable of should they not be paid off. At the same time, the police are to some extent constrained by public and political opinion: they must act in some cases (when a drug-addicted killer 'squeals', for example, or when there is mass violence).

In this symbiotic pairing, targeted killing is a tool whose benefits are shared in a blurred way by criminal gangs and the police. This occurs through a complex interaction between them, each party calculating its own interests. For example, gang leaders and hitmen explained that the prison authorities and police may manipulate 'assassins' to target certain gang members as a means of enforcement. Thus, in the words of one gang boss, 'when a gang becomes a problem for the prison staff, the head will use the assassins in a way that they manipulate wars between the various prison Number gangs'.[40]

This is disturbing stuff if you hold that old-fashioned view (which was probably never true) that the police are the thin blue line between order and the criminal world. In reality, in the South African context, the police are negotiators or gatekeepers of the boundaries between the upper and the underworld.

We'll explore the issue of the symbiotic relations between the police and organised crime later, specifically in relation to the use of police informers, but in the next chapters we first turn to an overview of how the underworld in South Africa has developed and how it has shaped the markets for violence.

# 3

# Rank and file: Life and death in South Africa's taxi industry

By all accounts, taxi boss Victor Nbulelo, nicknamed 'Small', was a colourful character. His mother was from the tough Coloured township of Elsies River, Cape Town, his father a Xhosa from the Eastern Cape. Victor married Thelma, a woman from the Cape Flats, and they had a child in 1997. It was a story of rags to (at least some) riches. In March 1991 he and Thelma bought a taxi, having won a cash prize from a charity lottery ticket. It was enough for a deposit on a minibus and the start of a new business.

The business did well and grew to the point where Thelma and Victor owned nine taxis, and Victor rose through the ranks of various taxi associations, eventually becoming, in the words of relatives and associates, the 'warlord' of the Cape Amalgamated Taxi Association (CATA). He must have been a tough nut, for running a taxi organisation demands a nose for business opportunity and a degree of ruthlessness. CATA and a rival taxi association, the Cape Organisation of Democratic Taxi Associations (CODETA), were engaged in a vicious taxi war in the Cape from the mid- to late 1990s. Victor's opposite number, the self-styled warlord for CODETA, was David Jezile.

As the number of taxis on the road, and hence the competition, continued to grow, people close to Small reported that he was increasingly concerned that there would not be enough business for everyone. He suggested limiting the number of taxis each person in the association owned to six. That way, the competition would be reduced and taxi owners would still make money.

## Kentucky fried killing

Victor's seemingly well-intentioned suggestion, however, proved to be his undoing. In October 2000 Victor was lured by one of his business partners to what was purportedly a meeting. Several men emerged from a shipping container and others from surrounding buildings. Victor was shot multiple times.

In the immediate aftermath of his death, suspicion first fell on Victor's arch-rivals in the taxi business, particularly Jezile. But the truth, it turned out, was messier, and a testament to the cruelty and greed that are hallmarks of the senior operators in South Africa's taxi industry. While several explanations have been advanced, the most plausible seems to be that Victor's murder had in fact been arranged by members of his own association. While there may also have been a connection to politics (Victor having recently been enlisted to stand as a candidate for the United Democratic Movement), several opponents within CATA had been drumming up opposition to him for some time, and his proposal to limit the number of taxis per owner was the last straw for his rivals. Senior members of the organisation arranged a collection to hire a hitman, Siyabulela Khobe, who then reportedly brought on board four accomplices. The order they were given was to be sure to kill Victor good and proper. Fulfilling their brief to the letter, they pumped him full of bullets.

Khobe was a well-known taxi hitman – a professional killer who sells his services to taxi owners, a job still in its infancy then. Khobe also operated a profitable side line in armed robbery in the Cape Peninsula. Nurtured by the taxi industry for a career in violence, he branched out into a range of other violent crimes. On his arrest, the police reported that he was one of the most wanted men in the country.

But Victor was no innocent man himself. It transpired in investigations that he had previously hired Khobe to terrorise a bus company, Golden Arrow, so that commuters would be forced to switch to taxis. Khobe, it was said, had not received his money. He bore an enduring grudge against Victor.

When Khobe was arrested, his four accomplices in the murder turned state witnesses and all were killed. And then the bodies started piling up in revenge. Everyone who had been involved in hiring Khobe to take out Victor was killed over a period of five years. Thelma would receive a celebratory bucket of Kentucky Fried Chicken from her family after each one was dispatched. There were nine corpses.

But the truth is stranger still. In a twist that few would believe – and it was not picked up in the court proceedings of the time – it turned out that at the age of 14, Khobe had been abducted on 12 May 1993, by none other than a man he identified as Small Victor. Over two decades later, the motives for the abduction are difficult to discern, lost in the violent conflagration that preceded democracy. The most plausible explanation appears to be that Khobe may have been involved with the wrong political people – meaning the young lions of the ANC – and needed to be set right.

At the time of Khobe's abduction, Victor seems to have been a member of the Big Eight, a criminal gang with links to the police and the taxi industry. Khobe was tortured by Victor and a member of the police's then elite Internal Stability Unit. Victor found himself in court defending the charge. The magistrate ruled (in a judgment that suggested it might have been influenced by the authorities) that Victor had been in his right to make a citizen's arrest of Khobe, and the torture allegations were overlooked.[1]

The brutal murder of Victor Nbulelo and the story of his assassin provide a window on the violence that has engulfed South Africa's taxi industry. Khobe, once a youth abused now turned killer, was a product of the vicious conflicts in the Western Cape in the days before democracy had dawned. His victim had previously tortured him and then hired him to inflict violence on others (and never paid), so when Khobe was approached by the taxi association to rid them of Victor, he must have been happy to oblige.

## A violent industry in changing times: The emergence of the taxi business

Today, in any South African town, the white Toyota 16-seater minibus taxi, weaving between the lanes and hooting for passengers, is a ubiquitous sight. Yet the so-called township taxi industry is a fairly recent phenomenon. But despite its short history, the development of the taxi industry in South Africa reveals a complex narrative characterised by a mix of brutal violence, politics and fierce competition.

Before 1977 in South Africa, the transport of people or goods was run by a state-controlled monopoly. Every driver needed a permit and these were in short supply, released under a strict quota system. The lucrative permits were divided into short-distance licences and the more profitable and sought-after ones for long-distance intercity or rural-to-urban routes.

For would-be taxi entrepreneurs, obtaining a permit was almost impossible under apartheid legislation if you were black, and 90 per cent of applications by black drivers were rejected.[2] But with South Africa's economy booming in the early 1970s, and because alternative forms of public transport were inadequate and prohibitively expensive, the state-controlled transport system was struggling to keep pace with the demand. Consequently, an informal system began to develop alongside the official registered taxis, with black taxi operators running taxi services using private vehicles. This morphed into a network of 'kombi-buses' (named after the Volkswagen Kombi model), which could carry up to 15 people. These became heavily sought after by commuters because they were affordable, they serviced remote areas and outlying settlements, made house stops and provided late-night services.

To protect themselves in an environment where transport regulators would fine unlicensed taxi drivers and often confiscate their vehicles, and where there was the simultaneous threat of being caught up in the political upheaval sweeping through the South African townships in the late 1970s, drivers organised themselves into taxi associations. These provided physical security and a pool of cash for paying fines – and bribes. Documents given to me from early meetings of one of these associations show that they were also formed as a means to regulate tariffs and loading practices at the taxi ranks.[3] Local governments sought to challenge the informal taxi industry by closing down taxi ranks, which prompted greater self-organisation on the part of the burgeoning industry.

The South African informal taxi industry began to materialise in an atmosphere of intense political conflict. Operating – or even using – unregistered minibuses, as opposed to the regulated transport services provided by the apartheid state, was tantamount to an act of political protest, part of the movement of consumer boycotts that were applied in the townships to pressure the racist councils. This strategy of boycotts had been born in the early anti-apartheid struggle, and the state transport industry was a popular target. One woman described the militant nature of a bus boy-cott in Port Elizabeth in 1987: 'We were throwing stones, throwing petrol bombs, stopping the buses coming from town, putting big trees on the road, big drums. And we used to hit people who were using the buses that time, hit them with sjamboks.'[4]

Spooked by the Soweto uprising and buckling under the pressure of operating a state transport system that was haemorrhaging money, the government appointed a commission of inquiry, which recommended a move towards free-market competition and the end to state control of the taxi industry. It was the start of the formal deregulation of the industry.

When it finally came much later, deregulation merely rubber-stamped what had already been the status quo in the taxi industry for a number of years, or, as one taxi operator put it, 'They deregulated it without ever regulating it.'[5] Although there was still, at least on paper, a permit system for taxi operators, it did little to control the industry – the apartheid gov-ernment had far more pressing problems to deal with in the late 1980s than to worry about taxi drivers' documents.

As state control weakened, the informal taxi industry expanded rap-idly, in part because the barrier to entry in the market was low. One Cape Town-based taxi driver told me that he used to drive an old Cressida – the sort of car referred to in township parlance as a cockroach (because they refuse to die). His vehicle displayed a sign brazenly indicating that his services were for 'non-white passengers only' – this as a stern apart-heid government official policed his taxi rank. 'And then, suddenly,' he explained, 'in about 1988 or 1989 it became a free-for-all. There was a mas-sive growth in the number of operators. I purchased my first minibus taxi, and after I had made some money I bought a few more. It was crazy.'[6]

His story is not unusual. The taxi industry became a source of business opportunities for people who had previously been excluded from enter-prise. Its impact was in this respect positive, providing, as it did, a source of transport and income for thousands. The industry empowered a generation of men at a time when jobs were drying up. This Cape Town taxi owner was able to send two children to university on the proceeds of his business; the eldest is now an ophthalmologist.

But the industry also has a dark side. As the same taxi owner put it, 'My daughter tells me I should get out, and my son says that he has no interest in the industry because there is too much violence.'[7] His words illustrate the contradictory nature of the South African taxi industry, one that, as Thomas Blom Hansen notes, has 'become a metonym of the underworld as well as a powerful symbol of post-apartheid economic freedom'.[8] The taxi business has brought both great wealth and great suffering.[9]

Various reasons for this dichotomy can be identified in the industry's genesis and development. Having been born out of South Africa's political struggle, the taxi industry was christened with the levels of violence that characterised the uprisings of the 1980s. Furthermore, when the government passed the Transport Deregulation Act in 1988, which opened the way for the dramatic growth of the private taxi industry, all of a sudden there was ferocious competition.[10] The taxi associations had begun to organise themselves more effectively. They entered into aggressive negotiations with government and other emerging associations. The industry's commercial interests were now taking precedence over service provision and political ideology.

Local authorities were inundated with drivers keen to buy into the taxi industry. It was, in many ways, a modern-day gold rush. There was a real possibility, as the experience of the Cape Town driver shows, of earning enough to change one's fortunes. Under deregulation, prospective drivers were no longer required to demonstrate a need for their services or to provide any sort of professional qualifications or vehicle roadworthiness documents to acquire permits. They were issued 'like confetti'; aspiring drivers just needed to pay the fee.[11]

The result was an excess of taxis on the roads (including pirate taxis that operated outside of the formal permit system). Between the registered and the illegal operators, there was a combined level of supply that far outweighed demand. By 1989, there were an estimated 50 000 kombi taxis operating in South Africa.[12] Competition had heightened sharply for passengers and routes and, like any emerging and rapidly expanding market, the taxi industry became volatile, capricious and highly competitive.

Hence, by flooding the market, deregulation greatly increased the incentives for violence: with so much competition within an environment of limited economic opportunities, violence became a tool to use against the competition.

Without any form of meaningful regulation by the state, the taxi associations became the industry's attempt at self-regulation. The myriad of associations that sprang up in the mid- to late 1980s sought to form strategic alliances among themselves and with a wider network of political partners – the aim being to strengthen their capacity to capture key routes. By the mid-1990s, some 1 300 taxi associations were in existence, and these local associations affiliated themselves with a number of umbrella or 'mother' associations to gain wider geographic coverage.

This two-tiered structure – local associations and national umbrella mother bodies – provided key roles at the two points where the owners and drivers needed support and protection. At the local level, associations helped secure routes and places in the taxi ranks. Nationally, the mother bodies helped access licences, which were increasingly being distributed on the basis of privileged, and often corrupt, relationships, in particular for the more lucrative long-distance taxi routes. As the number of unlicensed operators had grown rapidly, obtaining a licence remained a useful way for an operator to secure a position in the industry and to avoid being harassed by the traffic authorities.

Interestingly, unlike the development of other criminal markets ana-lysed in this book, there was no fundamental reason why the taxi industry needed to have become as violent as it did. In fact, even though taxis were a resource for political mobilisation, in the early years of deregulation the industry also operated with a degree of community spirit. According to taxi owners I spoke to, in the late 1980s, some taxis even put profit aside and were happy to transport political protestors, pensioners, schoolchil-dren, soccer fans, funeral-goers and the like for free or at reduced prices.

But, for two reasons, such benevolence was not to last long. First, as the market became increasingly oversubscribed and profit margins squeezed, altruism became largely unaffordable in an intensely dog-eat-dog environ-ment. Secondly, the deregulation of the taxi industry occurred at a time of significant political change and growing levels of political violence across the country. This was to have major implications in shaping the nature and types of violence associated with the industry. Violence therefore became grafted onto the taxi business from an early stage; it was part of its DNA.

Competing taxi associations were quick to take advantage of these reservoirs of violence within the communities they were servicing, recruit-ing hitmen and heavies to protect their turf, resolve disputes and promote commercial interests. And from there it did not take long before a classic mafia-type system began to take hold as the associations used their organi-sational strength and access to violence to not only defend their interests but also to extract new sources of income through extortion and protectionism. In a period of intense competition, a predatory attitude towards commuters and the violent protection of routes became the norm.[13]

Consistent with the long-standing tradition of politicisation in the transport industry, the mother associations developed close affiliations with the political parties. In ANC-controlled areas, taxi associations were not only seen as party allies, but their vehicles were also chartered to transport ANC supporters from the townships to rallies and other events.

Thus, even where the competition was predominantly for economic control, the pre-1994 taxi conflicts were marked by high levels of violence that took on a political tone, often descending into military-style engagements between the various associations.[14] In the Western Cape, for example, in the kind of taxi violence in which Victor Small became embroiled, political alignment coloured the conflict.

Of greater concern, and with significant implications for the post-apartheid state, was the extent to which the political parties and the police used the violent competition within the taxi industry in the period between 1987 and 1994 as a proxy battle for their own power struggles. 'Violence between associations,' concluded Jackie Dugard, who conducted a seminal study on taxi violence during the transition period, 'if not comprehensively encouraged by the apartheid regime, was ignored, allowing taxi associations to expand and proliferate unchecked.'[15]

Dugard documents cases in which the police used their positions of authority to provoke and promote rifts between the associations to destabilise black communities. As was the case with Victor Small and his assassin, they allied with taxi-industry warlords to target political actors or local troublemakers. And even where the police did not directly intervene, calculated inaction allowed the often military-style conflict between opposing associations to rage unchecked.[16]

## KwaSicily-Natal

The complex relationship between taxis and politics is well illustrated by the case of Elias 'Sputla' Mpungose, a former provincial politician who controls the second-largest taxi-industry association in KwaZulu-Natal. Mpungose was alleged to have been a member of the hit squads operating for the Inkatha Freedom Party in KwaZulu-Natal and Gauteng. Having been accused of countless murders, Mpungose has never been convicted, and witnesses are said to have been intimidated or have disappeared before they could testify.

In the late 1990s, Mpungose switched political allegiance, joining the ANC as a regional political leader. In 2007 he was sentenced to life imprisonment for raping a 14-year-old girl, who was mysteriously murdered a week before the trial began. He was later charged with the murder of the girl, her mother and a cousin, but a series of discrepancies in the witness statements led to the charges being dropped. In 2011 he was released when the Supreme Court of Appeal overturned the rape judgment against him. He received a hero's welcome on his return home.

In 2012 Mpungose was again charged with murder, this time that of a rival taxi boss, but the charges were withdrawn when the main witness to the murder disappeared. In 2015 he was under investigation for another killing, again of a rival taxi boss. It is said that R1.2 million was offered to a hitman to kill the leading police investigator in the case.[17] Mpungose's is a story that would not have been out of place in accounts of organised crime in 1930s Sicily.[18]

In this symbiotic relationship, Mpungose used his political connections and, allegedly, ties to senior police officers, to protect and expand his business. But, as a rich man, and one with the capacity to commission violence, he is now an indispensable ally for many. Among taxi operators, political affiliation, as is the case with Mpungose, is used as a protection strategy and as a way to secure a customer base. In the period of political transition and the last days of white rule, the politicians held the upper hand. It was not long, however, before increasingly wealthy taxi bosses were calling the shots by funding or supporting local politicians. The balance of power had switched.

The levels of politically related violence in the industry began to decline after the first democratic elections but, meanwhile, shoot-outs at taxi ranks and the targeting of innocent commuters became increasingly the stuff of day-to-day news reporting in the first years of the new democracy.[19] Taxi wars flared up in townships across the country, though KwaZulu-Natal has had a particularly large slice of the conflict. Whether motivated by political conflict or vicious commercial competition within the industry, violence in the taxi industry has become a feature of almost every town in the country and has scarred many lives.

Looking to explore one taxi conflict in greater detail, I made arrangements to speak to both sides of a long-standing violently competitive taxi dispute in Soweto. This taxi war is a microcosm of how a combination of poor regulation and greed drives violence. The conflict at its heart is about route allocation and the reality that there are a growing number of taxis serving a shrinking market. 'We do not make money like we used to,' said one taxi boss. 'There is much less to go around.' Both sides point to corruption in the allocation of routes by the Gauteng provincial government. Out of these declining opportunities have come a vicious and high-stakes competition, with assassinations of drivers and taxi bosses on both sides over the past few years.[20] One taxi official who monitors a local rank in Soweto told me: 'I don't sit and read the *The Sowetan*. I watch carefully. The hitmen come.'[21]

Assassinations have become standard practice. As Alpheus Mlalazi, National Taxi Association Secretary General reported in March 2016: '[T]axi operators are greedy, which leads them to commit horrendous murders ... For the past four months, every day a taxi driver, operator and commuter was killed – most in assassination fashion ... [our] graves are littered with the bodies of taxi leaders but the killers continue to roam our streets.'[22]

From our database, we attributed 484 professional hits to the taxi industry over the 17-year period we analysed, and these are only those murders that are confirmed and have been reported, so the figure is more than likely to be an underestimate. It's about route control, extortion and the positioning within associations – quite literally mafia stuff. In just one industry, this figure puts South Africa up there with places like Mexico, where hits related to the drugs market are commonplace.

What may seem remarkable, however, is the degree to which hitmen recruited from within the taxi industry are active outside of it. In the Wandile Bozwana case, for example (see the concluding chapter), the hitmen involved were alleged to have been recruited from the taxi world. Our interviews with taxi-affiliated hitmen also suggested this to be the case. And Radovan Krejcir, whom we will meet later, also used a killer recruited from the taxi business.

That the taxi industry is the source of easily hired killers was documented in a memorable newspaper headline: 'It's easy to hire a hitman. Just ask around at a taxi rank'.[23] Like their counterparts in the gangs, taxi hitmen are often preferred recruits for contract killing outside of their own industry. People source them through taxi bosses or operators, said one former taxi owner.[24] One hitman, speaking about his role in the taxi industry, even referred to his commissions as 'call-outs'.[25]

However, fully understanding the high levels of taxi conflict is a challenge in an industry shrouded in a conspiracy of silence. As one report put it, 'Nobody is willing to talk about the causes of the bloodletting. Inquiries about the killing are met with stony silence.'[26] A recent, moving account of an attempt by a young writer to trace why and how his father was killed in taxi violence in a small rural town is revealingly entitled *Nobody's Business*.[27] It is difficult to penetrate this industry, so taxi killings remain under-researched and little analysed.[28]

As mentioned, violence in the taxi industry from the late 1980s to the early 1990s had become inextricably enmeshed with the political landscape of the time. And while society might have hoped that the state would have quelled the violence, instead it escalated – a phenomenon that can be attributed almost entirely to the predatory role played by the mother associations, particularly those controlling the longer routes.

Most taxi owners are reluctant to talk publicly about the role that the mother association bodies play, but of the little that is known about them, there is a consensus that this is where the real money is made in the industry. A taxi owner from Newcastle in KwaZulu-Natal, one of the few who was prepared to discuss things, said:

> We pay every week to the association. We can see that they give us security guys, but we don't know what happens with all of the money. And there are lots of us owners paying. It's a lot of cash. The fees keep going up and up, and we are too frightened to say anything. I know owners who made a big noise and two of them were killed.[29]

They are an 'extortion racket,' said a veteran taxi owner in Cape Town. 'I try not to pay, but sometimes it is very difficult.'[30]

This system of extortion is enforced by both the threat and practice of violence. As Dugard puts it, '[T]he only real common denominators among mother bodies are their focus on violent protection of spheres of interest ... Whereas local associations provide an invaluable service to taxi operators, mother bodies focus on appropriating money and organising the violence.'[31]

The local taxi associations levy from taxi operators two fees: a membership fee, used to finance services, like policing the ranks, and a second fee, which fills the coffers of the mother bodies. How the latter disburse this cash lies at the heart of the violence that is so endemic in the taxi industry. The money is extorted through the constant fear of heavily armed private-security operatives deployed by the mother bodies. This makes them classic racketeering organisations, collecting funds ostensibly to provide security, while threatening with force those who do not pay or who are seen as a threat. Hence they perform no real service. The money is used to conduct operations against rival taxi associations and to hire hitmen to take out competitors or 'obstacles' – as was the case with Victor Small. Theirs is a modus operandi that perfectly fits the definition of a mafia industry – and elsewhere it would be called that.

How much money they extort varies between associations. But it is quite possible in some cases for R100 000 to be collected from affiliates every month, resulting in mother bodies being the recipients of huge sums of cash. With such large revenue streams, it is no surprise that positions within these organisations are highly coveted. Money is accumulated quickly by a small number of individuals who are allowed to rise to the top.[32] Several participants whom we interviewed suggested that it may be more profitable to have a top position in a mother body racket than to operate a taxi business. It is a route to influence and money.[33]

However, people in such positions are also acutely aware that their lives are in danger and that they live in constant fear of being violently displaced in the power struggle: 'It is a sort of arms race, with money being accumulated as quickly as possible and everybody weaponing up,' explained a consultant working on transformation issues in the industry.[34]

It's a precarious existence. A police officer investigating taxi killings in KwaZulu-Natal said that, bizarrely, taxi bosses 'know exactly where they are in the line of succession and how close they are to being the next target on the hit list. Can you believe that they even get upset if someone lower-ranking than them gets killed first? They also usually know exactly when they will die. It is weird.'[35]

The mother associations also act as quasi-regulators, which is evident in their use of violence against competing forms of public transport, such as trains and buses. There has been a spate of attacks, for example, on Golden

Arrow buses and the MyCiti rapid-bus transport network in Cape Town. In the case of the former, taxi bosses told me a hitman had been hired to assassinate drivers and commuters. And in a recent case in Chatsworth, Durban, taxi operators publicly issued threats to local school lift clubs, warning them to stop operating.[36]

Across the country, as the taxi associations increasingly embodied the spirit of organised crime, they found themselves having to come to terms with other elements of South Africa's post-apartheid underworld, namely the criminal gangs. Power-sharing agreements were reached, the character of which depended on the strength of the two parties and their capacity to achieve a *pax mafiosa* accommodation.

In the Western Cape, for example, certain taxi associations are 'gang-aligned' and owners regularly have to pay protection fees to gangs who control the routes.[37] Gangs therefore provide a system of regulation, with taxi associations operating under their (criminalised) governance. Taxi owners who work in these areas are understandably reluctant to discuss the links in detail, but intimated that paying tribute fees to gangs was something that all business people had to deal with in that part of the world, and the taxi industry appears to be no exception.[38]

It is significant how, in many respects, these two criminal industries have become inextricably linked, each reinforcing the other, sustaining each other and exploiting a number of operational synergies. The taxi industry provides the criminal gangs and their drug-trafficking businesses convenient access to clientele – taxi ranks are prime markets for the sale of drugs – while taxis provide an ideal means of drug distribution. Meanwhile, investing in the taxi industry is an easy way for gangs to launder money in an industry with high cash turnover and little oversight.

Perhaps the synergy is not surprising. As a former government security official explained: 'For the "taxi mafia", which is involved in violence, intimidation and running protection rackets, the transition to dealing in other illicit activities is not necessarily a big leap to make, particularly if they make money.'[39]

It has always been the case that the long-distance routes have been the money spinners. These routes have for many years linked the rural and urban communities, and provided the movement of labour from out-lying townships to the cities. However, as organised-crime groups and taxi associations became more enmeshed, long-distance taxi operations became profitable for another reason – the transport of illegal com-modities. According to Charles Goredema, long-distance taxi operators 'provide a means by which to transport contraband from points of supply to markets rapidly, and in a relatively inconspicuous manner'.[40] From the late 1980s, long-distance taxi operators became critically important in dis-tributing illicit products, most notably cannabis, transporting the weed from source markets, such as Lesotho, Swaziland, the Eastern Cape and KwaZulu-Natal, to the Gauteng conurbation.[41]

As the taxi industry got into bed with the drug trade, a dramatic increase in levels of armed security became essential to protect its members. Money also had to be ring-fenced by operators for bribing police and traffic offic-ers along the routes.[42] As a consequence, in the period from 1994 to 1997, the murder toll related to taxi wars reached a peak, with an estimated 250 homicides a year – though it is difficult to determine whether these figures are linked to commercial competition for taxi routes, or contraband – if the two services can indeed be disentwined.

Counter-intuitively perhaps, this affiliation with the criminal fraternity did not sever the ties that the taxi industry has always had with local poli-tics. If anything, it served to strengthen the taxi industry's unofficial role as the neighbourhood provider of violence and protection. Taxi bosses, have often been, for example, at the centre of vigilante-style responses to crime in the local community. Yet despite this unofficial 'protection' role they play, there is recent evidence of conflict between communities and taxi organisations. In Masiphumelele, an informal settlement in Cape Town, residents and taxi owners clashed violently on several occasions in 2016 when taxis failed to support residents' boycotts and protests.[43]

Since the late 1990s, with the increasingly violent trajectory of the taxi industry – and its integration with criminal activity – there emerged within it a new business line: professional killing.

This began as a form of moonlighting – the muscle of the taxi industry would hire out the service to whomever might need it. As the case of Victor Small shows, the taxi bosses themselves did not mind rolling up their sleeves to spill some blood. Today, however, this is less often the case: the killing has become more specialised and more targeted, and the professional outsourced taxi hitman has emerged, hired by the warlords to eliminate unwanted enemies. A 2005 Committee of Inquiry into taxi violence in the Western Cape concluded: 'Previous taxi wars were characterised by the taxi owners themselves taking part in the shootings. It is a recent development of the last nine years that hitmen were hired.'[44] The likes of Simon (whom we met in the previous chapter) now fulfil that role.

The older cadre of taxi hitmen have largely been replaced by a younger, and in some ways more violent group, more profit-orientated, and willing to sell their skills. In the past, taxi hits often took the form of ambushes, with the target dying in public view in a hail of bullets, with passers-by likely to be caught in the crossfire. As a consultant who works for local government explained, the application of violence has become more discreet over time – it is less conspicuous than the taxi-war shoot-outs of the past. Today, the preference is for an assassination rather than a massacre, a transaction rather than a blood feud.[45]

Two factors appear to be behind the shift in the way assassinations are conducted. First, say some people in the industry, there is the sense that overt acts of public violence may attract too much attention. High-profile arrests made in central Durban in 2016, for example, have led to a growing reluctance to engage in public shoot-outs.

But perhaps the main reason for the shift is that taxi bosses often sur-round themselves with high levels of security to protect their interests. This has meant that hits have by necessity become increasingly sophis-ticated and professional, including drive-by shootings. In these cases, as one police officer said, there is a common pattern – usually a driver, who is unarmed, and a shooter, often with an AK-47. 'These guys would have received surveillance information … showing when their targets are most vulnerable. That is when they kill him – usually as he is arriving home or leaving; and the *izinkabi* don't care about killing whoever happens to be in the car with the target. Even his wife, or children,' he said.[46]

In short, the development of the taxi industry's hit culture has followed a growing commercialisation of violence. The hit is contracted out because it is easier, 'cleaner', that way. It resembles a business relationship, a service that is paid for to protect the taxi bosses and one that simultaneously sus-tains professional hitmen, like Simon.

The earlier generalised violence in the industry has evolved into this more specialised contracted mode, and driving the process is fear. 'Crossing the top bosses who sit in the mother body is not a healthy idea,' observed a former Johannesburg taxi boss.[47] Indeed, one of the more star-tling outcomes of this research is just how feared taxi bosses are. In the course of writing this book, it emerged that taxi bosses seem to be the underworld group who instil the most fear. Taxi owners and operators were clear why: taxi bosses use violence with abandon, on each other and on anyone who crosses their path to profit.

Subcontracted violence in the context of the taxi industry has been described as a commercial aspect of the business, like any other input. 'In the same way that you would replace tyres, or service vehicles, you need to kill people,' a former taxi boss, who has withdrawn from the industry fearing for his life, explained nonchalantly.[48]

And, more broadly, the taxi industry has, through a system of paying for violence (essentially a mafia-style commercialisation crime), been central to the expansion of violence to other parts of the underworld. Taxi hitmen are often part of the same networks as those involved in political and other assassinations, and have strong connections with armed robbery, cash-in-transit heists and other forms of violent organised crime. In effect, by having paid hitmen who are waiting on call, the taxi industry has sustained a pool of violent entrepreneurs. Understanding this is crucial to exposing the shape, evolution and violent nature of the South African underworld.

A key element in maintaining this system of violence is ready access to sophisticated firepower. In a recent raid conducted by police in Stanger and Kranskop, for example, of individuals linked to taxi associations 15 unlicensed firearms, including AK-47s, semi-automatic rifles and nine-millimetre pistols were seized, along with army and police bullet-proof vests.[49]

Guns stolen from police stations continue to find their way into the hands of taxi hitmen and it is reported that some policemen may be willing to 'hire out' weapons for a fee. The situation has been exacerbated by widespread corruption in the process of issuing registered firearms, with powerful taxi bosses, according to people close to the industry, arranging for licences for firearms for their drivers and the security companies guarding the taxi ranks.

The taxi industry in South Africa is a formidable case study in the formation of a mafia system. It was born in a period of enormous violence, linked to the turbulent politics of the day, and quickly became associated with criminal gangs, generating large numbers of violent individuals whose influence extends into the contemporary democracy.

Understanding some of the dynamics behind this trajectory can be informative in answering two important questions. Firstly, how has an industry that has done so much to provide mobility for the masses and wealth also became the source of so much violence? And, secondly, why and how has the industry become a nursery of a wider set of violent activities associated with organised crime in South Africa? To answer these questions requires looking at some of the basic principles about how mafia control begins.

Comparative analysis of the growth of mafia-like protection rackets suggests that some industries are more attractive to criminals than others. One of the most compelling features to organised crime groups, in any industry, however, is the ability to identify and control key choke points – or areas of vulnerability – in a market. James Cockayne, in his masterly study of the development of organised crime in New York, gives the example of truckers and stevedores, who were major entry points for the mafia in the 1930s because they were in a position to control the movement of goods, making companies highly vulnerable to extortion. The organised-crime mobs effectively forced corporations to pay a fee to keep their businesses afloat.[50]

Where a situation of extortion such as this is applied by criminal groups, it is almost impossible to resist without going out of business. Over time, acquiescence allows mafia groups to penetrate the very sinews of the economy, proving extremely difficult to eradicate.

The taxi industry in South Africa provided the same opportunity for organised crime to take control. Since the era of political turmoil and social uprisings, the taxi industry has been a foundational driver of the South African economy. In addition, it had no effective regulation, making it a soft touch with few barriers to prevent criminal interests from entering. It therefore presented an attractive prospect for mafia-like control. And it offers an additional layer of appeal to organised crime, as it provides an easy means of laundering criminal proceeds.

But although the entry points in this industry may have made it readily accessible by mafia-type control, the sheer level of violence generated by the taxi industry is bewildering. Mafia-type systems, all over the world, rely on the deployment – or threat – of violence. However, the extraordinary levels of violence and the development of a contract-killing culture arguably make South Africa's taxi industry stand out. These features are by-products of the violent period of South Africa's political transition into which the industry was born. The presence of a violent political process, armed men and organised criminal operations were defining factors of the environment in which the industry developed. It was perhaps this that caused the industry to evolve into its current iteration, where it now provides resources and infrastructure to other political and criminal activities.

The taxi industry continues to evolve, but it still remains central to the South African economy and life of the community. Minibus taxis are estimated to transport 60 per cent of the total South African workforce from home to work and back. In 2013 the Gauteng Department of Roads and Transport alone had 180 registered taxi associations and 62 500 taxi operators. The scale of the industry and its importance make it perpetually hard to regulate and constantly vulnerable to criminal control. In the 17-year period for which we have data, the highest number of taxi-related hits occurred in 2016. Despite nearly two decades of efforts by government, the industry remains predominantly criminally governed and extremely violent, and this will leave a lasting legacy in the country and hamper its efforts to achieve the rule of law and a stable democracy.

Taxi bosses are often powerful community figures, enmeshed in local politics. Although that is not necessarily a bad thing, it is worrying that the mafia-like attributes of the taxi business and its linkages to local politics subvert the operation of municipal-level democracy and replace it with the threat of violence.

To portray the taxi industry as exclusively a negative phenomenon would be disingenuous, however. It remains a critical artery in the lives of many communities. The majority of pupils who attend school outside of their immediate neighbourhoods use taxis.[51] The industry has provided enormous opportunities for individual entrepreneurship and enrichment, and has played an iconic role in South Africa's political and economic transition. Taxi bosses are often people who have made good in trying circumstances. Owning a taxi is often the first step on the economic ladder for many of the country's poor. The stakes are often high: an all-or-nothing struggle to make it as a local 'big man'.

It has been shown elsewhere, notably in the study of the mafia in Italy, that how local forms of governance evolve is crucial to the shaping of later forms of organised crime, and thereby the nature of the relationships between the upper and underworld.[52] The newly emergent taxi bosses (and we will come back to this later) have formed alliances with local political figures across the country. At the same time, they have brought with them the tools of the taxi trade, including the practice of eliminating those who stand in their way.

# 4

## Cyril Beeka:
## Clubs, drugs and the ultimate hit

odderdam Road, a busy Cape Town thoroughfare, was renamed Robert Sobukwe Road in honour of the anti-apartheid activist and founder of the Pan Africanist Congress. The name change took place exactly two years to the day – 21 March 2013 – after the road had been the scene of one of the most notorious underworld assassinations of South Africa's democratic era: the killing of criminal boss Cyril Beeka.

The name changes that were applied to several major Cape Town roads marked a symbolic shedding of apartheid-era labels in a move towards honouring people more widely representative of the city. Beeka would have welcomed the name change. He had established himself in the criminal economy as one political era was ending and a new one was being constructed – and he seemed to cross effortlessly from one regime to the next.

It was a Monday afternoon. Beeka was on one of his periodic business visits to the city. He had been spending more and more time away from the Cape at his place in Pretoria, but there were reports that he intended to move back to the city of his birth. On this occasion he was visiting Jerome 'Donkie' Booysen, the infamous leader of the Sexy Boys gang. Since Beeka had moved up-country ten years earlier, there had been major changes in the underworld, including the emergence of some powerful criminal networks with whom Beeka seems to have been associated. Booysen was the leader of one of them and a man whose power had been growing.

Beeka's driver, Dobrosav Gavrić, had just brought the BMW 4 x 4 to a halt at traffic lights in Belville South, not far from Donkie Booysen's home, when a motorbike with two men on it pulled up alongside. There was a flurry of gunfire – some reports saying as many as 30 shots were fired. Beeka, who appeared to be the target, was hit in the chest, arms and head. Gavrić described the incident as follows:

> Cyril had turned in his seat … facing the driver's side window. … I saw something stop but it was out of the corner of my eye. The next thing I recall was hearing two loud bangs going off. I was hit in my right arm as well as my left one and I noticed that Cyril had been hit in the chest. It sounded like a shotgun went off. There was smoke and glass and I was a bit confused. Then I came to my senses and I noticed a motorbike on my right-hand side. Then more shots were fired in succession.[1]

Gavrić's immediate reaction was to slam the car into reverse – a smart move given how difficult it would be for a motorbike with two people on it to reverse or turn around to chase the BMW. When the bike sped off, he chased it down Modderdam Road, despite his wounds, firing shots at the two riders, but apparently without hitting them. Things seemed to get hazy after that: 'The next thing I recall was my motor vehicle lifting off the ground and I lost control.' The BMW rolled, coming to a stop outside the University of the Western Cape. Beeka died shortly afterwards.

A hammerman from the Cape Flats, who appeared to have been involved in Beeka's death, or at least knew who was, was later killed in what appears to have been a deliberate hit. He was about to turn state witness. By all accounts, it looked like a case of dead men don't talk.

After the shooting in Modderdam Road, the foreign driver of the car gave a false name to the police. His real identity emerged only later. Mysteriously, and in a detail that would not be amiss in a Cold War spy novel, Gavrić turned out to be a Serbian fugitive from justice. A former police officer with close ties to the Serbian underworld, Gavrić had been responsible for perhaps the most prominent assassination in post-war Serbia – the killing of a paramilitary commander, Željko Ražnatović, known as Arkan. Ražnatović had been indicted by the International Criminal Tribunal of the former Yugoslavia for crimes against humanity. Gavrić was reputed to have links to the Serbian intelligence service, and may well have been acting on their instruction in the murder of Arkan. By the time his 35-year sentence was handed down, Gavrić had simply vanished – reappearing again as Beeka's driver in the Belville shoot-out.

And, just like his driver, Beeka also occupied the shadowy zone where the underworld meets the state. He was understood to have been an informer for the apartheid-era Security Branch and later for the post-apartheid National Intelligence Agency.

Whatever the truth about Beeka's murder, there are interesting parallels between the evolution of the Serbian and South African underworlds, with both countries undergoing political transition and with criminal linkages to state-security structures. Those connections could not have been better symbolised than by these two men trapped in a car with multiple bullet holes. In different ways, they both represented the evolution of the South African underworld, and its connections to global illicit networks. The violent market where these connections coalesced was in the booming night-time economy. Paralleling the taxi business, the clubs and drugs scene in South Africa grew rapidly, attracting a set of violent entre-preneurs who sought to profit from its regulation.

## A tale of two cities:
## Markets for violence in Cape Town and Johannesburg

Beeka's was a story of a lower-middle-class boy who made it. But it was an upward trajectory soaked in blood. Although he was involved in several criminal markets, Beeka's core business model was one built on violence – or its threat. He targeted the burgeoning club and drugs market in Cape Town, extorting business owners into paying for protection. Those who failed to do so faced the brutal consequences: smashed-up establishments and injured staff.

Interestingly, Beeka was not, as might be expected, a product of the gangs of the Cape Flats. One of eight children, whose father was the principal of the school that he attended, he graduated with a degree in mechanical engineering from the Cape Peninsula University of Technology. Cyril's early love was karate, for which he had a black belt. Karate and sports clubs were his opening – as is the case with entrepreneurs of violence in several other places – to the world of protection rackets.

He was characterised by a contradictory personality – both highly social but prone to bouts of violence. 'He was absolutely ruthless,' said one source, 'and often unpredictable.'² By the end of his life, Beeka had gathered around him a network of contacts spanning the upper and underworlds. This was nowhere more evident than at his funeral, which was attended by an assortment of gangsters, state intelligence officers, members of the Hell's Angels Motorcycle Club, and prominent ex-Springbok rugby players. What's more, the funeral was conducted as if it were an official ANC event, with Beeka's coffin draped in the party colours, a clear sign of his allegiance to his political masters in the new regime.[3]

At the time of his death, it was said that he was involved in a high-level entrapment operation involving the drug trade.[4] Beeka had also been quoted publicly as saying that he acted as a bodyguard for prominent ANC, and later government, intelligence figure Mo Shaik.[5]

The funeral was the end of an era in the underworld, and Beeka's killing one of the most sensational hits that the post-apartheid underworld has seen, ending his reign of terror. This is because Beeka was a definitive figure in the early post-apartheid criminal economy, a man of notorious repute, who, by using his state and criminal connections to shape a protection business, opened the way for others to follow.

Beeka established a wide network of underworld linkages – including a relationship with another Serb, Radovan Krejcir, whom we will meet again later in the book. His murder was part of a major realignment of power among a network of some of the underworld's most well-known and ruthless operators, whose criminal origins, like Beeka's, could be traced to the violent days of late-apartheid and the first uncertain days of the new order.

Entrepreneurs of violence, like Beeka, emerge in environments where there are opportunities for violence to be bought and sold. Such opportunities had unquestionably existed before in South African history, but new openings for the violent entrepreneur began to emerge in the late 1980s in several South African cities.

This pattern began to take shape in Johannesburg, when a group of white nightclub bouncers moved into the market to take advantage of the burgeoning night-time entertainment economy. These were the years of the state of emergency, declared in 1985, and the final decade of the apartheid order. The white regime was still in control, but that control was slipping, the changing order in the upperworld being reflected down under too.

Meanwhile, there were other changes under way as the country's illegal drugs market evolved. In the late 1990s, drug addiction was becoming rampant on the Cape Flats, with disastrous social consequences.[6] Control over drug distribution fuelled vicious conflicts between the gangs, exacerbated by an influx of illegal firearms. Today this ongoing drug conflict is reflected in the city's astronomical homicide rate.[7] As we will see in the following chapter, Cape Town's murder rate places it on a par with urban complexes in Central and Latin America, where forms of violent entrepreneurship are central to controlling drugs and extortion-based criminal economies.

In Cape Town's inner city, the club scene had been controlled since around the late 1980s by a network of white bouncers – who also cornered the lucrative distribution of drugs in the clubs – following much the same pattern as in Johannesburg. According to interviews with people familiar with the period,[8] lack of security in the inner city and the inability of the police to control crime provided an opportunity for the development of this bouncer system of control, which was linked to the gangs of the Cape Flats.

After the end of white rule in 1994, the Mother City became a major pull for both locals and foreign tourists, eager to sample the urban attractions of the new South Africa.[9] Cape Town's night-time economy had two main centres: the central business district, and the entertainment venues of the northern suburbs, which catered largely for the burgeoning white middle-class suburban developments there.

For these entertainment businesses, Cyril Beeka established a mafia-type system of violent extortion protection in the 1990s. Beeka had spotted a gap in the protection market – a strategy that he may have owed to Vito Palazzolo, an Italian mafia figure then resident in Cape Town, whom we will encounter again in Chapter 6. Palazzolo is said to have suggested to Beeka that the Italian system of '*pizzo*', or forced protection payments, might work nicely in the Cape club scene.[10] Beeka's approach was to enforce an 'exclusive contract', whereby his clients would feel less threatened by the gangs, but would be locked into a deal for protection with Beeka's security company. It was an innovative idea – the inner city was seen as unsafe, plagued by violent crime perpetrated by gangs, and meanwhile the police had bigger priorities. But it was an operation based on violence and the threat of it – something in which Beeka and his men became practised experts.

Beeka operated through his two security companies, Pro Access and Red Security, which approached entertainment outfits offering to provide 'protection' for a fee. Businesses that refused the service deeply regretted it. They would be trashed and their staff assaulted. 'These guys would just come in,' an owner of a bar on Long Street told me, 'and smash the place up. There was not much that you could do. The patrons would flee – and business would turn bad. Nobody would want to drink in a place where things would get nasty. It was better to pay. We almost all did.'[11]

People I spoke to recounted how intimidation was applied to best effect when venues were full, so as to achieve maximum impact. Patrons would then witness the destruction as Beeka's security men would 'throw glasses around and break everything'.[12]

The police seldom, if ever, arrived on time, almost deliberately, it seemed, so as to avoid confrontation.[13] When a club had been roughed up, any charges that had been laid with the police would 'disappear' and, in several cases, CCTV footage that the police had acquired would not see the light of day.[14] It was to become an all-too-familiar pattern and soon entertainment venues in the city centre could do little to avoid protection payments to Beeka's security companies.[15] Beeka's approach incorporated a toxic mix of real and symbolic violence. A business owner in central Cape Town told me that the arrangement was driven by fear, and nobody, it appeared, was willing to stand up and be counted. It was just easier to pay.[16] The power of the protection economy seemed greater than that of the state.

Meanwhile, Beeka negotiated a strategic agreement with the Cape Flats gangs, whereby the city centre was off limits to them and, in return, they would receive a share of the proceeds to keep out of his lucrative territory.[17]

Beeka's links to the state appeared to provide him with impunity. Even though a long list of police cases against him mounted over the years, from petty theft to murder, he never served a day in prison. As mentioned, before 1994 Beeka seemed to have been an informer for the apartheid police's Security Branch and was described by an ANC politician quoted in the press as a 'low-level courier' for the liberation movement.[18] What this means exactly is unclear, although presumably it entailed transporting money, documents or guns that were needed at various places.

But, as in all such arrangements, there must have been some reciprocity between Beeka and his partners in the state and the ANC, most notably in terms of keeping him out of jail. The same politician, who spoke on condition of anonymity, said: 'It soon became apparent that he was involved in drug smuggling and other shady dealings. Everyone knew he was an informer for the old intelligence service. ... He seemed to be protected.'[19]

Beeka gained this extraordinary degree of immunity from the law through the links he established with the police and the intelligence service. On one occasion after having been arrested, Beeka simply phoned his intelligence handler and pointed out to the police a file of 'intelligence reports' in his car to show that he worked for the state and could not be arrested.

But he also made sure he protected himself through his own mechanisms of violence. As Beeka ascended to power in the underworld, various players rose up to challenge him. One gang leader said: 'They were almost all taken out or assimilated. If they were assimilated they were watched closely, as they were never trusted.'[20]

When the newly formed law-enforcement unit, the Scorpions, made a point of trying to crack down on extortion in Cape Town, eager to demonstrate that the democratic government could fight the growing scourge of organised crime, they ran into a wall not of bouncers, but of lawyers – also forced onto the businesses by Beeka. When the Scorpions tried to interview business owners, the lawyers would sit in. A former member of the Scorpions said: 'All the statements ended up saying that there had been no coercion … that the people had agreed to [Beeka's protection] voluntarily.'[21] It was simply too dangerous to resist, a former bar owner told me.[22]

Another innovative technique of Beeka's was to use his private-security operation as an umbrella for a range of other criminal activities, such as drug trafficking, prostitution, the disposal of stolen goods and violently enforced debt collection.[23] An officially registered company provided not only a way to legitimise ill-gotten gains, but also a veneer of respectability to what was essentially a mafia operation.

In direct competition with Beeka's Pro Access Security, a former military officer, Andre Naudé, allegedly started up a similar extortion racket, Professional Protection Services, which operated in parts of the city's northern, predominantly white, suburbs.[24] Ironically, and this is an example of the power of criminal money to break down racial boundaries, Professional Protection Services drew its muscle from Donkie Booysen's Sexy Boys, a Cape Flats gang of violent repute. The gang was commandeered when violence was needed to maintain control.

In the Cape Town extortion economy, the provision of 'muscle' existed at two levels. At the door of the clubs were the bouncers, many of Congolese origin,[25] men who were less expensive to hire than the original white bouncer brigade, and many of them refugees from the war in the Congo keen to find work. Even when clubs employed their own bouncers, they were still locked into the 'services' of the security company. That service was offered, or more precisely enforced, as a backup. The security companies made it clear to the club bouncers who called the shots (quite literally). Under Beeka, one bouncer told me, the message was clear: 'While you are paid by the club, you work for us. You can keep your job, but we make the rules.'[26] This way, the bouncers were drawn into the network of violent control. The extortion racket could still function, as could the control of drug sales, even where bouncers were on contract to the club. It can be seen as a staged process of takeover of the club market by the security companies, with extortion being the central tool of enforcement.

Then, there were groups of enforcers, who provided stand-by support, appearing only when the application of violence was necessary. In the case of Beeka's Pro Access Security, these men were recruited from the Moroccans gang (named after their leader's nationality). These enforcers were the front end of the extortion business.[27] (The Moroccans also provided security to Palazzolo.)

The Cape Town protection rackets relied therefore on a supply chain of violence commissioned from the gangs on the city's periphery and applied in their city-centre operations. This was in marked contrast to the way things developed in Johannesburg – with significant implications for the long-term survival of the criminal enterprise in that city.

Although Beeka was a criminal innovator, his position was always precarious. According to several sources, various attempts were made on his life. It is said that Beeka had moved to Johannesburg in part to evade the threat posed by his underworld opponents as his Cape Town business grew. He is said to have tried a similar formula up-country, but was beaten back.[28] The threats he experienced on his home turf and the attempts on his life show the fragility of senior figures within the South African underworld – a theme that we will come back to again.

The fight for control of the extortion, prostitution and drug-distribution businesses in Cape Town had seen a prominent hit in 2007. Yuri Ulianitski, known in Cape Town as Yuri the Russian (he was Ukrainian) was murdered on his birthday on 29 May 2007, along with his daughter. Ulianitski had arrived in Cape Town in the 1990s, where he forged contacts with the local underworld and worked as the bodyguard for a powerful gang leader, Rashied Staggie of the Hard Livings (whose twin brother, Rashaad, was killed by vigilantes in 1996 in a spate of hits targeted at Cape Town's criminal elite). Ulianitski graduated over time into the local extortion business.[29]

By the time of his death, Ulianitski was said to be the 'don' of the downtown area, having joined forces with Beeka. In the complicated overlaying sets of allegiances that characterised the underworld, however, Ulianitski was also a business partner with an up-and-coming and widely feared businessman who had strong links to the underworld – Mark Lifman. He and Lifman were said to own a strip joint in the city centre.[30] They were also accused of using life threats and other forms of violence to fix horse races, for which Lifman received a life ban from the racing fraternity.[31]

After Ulianitski's death, Beeka is said to have become even more aware of the possibility that he might be next in line. In the months before he was murdered, he gathered around him a group of bodyguards. They were Serbs – presumably because they were more trustworthy than the local variety – among them the fugitive Dobrosav Gavrić, who would later be the driver of the ill-fated BMW on Modderdam Road.

Neither Ulianitski nor Beeka's deaths have been solved, and it is increasingly unlikely that Beeka's ever will. Leon Davids, a hitman said to have information on the Beeka case, presumably because he was somehow involved, was assassinated as he was on the verge of turning state witness and entering a witness-protection programme – another sign of how fragile the ecosystem of violence is. Their deaths nevertheless are two prominent reminders of the violent processes of criminal consolidation around the extortion economy in Cape Town.

Beeka's departure, given that he had controlled his empire with an iron fist, led to a short period of instability in the market, followed by a rapid – some might say too rapid – alignment of night-time security in the city under one umbrella service, Specialised Protection Services.[32] At the time of writing, this outfit currently dominates the market. Lifman and Booysen are said to be the men behind the operation – underworld innovators in their own right, like Beeka. Interviews with people close to the process suggest that they have attempted to legitimise their activities (if that can be possible), reduce the levels of violence and distance the main beneficiaries from the day-to-day functioning of the overt operations of the business.[33] Attempts to crack down on their private-security operations have largely failed.[34] Lifman, who has had several run-ins with the law, has also fallen afoul of the tax authorities and has of late assumed a lower profile.[35]

Whether their operations are sustainable is unclear. For one, in the context of a booming tourist economy, which the City of Cape Town authorities are eager to promote, Cape Town's city centre is now the most popular tourist attraction in the city, ahead of the Waterfront,[36] so it is unlikely that violence linked to the protection economy will be tolerated – especially given that the Democratic Alliance-controlled city government is well aware of the extortion market and keen to root it out. As we shall see, however, a recent spate of violence in early 2017 suggests that all is not well in the Cape underworld.

Turning to Johannesburg, it is interesting how the city, which initially spawned a similar violent extortion economy around the club scene, now looks so different from the Cape Town environment. The pre-1994 Johannesburg underworld was a place where the state-security apparatus, privatised entrepreneurs of violence, pimps and an emerging set of drug traffickers mixed freely.

Around the late 1980s and early 1990s, Johannesburg's white 'bouncer mafia' gained control of access to the clubs – many of them in Hillbrow at the time. Before the days of mobile phones, nightclubs were the main distribution channel for selling drugs. Increasingly, clubs depended on profits from the drugs sold within them, and those who controlled these venues were often well positioned to gain from the growing drug trade.[37]

The club owners needed security and the police were too overstretched to supply it, so they turned to networks of bouncers to provide the service. These white heavies generally had military experience. They constituted what they themselves have described as 'a tribe'. It says much about South Africa at the time that many were police officers moonlighting to supplement their wages.[38]

These bouncer networks, which purported to be private-security operations, were in reality little more than mafia protection rackets. Club owners were extorted into taking on their services – and, as in Cape Town, those who did not quickly found their clubs threatened or destroyed.[39]

Johannesburg's sprawling conurbation gave rise to several new centres for the night-time economy, which meant that various security providers emerged, competing for a slice of this large, geographically dispersed market. The violence associated with the city's drugs market was strongly associated with territorial control of the clubs.[40] For the most part, particularly from the early 2000s, this competition took the form of isolated shootings and assassination-style killings, but there were also several high-profile incidents where groups attacked each other warfare-style.

Eventually, Johannesburg's illicit drug trade fell under the control of three dominant security groups – Diplomat, EPS and Viper – who carved out the city's club-drugs market among themselves.[41] Their fiercely guarded territorial boundaries were tested on occasion, with predictably violent results, but remained broadly stable for about a decade. One bouncer recalled a particular club raid carried out by a competing group: 'They tried to take over Joburg one night. They came to a club called Vertigo in Illovo. They thought, "Fuck you, we're going to take over Joburg." But let me tell you, they got fucked up instead.' When an ambulance arrived to take the injured to hospital, a member of this bouncer's outfit took the ignition keys and threw them away.[42]

From the outside, this kind of violence could appear gratuitous, but it was closely linked to the control of turf. The Vertigo incident also illustrates a characteristic feature of the kind of violence adopted by the security companies in Johannesburg in those days. Guns would be largely absent, or at least hidden. But the level of violence was often extreme, with groups of bouncers piling into individuals and kicking them on the ground. People were seriously injured in these melees. Some former bouncers in interviews hark back to this as a 'golden age' – there was extreme violence but not in the shape of the coldly targeted assassinations that have developed more recently. This mirrors the phenomenon we saw in the taxi industry in the previous chapter, where there was a shift over time from more overt to covert violence. The assaults were bloody and people got badly hurt, but they occurred openly.

This open violence between the bouncer groups gradually gave way to a series of more targeted encounters. In one particular case in December 2002 a well-known bouncer, Patrick Caetano, was targeted in a revenge killing as the groups competed for turf. Caetano was brutally murdered with a butcher's knife in a parking lot in Kyalami, north of Johannesburg. As befitted the mafia style of the business, the police investigating officer was repeatedly harassed and threatened.[43] One of the suspects in the case was said to have links to the Israeli mafia, who were responsible for a spate of hits in the country in the early 2000s (we examine this briefly in Chapter 6).

The geographical territorial agreement – a *pax mafiosa* – that had been brokered by the three major security companies that controlled the Johannesburg night-time economy began to break down as a new entrant into the market appeared. The new group, Elite, deployed significantly higher levels of violence than its predecessors in its bid to take control of the whole Johannesburg club and drugs market. This disruption they managed to achieve fairly quickly. A former partner of Elite explained their undeniably pragmatic business model: 'We would tell club owners, "It's better you don't use your own security." We would send guys to make trouble if they didn't say yes. They didn't really have a choice.'[44]

The dominance that Elite managed to maintain over this market was shored up by high doses of violence, racial prejudice and extortion across Johannesburg. While at first it was impossible for any security group to enter the market during the period that Elite exerted its monopoly-like grip, by the early 2000s, however, its dominance had begun to slip. The group started to gain notoriety for acts of violence, as they diversified into murder, debt collecting or 'just sorting people out'.[45] Elite had crossed too many lines. Its expansion into the market for general violence led it to become vilified by the public and, more importantly for its demise, targeted by the police.

One of Elite's former partners, Mikey Schultz, would later confess to shooting and killing businessman Brett Kebble in 2005, in what was apparently set up to be a bizarre case of an arranged suicide. Kebble, entangled in a web of fraud and commercial crime that was progressively being exposed, appeared to have arranged his own murder partly to ensure a life-insurance payout to his family. Shultz (having by this stage left Elite), who was widely known in the Johannesburg bouncer community as having a propensity for violence, was approached to do the job. He and his two accomplices, Nigel McGurk and Faizel Smith, were given immunity from prosecution in exchange for testifying against drug trafficker Glenn Agliotti, the man who allegedly had masterminded Kebble's killing.[46]

The beginning of the end of Johannesburg's bouncer mafia was driven by a series of factors. The complexion of Johannesburg's night-time economy began to change as the club heartland shifted – as did the economic pulse of the city – away from the downtown area into the wealthier north-ern suburbs. That had implications for how bouncer 'crews' worked.

To protect the growing number of clubs under its charge, Elite had developed a mobile force of men, who could move to wherever trouble was brewing. In the end, however, the shifting terrain of the night-time venues across Greater Johannesburg made that strategy unsustainable. As the market's territory widened, Elite found that its zone of influence and capacity for violence were spread too thinly to be effective in an industry that depended on heavies exerting pressure.

Unlike in Cape Town, there was no possibility to contract in backup muscle in the form of township gangsters, with whom the white bouncers had little connection and whom they did not trust.[47] In many respects, then, racial boundaries were also part of the undoing of the white bouncer mafia in Johannesburg. Meanwhile, internal conflicts among the partners of Elite, often over the drug trade that they were overseeing, accelerated the firm's end.[48] Soon venues were recruiting their own protection services.

Interestingly, the decline of the bouncer mafia in Johannesburg mir-rored the drop in numbers of white police officers in the force. The easy relationship that these two groups had once enjoyed ended with apart-heid as a growing cadre of black police officers came onto the streets. Old cosy relations based on trust – and race – were now replaced by new ones based on financial exchange. For the cash-strapped and foundering Elite, this financial relationship proved untenable as new actors, offering greater sums, began to enter the market.

But there was another factor that had been thwarting the likes of Elite and the domination of the white mafia networks in Johannesburg. In the late 1990s and early 2000s Nigerian criminal networks started to infil-trate the drugs market (we will return to this later). Nigerians had been moving into Johannesburg during a period when the bouncer companies were finding it hard to recruit new white members prepared to do the job. So, increasingly, black men, many of them immigrant Nigerians, who were prepared to work for lower rates than their white counterparts, filled the vacuum. There was a ready network of Nigerian drug dealers eager to enter the club market and the nature of their close community connections with their compatriot bouncers supported them in this.

The owner of a private-security company that Elite had eviscerated may have had little respect for the opportunistic new entrants,[49] but it cannot be denied that their impact on the club and drugs markets, combined with redoubled police attention drawn by the horrific levels of violence meted out by Elite's men, helped spell the end of the once undisputed market leader. Violence in and around the clubs became increasingly bad for business and, say club owners from the time, it was increasingly clear that the problem lay, ironically, with the very people who claimed to be providing security. Elite, now weakened by internal conflict, was increasingly unable to police its turf. By the early 2000s, club owners began to turn to Nigerian bouncers to provide their security. With control much more in the hands of a network of Nigerian dealers, the days of the big security provider were over. This has meant a shift in the control of the city's drugs market and, simultaneously, a significant reduction in violence associated with 'protecting' the trade.

The Nigerian criminal networks are now well entrenched in Johannesburg, operating discreetly as they fill the gap left by the implosion of the white bouncer mafia. They have made some attempts to break into the market in Cape Town too, but, there, they have been rebuffed or are firmly controlled by other parties regulating the trade.[50] In Cape Town, Nigerian dealer networks are careful to align themselves with the existing protection order without assuming a dominant role. 'They know what they can do and what they can't,' said an ex-gang member, 'and they have formed alliances with the powers that be, rather than being able to control the place.'[51]

An intriguing question is why the Nigerians did not openly adopt the role of violent entrepreneurs in the manner of the white 'bouncer mafia' who had preceded them. As we will see later, Nigerian criminal networks can be extraordinarily violent, but that violence is generally carefully controlled and targeted at weak points in the criminal economy. Nigerian networks, at least in the early 2000s in Johannesburg, were too vulnerable to engage in public displays of violence in and around the club scene. Based on conversations with people close to and part of the networks, it appears that because Nigerians are outsiders, and therefore lack local roots, they are more vulnerable and more easily identifiable. That is a product of the xenophobic society in which they set up business. As a result, they are more likely to be targeted by the police if they behave violently (even if it is bribes that the police are after, as opposed to justice).[52]

In Johannesburg, according to former bouncers and current Nigerian ones, for Nigerians to threaten club owners with violence through the creation of a protection economy would have seen a counter-reaction, including a public outcry and resulting political and police responses. Effective systems of extortion almost always require a highly localised presence, embedded in local systems of power and politics. This is something that the Nigerians do not possess. Instead, they have chosen to play to their strengths, establishing an unrivalled capacity to network across the clubs through a system of drug dealers who moved easily and quickly where the supply was needed. If Elite's business model was high profile and violent, the Nigerian strategy was exactly the opposite.

It is a radically different approach from the top-down, highly structured system we see in the same Cape Town markets of violence, and it says much about how certain criminal groups may take control by stealth, as beneficiaries of changes in social, political and structural conditions.

The one exception to these developments in Johannesburg perhaps also reinforces the same conclusion. Along the mining towns stretching away to the east of the city, the bouncer networks tend to remain white-controlled. But the forces of social change are likely to sweep them away too. They are an ageing crowd and few these days are able to put solid security or military credentials on the table. When it comes to capacity for violence, the white Johannesburg underworld has largely moved on. When Radovan Krejcir's violent reign of terror got underway, the old bouncer network was too old or too distant to be recruited to conduct hits.[53] This group, many still involved in or connected to criminal networks, are increasingly purchasers of, and not practitioners in, the markets of violence.

## The conditions for mafia-style protection economies: A South African perspective

As I said in the Introduction, 'mafia' is not a term that is widely used in reference to South Africa's criminal world. Yet the stories of the development of violent men around the drug and club scene in Cape Town and Johannesburg suggest that perhaps it should be.

A significant body of work has now identified the core function of mafia groups as the provision of enforced protection to legal and illegal activities.[54] In short, mafia-style groups, through their capacity to engage in violence, or to assert the threat of violence, and their ability to leverage social and political influence, are well positioned to extort tributes or fees under the guise of protection.[55] An opening to do that occurs when the state is unable (given that the market is illegal) or too weak to assume that role. The hard men from the mafia markets are often drawn upon for contracted violence, including targeted murder, or 'really hurting someone so they can't feel the pain', as an ex-bouncer told me.

Mafia rackets therefore make money primarily from delivering protection as a commodity, or selling their capacity to be violent as a marketable product in its own right – or what we have encountered as the entrepreneurialism of violence.[56] What's interesting though is that most people who sell violence are not very good at selling other stuff. So, one can in most cases make a distinction between criminal entrepreneurs and violent entrepreneurs. In more academic language, that means that the provision of protection must be distinguished from a different set of transnational organised-criminal 'business' activities, such as illicit smuggling or trafficking, which involve a range of actors that mirror production and supply chains in the legitimate economy, with producers, processors, transporters and vendors.

The strongmen often make a mess of the business side of organised crime. For example, I have worked in the West African state of Guinea-Bissau. There the military (effectively the strongest men in town), who were paid by drug traffickers to protect their shipments and move them through the country, were onto something very profitable when they confined themselves only to the muscle side of things. The hard men got greedy, though, and tried to take over the trade itself, and that's when they made themselves vulnerable to the actions of the US Drug Enforcement Agency. On one occasion, for example, a member of the network was lured into international waters. He thought he was sailing out to sign a lucrative drug deal, but it turned out to be an entrapment operation and the would-be dealer ended up in a New York courtroom in handcuffs.[57] The sellers of violence are an exclusive group and it is often better for their business model if they don't diversify into other activities.

Being a strongman has another dimension too. They often need to operate close to home, or at least in a place where they have a strong local network. Although it does not focus on the South African context, a landmark study by Oxford University's Federico Varese seeks to understand how mafia groups move or expand their operations. Varese concludes that mafia organisations are essentially stationary and tied to a particular place:

[T]he service they provide is inherently local. They ensure selective access to resources in a given territory. In order to do so, they build a long-term relationship with the place in which they operate as well as with the people, officeholders and the police ... As a rule, political (and criminal) reputations are local and are the product of costly investments.[58]

Crime bosses therefore often have an ambit of influence that is confined to the local environment – or at least they start out that way. This means that protection rackets tend to be highly localised, concentrated where the bosses' recruiting networks and connections lie. As a study on trafficking highlights, the flows of illicit commodities may be transnational but their control is very much local.[59] That notion fits well with the experience of the protection rackets seen in South Africa, and says important things as to how and when foreign criminals may find opportunities in a new country (the theme of Chapter 6, which explores the way in which foreign criminal networks have established themselves in South Africa).

Specific sets of conditions must therefore be present to allow mafia groups to emerge, establish themselves and become rooted over time – and for them to sustain their position. I would suggest that four key criteria must exist simultaneously as preconditions for the establishment and growth of violent entrepreneurialism.

First, there needs to be a radical change in the structure of a market, or, as Varese puts it, a 'sudden boom in a market that is not governed by the state can lead to a demand for criminal protection'.[60] Such a market change is most apparent where a commodity is illegal, such as illicit drugs. As we have seen, the opportunities provided by the rapid and unregulated growth of the taxi industry had a similar impact in South Africa. But that change must take place against a broader set of factors related to how that commodity is distributed and sold, and most particularly where it can be safely marketed. In other words, specific markets must be secured for criminal activity.

Secondly, the development of mafia groups requires the presence of a network of individuals with the ability and predisposition to engage in violence, and a social and political context in which they can be recruited. This will often mean that they are drawn from a similar ethnic community or class or social group, like the mafia culture in the first waves of the Italian diaspora in the US, which *The Godfather* movies draw upon so vividly. To give another example, Vadim Volkov notes how in the former Soviet Union the criminal protection market grew out of a recruitment pool of young men who were members of boxing and martial-arts clubs (the same recruitment locations, interestingly, as some bouncer mobsters in South Africa).[61]

A third condition is that state institutions need to be weak or compromised, and unable to mount a response to the emerging criminal network until it is too late. In these circumstances, the state may choose to accommodate or collaborate with criminal organisations for its own ends. Such conditions may occur when agencies of the state are threatened or challenged by other forces and seek alliances with emerging criminal protection groups with the intention of shaping them for their own purposes. Beeka's relationship with the pre- and post-apartheid security establishment is a case in point.

The final factor that facilitates the development of mafia groups is that other (i.e. non-state) forces regulating the criminal market must not be present. This may include other criminal organisations that are already established, creating barriers to entry. New criminal networks entering criminal markets where there are established actors often do so by stealth, rather than by direct confrontation, and thus become well placed to assume market control when existing organisations weaken or fragment. How the Nigerians gained influence over the bouncer mafia in Johannesburg is one such example.

For these four conditions to be in place at the same time, there must be some significant disruptions or shifts in political, economic or social conditions. For this reason, political transitions, sustained periods of conflict or other dramatic system disruptors, such as major economic changes, like de-industrialisation, have the potential to give rise to new criminalised forces.[62]

In South Africa the necessary conditions for criminal opportunity were created by a number of such disruptors – the conflictual political transition, development of the night-time economy and growth of the drug markets in Johannesburg and Cape Town. While these provided the ideal preconditions – and many of these conditions were similar for both cities – the nature of local contexts has also been central to shaping the drugs market, and mafia groups, and, consequently, the way that organised crime has unfolded in both cities.

So, how can organised crime in the context of South Africa's two major cities be understood against the criteria identified as preconditions for the emergence of the mafia? At a macro level, two of these four preconditions were already present in both cities. The first was the disruptive nature of the political transition, both in the years leading up to 1994 and in the immediate aftermath, leading to weakened state institutions. Policing resources were focused elsewhere and the police had limited skills or legislative tools to deploy in the face of organised crime.

The second factor was the growth of the drugs market in South Africa, and the networks able to distribute them, which coincided with the political transition. Drugs first began appearing in the years before the end of white rule, but the market greatly increased in the immediate aftermath of the first democratic elections.[63] What is clear from my interviews in Johannesburg and Cape Town is how rapidly this process accelerated around 1995.

In both cities, the drug market was regulated by the strongest available set of muscle. And, in both cases, these groups had strong links to the state. In Cape Town, Cyril Beeka was reputed to have had links with both the old and new regimes, while the Johannesburg bouncer mafia had close connections to the apartheid police, and individuals who epitomised the most violent and depraved elements of the late-apartheid state. In both cases, private-security companies provided a useful cover in a period when city and police authorities were hard-pressed to do so, or were look-ing the other way.

The mafia groups in both cities therefore were able to establish them-selves because the state largely acquiesced, for political and practical reasons, in their formation and growth (that constitutes the third condi-tion – a weak state). The state later cracked down only when the violence perpetrated by the Johannesburg bouncer mafia became too conspicuous and destructive, but by then its dissolution was already under way.

In Cape Town, action was taken against the protection networks only after the death of Beeka. High-level state investigations into him ran into trouble and have borne little fruit. The protection economy in the city is now well established. Only recently, apparently as a warning to local establishments not to mess with the system, a well-known and well-liked bouncer was killed assassination-style by a group of gangsters in Long Street. The establishment where the bouncer was killed had been talking to the police. That cooperation ended with the hit.

The Cape Town violent criminal economy remains perennially unstable. The violence in the city is likely to continue to flare, as it did briefly in late 2016 and early 2017, as internal disagreements are resolved, and clubs and pubs are brought into line. As the story of Johannesburg shows, no crimi-nal hegemony lasts forever, least of all in the ebb and flow of South Africa's underworld. While the current criminal commanders of the city may feel secure, their control may be eroding. In the underworld, leadership is inherently fragile, it may make you rich – but it also makes you a target.

In April 2017 a spasm of violence ran through central Cape Town as a group of gangsters tried to overturn the existing violent hegemony over the clubs. It ended, predictably, with a hit. The barriers to entry to the markets of violence (the fourth precondition) are high – measured in blood.

The attempt to change the prevailing order of control appeared to be related to an internal disagreement, which spiralled quickly into a series of armed confrontations on the streets of Cape Town in the nightclub district. In one case, 30 armed men smashed up two clubs, although, predictably, police investigating officers report that few of the injured will speak. The armed group was led by one Nafiz Modack, said to be a naturalised South African of North African origin. While originally aligned with the Lifman-Booysen network, a falling-out over money apparently led him to challenge the prevailing order, leading him to target clubs owned by Lifman. The result was an immediate escalation of tensions as armed men camped outside houses across the city.

It seems impossible to believe that the assassination of a prominent gang leader a few days after this incident was not connected. Shamiel Eyssen, leader of the Fancy Boys gang, was gunned down by three men in what bore all the hallmarks of a professional hit. Either the Fancy Boys are reputed to have provided the manpower that Modack drew on when he disrupted the clubs or Eyssen had sought to take advantage of the openings that seemed to emerge as conflict spilled out into the open. The murder was a message: it signalled that a new period of instability in the Cape underworld was about to begin.

The murder of Cyril Beeka is the great unsolved crime of the South African underworld. But his shooting in March 2011 connects all the way to the hit on Shamiel Eyssen, six years later. Beeka's removal provided the space for the shaping of a new generation of powerful criminal figures. On 10 October 2013, another assassination linked to the Beeka shooting highlighted again the high-stakes game at play. A Cape Town hitman for the Sexy Boys, one Leon 'Lyons' Davids, was shot by two men during a braai at a house not far from where Beeka was killed. Sources suggested that Davids had been seeking a plea bargain in the Beeka case and may also have had information on the death of Yuri the Russian.[64] The story of the bouncer mafia is littered with a trail of bodies and it is a story, at least in Cape Town, that still has some way to run.

In any community, the presence of a cohesive group with a propensity for violence will offer the possibility to coalesce around an illicit activity, which can be 'taxed' as long as the right conditions are in place. Contextual factors are important in determining how such violent entrepreneurs take control and whether this control can be sustained. In the case of Johannesburg, the bouncer mafia lost ground because they lacked the manpower, ceding control to new Nigerian criminal networks. In Cape Town a more centralised system developed linked to a group of violent entrepreneurs from the Cape Flats (in the shape of the Sexy Boys), capable of drawing recruits and projecting violence where required. This proved to be a more sustainable model. In both cases, agreements around geographic turf were essential for stability and growth, although these inevitably disintegrated, as there is little honour among thieves.

What might this mean for the future development of mafia-style protection arrangements in South Africa? Like all social and political formations, mafia groups ebb and flow in line with a number of shaping factors. One of those is the strength and integrity of government institutions. Take just one historical case close to home. In a fascinating account, Charles van Onselen found that in Johannesburg at the turn of the 20th century, when underworld activity threatened the prevailing social norms, the political and economic elite panicked and pushed for a stronger police force to face the challenge.[65]

Similar fears of organised crime have gripped other countries, leading to attempts to strengthen the capacity and integrity of the state, not least in the US. If this occurs in contemporary South Africa, the impact of Cyril Beeka may become a thing of the past, just a curious subject for historians to analyse, rather than an ongoing concern to criminologists intent on finding a solution to organised crime.

However, the jury is still out over which way the chips may fall. Much, then, depends on how the state evolves. A corrupted state may seek even more common cause with the men of violence if this serves powerful political interests, thereby increasing the challenge of developing an effective response to organised crime.

On a perhaps more optimistic note, the more Cape Town relies on its city-centre tourism economy, the less likely it is that violence from the protection mobsters will be tolerated by the authorities. As elsewhere in the world, it is possible that if the state cannot end the reign of the mobsters, it will accommodate them – as long as the violence is kept to a minimum. As the next chapter argues, however, this will mean reducing the capacity for gang violence on the periphery of the city, the Cape Flats, where gangs are key in helping sustain the mafia-style protection economy at the city's core.

# 5

## Living by the sword:
## Gang bosses and their prey

O n Friday 15 January 2016, gang boss Nathaniel Moses, also known as 'Nigga', was about to pick up a rented car from the Avis offices in Strand. Situated on the city's southeastern outskirts and once a holiday mecca for the white lower-middle class, Strand is now a spruced-up cluster of apartment blocks that line a strip of the windswept False Bay coast where the Cape Flats give way to the Hottentots Holland mountains, a jagged barrier through which wind roads that lead to the Southern and Eastern Cape.

Moses planned to set route for Johannesburg to complete some business and his schedule was known to the gang members whom he had recruited into a criminal group he named the Mobsters. It was an appropriately chosen moniker given that he and his criminal network had over a period of several years caused considerable mayhem down under, largely unnoticed in the upperworld. Moses was in his early 30s; he was young for a gang boss. He had risen fast and furiously through the criminal ranks, leaving a score of dead bodies in his wake. They had been shot in all types of ways, in one case the victim forced to kneel as he took a bullet to the head.

On that January summer's day, Moses was reported to have been feeling nervous. Some of his gang members said that he seemed to have had a premonition of his own death. In the weeks before he was killed he had apparently been playing the guitar, and a source close to him described his mental state as peaceful. 'That guy knew he was on his way out,' he said. He must have known that various powerful people with criminal connections and the capacity for violence were now conspiring against him. Perhaps the underworld had already sent him a warning and he knew there was no way back. It was little wonder: Moses had been making the underworld angry.

For several years, Moses, who had been careful not to develop a public profile, had shaken up Cape Town's criminal economy. He had broken a set of unwritten underworld rules. Violence was integral to his strategy, and he had gathered around him a network of shooters from different parts of the city to form the Mobsters. His gang was described as a breakaway group from the 28s, a powerful prison-aligned Number gang, and many had previous criminal convictions and gang associations. The 28s and their affiliates had become powerful because of their ability to access guns. Moses, who had also acquired some firearms, wanted to rise up the slippery criminal hierarchy as quickly as he could, building on the business of killing by forcing his way into the city's drugs market.

Moses seemed to kill with abandon, but two documented cases provide insight into what seems to have been a well-defined strategy. He murdered serial-style a number of mid-level gang bosses, taking over their drug turf as he expanded. In May 2010 McNolan Koordom, who had developed a thriving drug business in Bonteheuwel, was assassinated. In August 2011 Mario Snell, who was operating a drug house, was shot dead in Eerste River. In both cases, Moses' men took over their operations, securing the drug houses with gunmen, and thus the Mobsters grew their market share.

This strategy was then repeated. A senior police officer estimates that

Moses and the Mobsters may have been involved in dozens of hits over a period of five to six years – all of this without attracting the attention of the authorities. But, eventually, the police became suspicious. 'We knew something was up,' said an investigating officer, 'because the same car was used in several cases and opposing gangsters seemed to have been killed by the same gunmen.' The police then opened an intelligence project on the Moses killings and witnesses began to speak. Within a short period, however, four of them had been killed, including one who had entered the police's witness-protection programme.

By January 2016 Moses had gained control of a number of drug sales points in Kraaifontein, Bishop Lavis, Belhar and Elsies River. He was nothing if not entrepreneurial, and quickly diversified beyond the drugs market. He developed a link to the Chinese triads in the Cape, which enabled him to break into the abalone trade. (Abalone is a prized shellfish, the exploitation of which is banned in South Africa, but it is considered a delicacy in Asia, and China in particular, and the illicit market is dominated by organised crime.) The triad connection allowed Moses to establish a business in which abalone was swapped for drugs sourced in China.

Moses also traded in violence as a service. He is said by police sources to have hired out his gunmen (40 to 50 in number at the height of his business) to other gangsters who wanted to conduct assassinations or engage in turf battles within the underworld – at a price of course. One of the biggest users of the Mobsters had been the notorious 28s gang kingpin, George 'Geweld' Thomas, who was sentenced in 2015 to seven life terms for a spate of violence and racketeering. The Mobsters had increasingly sought to be independent actors, and so the ties loosened as Geweld (his *nom de guerre* means violence in Afrikaans) disappeared into prison, although he and Moses stayed in touch. Moses had seemed to shake himself free from his former overseer – going 'AWOL', in the words of an observer. As always, in the complex and violent underworld of the gangs, it often seemed difficult to understand who he was working for.

Moses represented a wider and, for some underworld insiders, disturbing trend, one that had begun in the early years of South Africa's democracy and had been gaining momentum: in the new criminal economy, the traditional prison-based Number-gang culture was breaking down. Old allegiances were dying. Moses was, by membership, a 28, but, in the words of those who knew him, he represented a new class of criminal who had subverted the Number system. He was one of a group of gangsters who had not been initiated into prison-gang culture; he cared less about the old system than about the money that could be made outside of it. Moses, said one observer, was seen as a mongrel, lacking the credentials of a pure-bred Number man. Moses was part of an evolving criminal order, one that is more dynamic, increasingly violent and unpredictable.

Moses had been watched for weeks and members of his own inner circle had apparently reported on his movements to rivals. His death was cleanly executed. Three men approached him outside a car dealership on the outskirts of the town. Two of them shot him multiple times, checking that he was dead before fleeing the scene. No one else was killed or injured. Nobody has ever been arrested for the crime and a police-intelligence document concluded that the murder had been planned to perfection right down to the very last detail: 'It would most likely end up being an unsolved [case]', it stated.

According to police-intelligence sources, the killers were identified as being linked to the Sexy Boys, whom we met in the previous chapter. The Mobsters, it was reported, had been muscling in on the Sexy Boys' turf, particularly in their home base, Belhar. Although it is not known for certain who killed Moses, interviews with people in and close to the Cape Town underworld suggest that his death was the result of a complex piece of criminal cooperation. Members of his own gang provided information that led to his death, while the Sexy Boys allegedly hired another group of killers to do the work.

Their motive? Moses, it is said, had become disruptive, disrespectful and unwilling to share out the spoils of his activities. Those behind the killing seemed set to benefit, taking over Moses' network of gunmen and reinforcing their alliances with others in the criminal underworld who had sought to put an end to the Mobsters' reign of violence.[1] The Mobsters were essentially a gang of hitmen, having broken free from the underworld influence of other powerful players. They were willing to sell their services to the highest bidder and at the same time they began seeking to carve out for themselves a segment of the city's profitable drugs market.

The Mobsters, as a self-styled group of hitmen, spotted a market niche, a senior police officer told me. Although the police had noticed the same modus operandi in murders across the peninsula, he said that they had not anticipated that it was a gang itself doing the killing. 'It turned out to be a gang hired by other gangs. Then they went out of control,' he said.[2] The Mobsters fit the phenomenon of hitmen, only in a more sophisticated and organised form. But in pursuing that line of business, and more particularly by seeking to break directly into the drugs market, they became a threat to the very people who had hired them in the first place. Powerful interests in the underworld did not want a group of rogue killers on the loose, pursuing their own criminal profits in the same market in which they were already competing.

## Evolving hierarchies of violence and power

On other occasions, a killing spree by a group of outsiders like the Mobsters may well have led to widespread death on the streets as gangsters openly clashed in fierce displays of rivalry around turf. What is interesting and significant in this case is that the deaths attributed to the Mobsters preceding the assassination of Moses had not precipitated a wider gang war.[3] In April 2016, for example, in the gang-afflicted ghetto of Manenberg, 19 people died in the space of two weeks as enemy gangs engaged in a war. Although the reasons for the Manenberg conflict are hard to discern, it seems to have been sparked by a combination of elements, including historical grievances over past gang wars, gang members who had changed allegiance from one gang to another and the fear that drug turf was being captured.[4]

But in this case, the gangs had managed to contain the damage. Why is not entirely clear. One explanation is that the Mobsters were selling their services to a more powerful group of clients, but then started acting too often on their own initiative. Moses had been tolerated up to a certain point, but was then killed with what seems to have been assistance from his own people. 'It is the case of a mother killing [a] child,' said one businessman with connections to the gangs.[5]

The question of gang governance, and the fragile role and lives of gangsters in the complex, increasingly violent and evolving context of organised crime in Cape Town are the subject of this chapter. As we have seen, however, one needs to distinguish between the open form of warlike conflict seen in the Manenberg clashes, and the more discreet, systematic use of assassinations – as in the case of the carefully planned shooting that ended the life of Nathaniel Moses. Both forms serve a purpose and in some ways they are interrelated. Unfettered gang violence precipitated by the ready availability of firearms increases the need for targeted hits that enable gang bosses to retain control. It's a kind of vicious cycle.

While gang bosses increasingly prefer to avoid open conflict, they are aware, it seems, that gang warfare may sometimes be a requirement. This kind of violence is critical to maintaining the recruitment and discipline systems for the largely young male gang members. The nascent threat of violence in communities where gangs are present is vital to the business strategy of extortion and drug sales. Ironically, then, open conflict Manenberg-style may not be welcomed by gang bosses, but is seen as a necessary evil. Meanwhile, discreet, covert assassinations are used to manage problems inside and outside the gang, as the case of Moses illustrates.

Moses' death seems to illustrate rather well an adage often applied to the criminal underworld: 'You live by the sword and you die by the sword'. While Moses' life and death validates this truism, his and the Mobsters' story also provides some insight into the changing nature of the Western Cape gangs and their linkages to the communities in which they are situated and which they often dominate.

The Cape gangs exist in and relate to these communities in sometimes paradoxical ways. They are both drivers of violence and fear, and providers of social services and security. And they can be a source of community pride. Gangs in the context of Cape Town are products of 'history, identity and necessity'.[6] The causal factors for gang-related violence in Cape Town are a complex intermeshing of historical and contemporary phenomena, including a surge in drug use since the early 1990s and the resulting struggle for control of local drug markets.

By the late 1990s it was estimated that there were some 130 gangs in the city, several of them widely known and part of daily public discourse, such as the Americans, the Hard Livings, the Sexy Boys, the Mongrels, the Clever Kids and the Junky Funky Kids. Gang membership in Cape Town has been estimated at around 100 000, with the larger gangs having as many as 5 000 members.[7] Gangs are so pervasive in some communities that young people join them as a means of protection. Many adolescents from fractured homes are also in desperate need of a metaphorical home and a set of role models, and that is why they turn to the gangs. In scores of discussions that I have conducted with gang members, joining the local gangs is often described as a necessity, something that is almost pre-ordained.

Since the start of democracy, the city has seen a series of vicious con-flicts among gangs. Gang violence has had a significant impact on ordinary people's lives, predominantly in various marginalised so-called Coloured communities on the city's periphery. Here, people express a strong fear of gang-related violence and are often forced to pay money to the gangs to protect themselves and their property. Protection racketeering in Cape Town has not been confined to the central business district, an issue we saw in the previous chapter. Don Pinnock notes that the protection mar-ket is a criminal activity that can be dated back to the District Six gangs in the 1940s and 1950s.[8] That criminal market continues today, and busi-nesses in many parts of the city, but primarily on the Cape Flats and in areas that verge on the ganglands, have to pay tribute to the entrepreneurs of violence.[9]

Extortion is integral to the way the gangs operate, as a gang boss in Manenberg explained: 'In Manenberg, the Clever Kids and the Dixies [two local gangs] were not [originally] involved in drug trafficking because their main business was protection: they would charge a protection tariff from everyone and anyone who moved commodities inside their turf. We are speaking about charging taxi drivers, hawkers, church officials, small-business owners – anyone.'[10]

Because of the hefty profits to be made from the growing drugs market, however, these gangs gravitated towards controlling drug trafficking and dealing. In the late 1980s, the bigger gangs, such as the Manenberg-based Americans, spread their influence across the wider Cape metro by provid-ing protection for drug dealers who did not have the capacity for violence and needed to outsource it.[11]

Extortion is, however, still a major revenue stream for city gangs and it intersects now with the control of drug markets and the associated battle for drug territory. A member of the Hard Livings gang described the way the system works in no uncertain terms:

When you come to Manenberg you find that everyone must pay to do business here. It doesn't matter if you belong to the church or even the council, we will fucking make you pay if you want to do business here. If you don't pay we will fuck you up or we will fucking kill you. And don't mess with our drug business ... there is so much money to be made with drugs here so gangs are always fighting over who can [sell] drugs where.[12]

The extraction of payments from local communities and the control of places where drugs are sold mean that there is a strong geographic imprint to the gangs and their identity. The struggle over territory has had a huge impact on the nature of violence in Cape Town. With a murder rate of 60 per 100 000, the city has higher levels of violence than any other city in the country, and double the level of Johannesburg.[13] In fact, Cape Town is now reported to be among the ten most violent urban complexes in the world.[14] The number of reported murders in the city has increased by around 60 per cent since 2009, with steep increases from 2009 to 2015 (as illustrated in Figure 3 – *see the appendix*). Based on these figures, in Cape Town in 2015/16 an average of 40 people were murdered every week.

Although not all of this killing can be laid solely at the door of the city's gangs, a substantial portion can be. If homicide figures for each of the city's police stations are disaggregated and numbers of homicides compared across the five-year period in which the greatest increases have been seen – between 2011 and 2015 (*see Figure 3*) – those areas on the Cape Flats with high levels of gang activity show consistent increases. In fact, no area where gangs are active showed a decline.[15] According to the cluster chairman of a community policing forum working on the Cape Flats, Hanif Loonat, the situation is worse than it's ever been. 'The gang violence has reached national crisis level and the truth is SAPS [the South African

Police Service] has lost its grip because they are too understaffed to man this area,' said Loonat.[16]

How has the crisis reached this stage? Several intertwined trends have marked the development of the gangs in Cape Town over the last decade. The first is the increasing sophistication of their leadership structures. Before the early 1990s, the Cape Town gangs were more fragmented than at present, and largely dealt in Mandrax (methaqualone). That changed and gang supremacy emerged as more lucrative imported drugs entered the scene. As we saw in the previous chapter, increases in the trafficking of drugs to South Africa in the 1990s had a big impact on local drug markets,[17] particularly the trade in cocaine and heroin. The rapid influx of crystal methamphetamine (known locally as tik, whose use has reached alarmingly high levels) also reaped enormous profits for certain gang leaders. Although there are still numerous gangs across the city, there emerged a smaller number of more powerful (and visible) gang bosses in Cape Town as a consequence of the growing drugs market.[18]

The second trend, although related to the first, is the degree to which drug use has escalated in marginalised communities in the Western Cape. Although there is no single measure for the extent of drug availability and use, a combination of proxy measures suggests a trend. One is the dramatic increase in drug-related crimes detected as a result of police action. In Cape Town this type of crime increased by a remarkable 469 per cent between 2000 and 2015.[19] Figure 4 (*see the appendix*) compares this data for the Western Cape with that of South Africa as a whole since 2005. The rate of the increase over the last few years provides an indication of the degree to which drugs have become a key challenge for policing in the Western Cape.

Another proxy is the number of people presenting at drug clinics in the Western Cape. The South African Community Epidemiology Network on Drug Use noted that the Western Cape is heavily affected by drug-related problems.[20] Drug-use surveys also show that the overall price of illicit drugs continues to decline, suggesting greater availability.[21]

Thirdly, there have been changes in the nature of gang formation and mythology, as illustrated by the career of Nathaniel Moses. Historically, South Africa has seen two broad types of gang formation: prison gangs and street gangs. The prison, or Number, gangs traditionally performed specific functions only within the prison system and membership used to be confined to sentenced prisoners.[22] However, as the South African drug economy grew, prison gangs became aligned with street gangs, and vice versa. The increasing integration of these once separate spheres is said to have bred a greater culture of assassination on the streets.

There remain, however, certain significant differences between the two. Some gangs make it a point to reject altogether the ordering principle of the Number as something of the past. A member of the Clever Kids, a hard-core and violent gang in Manenberg, described the position to me as follows:

> Here we don't give a fuck about the Number! We will kill you if you are not a Clever Kid. You must *raak wys* [get wise] because, see, this is not prison, so these rules don't mean anything here. If it's gang war and you take the side of the HLs [Hard Livings gang], we hunt you, and if you are stupid and come into our area it's lights out for you.[23]

The final thread explaining the ascendancy of gang culture in the Cape is the fact that the nature of policing has shifted since the transition to democracy. Whereas gangs in and around Cape Town were previously used in ways that were beneficial to the apartheid state, the connections between gangs and the police are today more about contractual arrangements concerning protection and profit.[24] The gangs are said to pay the police for protection and, in return, they operate with a degree of impunity. That impunity is, however, not taken for granted. An uneasy truce exists between the police and gangsters in many areas. In this sense, the relationship between gangs and the police often takes on a commercial colour, a theme we come back to in more detail in Chapter 8.

There is perhaps no better example than the following to illustrate the link between the police and the gangs, one that lies at the heart of Cape Town's gangland violence. Between 2007 and 2015 a senior police officer, an expert on ballistics who was in charge of the service's main armoury, sold enormous numbers of confiscated guns to an intermediary, who then sold them on to the gangs. The ex-officer in question, one Colonel Christiaan Lodewyk Prinsloo, used the money to travel overseas, to fund his children's university fees and to buy himself a fancy house.[25] If you get the time to page through the list of firearms contained in the court documentation, you will find it is a staggering catalogue of weaponry – some 2 400 items, easily enough to outfit a small army.[26]

Thanks to Prinsloo's supply chain, the gangs were able to gun themselves up to an extent never previously seen, and from around 2010, as the homicide figures for Cape Town show, the killing then intensified. The exact link between the flood of firearms and the increasing homicide in the gang wars is hard to establish statistically, but, according to one account, 'the number of firearms in circulation, and illegally obtained firearms in particular, may explain the latest increases in the Western Cape homicide rates'.[27] It is also clear from the interviews we conducted with gang bosses and senior police officers that violence began to soar around that point. It was just hard at the time to see why.[28]

When the police confiscated guns, it seems it did not take long before they found their way back onto the streets. A member of the Hard Livings explained: 'We got a way with the cops … they are fucking corrupt, so they will take the money. So the gun with the serial number off gets sold back to us … so they *mung* [arrest] you with a gun, but then the gun comes back onto the street, you see?'[29]

The guns entered and spread through the Cape's gangland like water flowing through a series of interconnected channels, an illustration of how interlinked are the players in this violent ecosystem. One gang boss said that the firearms initially entered the system through a gun-licensing racket run by Ralph Stanfield, the leader of the 28s: 'You could pick up an automatic like an AK for about R3 500,' he said.[30] Other interviews revealed the guns soon began to pile up among various opposing gangs.[31] As a member of the Ghetto Kids, one of the first recipients, said: 'My broer, we now got so much guns no one will fuck with us cos they are too scared.'[32]

Soon there was an arms race. As one gang 'armed up', it disrupted the local balance of power and others also went in search of weaponry. A senior police officer explained how the supply of guns meant that even smaller gangs, such as the Corner Boys, for example, became empowered. The firearms were sold in packs of ten for around R40 000. Once a gang had sufficient guns, they were able to control more drug-market turf. Hence, guns made profit, and the profits bought more guns.[33] The effect was that recruitment also picked up because, now, bosses could offer gang membership with a gun – a huge status symbol in gangland, much like a company car in the upperworld economy.[34]

The illicit introduction of such a vast quantity of firearms – arguably one of the single most deadly crimes in post-apartheid South Africa – led to a fragmentation of conflict among the gangs from 2010 and halted what analysts had seen as a period of criminal consolidation. The gang environment saw what seemed like a series of unconnected but increasingly vicious shoot-outs as gangs fought one other. There was also a marked increase in the number of assassinations of mid- and senior-level gangsters. This is clearly evidenced by the increasing homicide rate, and rising proportion of people in the city dying of gunshot wounds. The head of forensic pathology at one of the main city mortuaries, that at Salt River, where many of the victims of gang conflicts are brought, said exasperatedly early in 2016: 'We are now in a state of crisis. Murders – most notably by gun-shot – are bringing in more and more bodies each year, and the morgue cannot cope.' The number of gunshot victims presented to the mortuary in 2010 was 290; by 2015 it was 695, an increase of some 140 per cent.[35]

The introduction of guns into the gang system meanwhile appears to have had a side effect: it increased the need for internal assassinations – simply so that gang bosses could maintain control. The murder of Nathaniel Moses is a classic case of this. The availability of guns allowed the ascendancy of his gang, the Mobsters, in a way that would not have been possible in the past without firearms. The gangs resolved to end the disruption caused by Moses by eliminating the leader and buying off the gang members. Elimination in this case meant contracting out his assassination.

While the flow of guns spurred the growth of the gangs, gang bosses, as mentioned, are not necessarily supporters of open conflict between gangsters on the streets. 'Peace is in fact beneficial to gang operations,' explained a church leader in Manenberg. 'The gangs breathe easier when there is peace because there is less police focus on their activities. The gangs have trouble dealing in drugs and their other operations come to a halt when there is too much police presence, especially in times of gang war.'[36] If there is to be 'war', explained one mid-level gang boss, it is better that the leaders of the gangs control it.[37] One of the best ways of doing that, it seems, is to control the flow of weapons to gangsters. Because there is now widespread weapon possession among gangsters, however, bosses are not always in control of what happens on the ground.

Understanding the relationship between gang bosses and rank-and-file members is critical to determining when and how violence occurs, and how the bosses in particular seek to benefit from violence, even when they recognise that it has costs for business. The reality is that there is a layer of organised-crime hierarchies in the city, with several powerful figures playing critical roles within the wider network.[38]

At the apex of the system of gangs in the Western Cape are a relatively small number of gang bosses – perhaps about 20. Several key figures stand out here, partly because they have received more publicity, and because they belong to criminal networks that extend nationally, and, to some extent, internationally. These are people like the three Booysen brothers, who run the Sexy Boys gang, with Jerome Booysen an allegedly close associate of Cape Town businessman Mark Lifman. Rashied Staggie is said to continue to control the Hard Livings through two intermediaries (although he is restricted by a monitoring device he wears as a parole condition since his release from prison in 2013). Ernie Lastig Solomon, having branched out into a career in acting and music, is said to still control much of the abalone business in the Southern Cape. Ralph Stanfield is a big name in the 28s gang, whose networks extend from a base in Mitchells Plain. Igshaan Davids – aka Sanie the American – is the leader of Cape Town's biggest street gang, the 5 000-strong Americans. What many of the senior gang leaders now have in common is a desire to legitimise themselves and the money they have made.[39]

Below those who occupy the top of the command-chain hierarchy are groups of mid-level gang bosses and leaders of smaller gangs – much like Nathaniel Moses, murdered because he had dared disrupt the underworld order. The term 'gang boss', as it is widely used in Cape Town, subsumes both of these categories, the elite top rank and the 'middle managers', into one broad group. Underneath this rank are the faceless grass-roots gang members who belong to the numerous gangs across the Cape.

Several powerful gangs also have junior divisions, which recruit children as young as ten and provide them with a criminal career path into the senior structures of the gangs. One can see these as a form of youth league supporting the gang's future operational strategy. Even at the lower end of the gang, said a leader of a junior gang, the No Fears, which is linked to the Americans, children are encouraged to engage in violence, enticed by promises of new takkies or clothes and the like. 'But they won't just get anything,' he added. 'You must keep them *vaal* [ignorant].'[40]

Promotion through the ranks is a ruthless business, and by far the majority of gang members remain at the bottom of the system, often marginalised and unaware of the main workings of the gang. At the bottom end, members do work such as selling drugs or killing people for a very small fee, although what they earn from performing such tasks for the gang may well be greater than what they would be able to acquire in the formal legal economy, hence the attraction of joining the gang in the first place.

Once a member, always a member. It's a calling for life (although on the Cape Flats that life may well be very short) because getting out of the gang can be an enormously difficult process. Oddly, as we saw earlier when speaking to hitmen, one way out that seems to be honoured by several gangs is when members choose to curtail their involvement on the basis of finding God and joining the church.[41]

The relationship between gang bosses and the gangs as organisations has been too little explored in the literature, which has generally focused on the experience of lower-level gangsters. Gang bosses are characters who fascinate as much as they repel. They manage the difficult task of retaining their influence over the gang while seeking to enrich themselves. They feed their members scraps while creaming off most of the profits for themselves. It means maintaining a base within the gang areas, while building a life outside. Although they often own properties outside the gang's territory, they need to keep a foothold in their members' home turf to maintain credibility, presence and control, visiting the gangs, giving instructions and assessing business.

How they balance a process whereby they are proponents of violence while at the same time being caught up themselves in the dynamics of gang violence, says much about the fragility of their positions. A list of top gang leaders from several years ago would look rather different today.[42] And a violent campaign that led to some 30 assassinations of gang leaders conducted by vigilante group PAGAD in the late 1990s in Cape Town caused major disruption in the underworld. The senior leaders, however, were quickly replaced to ensure the ongoing stability of the organisations.

I was interviewing some young gangsters in an area of Cape Town dominated by a particular gang when the gang boss arrived in an expensive car. The difference between the unkempt, drug-addicted youngsters and the well-dressed, gold-chained boss was striking. What was also clear, however, was the degree to which the boss was both respected and feared. 'Bosses must not be crossed – you will die,' is how a religious leader working in gang-dominated Hanover Park described the situation.[43] Maintaining leadership over a gang is a complex process of manipulating the members, promising rewards and 'drip-feeding goodies to them down the system'.[44]

In Manenberg, a mid-level drug dealer was more critical in his assessment:

> The drug lords get richer and buy more properties and cars while the families and the very communities are torn apart. Honestly, it's like a zombie nation … it is scary to see, but people outside of these communities do not understand what is really happening here … if you came here for a day or two, you will see that it is hell here on earth.[45]

There are two reasons why gang bosses maintain that 'hell on earth'. The first, as the words of the drug dealer suggest, is that underlying the nature of gang rule is the propagation of fear. Social support and the distribution of resources play a part but, ultimately, maintaining control over a gang is about instilling fear. As an ex-gang member told me: 'Putting the community in fear is central to maintaining business. People are compromised in all sorts of ways … they have to store drugs at home, must support businesses owned by drug bosses. [The gang bosses] can execute what they want – as long as there is fear.' Fear is based on the capacity for or threat of violence, and violence is the route to power in the universe of the gangs: 'Power is more important than money. You can always acquire money if you have power. You need to get power – and power comes from having *laaities* [young men] on your side, and guns.'[46]

The second reason is that violence is part of the recruitment strategy and a way to ensure that gangs maintain territorial boundaries for drug dealing and extortion rackets. The recruitment of gun carriers and low-level drug peddlers is essential to gang operations – and violence remains a way of controlling those operations.

Violence is therefore a recruitment strategy, a mark of passage within gangs, and a way of maintaining control over the gang's contours and operations, and the associated drug and extortion markets that feed them. It is not for nothing that violence is at its most intense in those areas of the city where gangs operate close to each other's territories and tear each other apart – 'like piranhas in a small fish bowl', as it has been appositely phrased.[47] Violence also serves the useful defusing function of focusing the youthful aggression of gang members outwards rather than inwards or up the gang hierarchy.

At the base of the system, the boundaries between the gangs may blur as members switch allegiance from one gang to another, attracted by better benefits – a fact that any self-respecting gang must respond to with violence if it is to maintain its integrity. In the deadly conflict in Manenberg, which has rumbled on and off over the past few years, the Hard Livings, which dominated the area, saw large numbers defect to the Americans. That betrayal resulted in a spate of killings. In 2016 the former defectors then switched back to their original camp. These shifting allegiances and resulting confusion in the neighbourhood's day-to-day gang violence resulted in all-out mayhem. In one incident, a member of the Clever Kids was mistaken for an Americans gang member and gunned down by a member of the Hard Livings. The Clever Kids responded by rallying with the Dixie Boys and the Americans against the Hard Livings.[48]

Such acts of betrayal and violence are long held in the collective memory of the gangs. Disrespect necessitates revenge. This is why gang wars are cyclical and may often be accepted as a necessary evil by gang bosses. A failure to crack down may mean the loss of respect, and ultimately losing new recruits and drug turf. The crucial skill here, an ex-gangster said, is to be able to use violence but end it when things 'get too hot'.[49] Violence is tolerated, because while it may be temporarily disruptive and conflict with the smooth running of the criminal economy, it is sometimes necessary to help maintain long-term control.

## The utility of assassinations

Targeted killing is a relatively clean way of maintaining relationships and enforcing transactions between gangs, within gangs, with the wider public (most clearly in the case of extortion) and between the authorities and the gangs. Assassinations perform a clear function: they provide a potent demonstration effect, while, perhaps ironically, containing the impact of the act of violence itself. Assassination is a specialised function; it is essential, both practically and symbolically, to maintaining the system of gangsterism in Cape Town.

If open violence is accepted as a necessary evil, far more efficient, as the case of Nathaniel Moses shows, is the use of targeted killing as a form of regulation. While it is not possible to know what proportion of gang violence takes the form of assassination, interviews suggest that such focused acts of violence are a key instrument in the management toolbox of gang bosses. Individual killings, if carefully undertaken and when the protagonist's identity is concealed, may prevent wider gang wars, allowing gang bosses to maintain internal control in their organisations, while seeking to advance the frontiers of their geographic control.

Such targeted violence reflects the fact that competition between gang bosses is intense and the top of the criminal hierarchy is perennially unstable. Their lives are constantly under threat, both from the competition and from potential challengers in their own gangs. 'It's a paranoid existence,' said one observer, recounting how the city's criminal leaders sleep with a gun under their pillow.[50]

And, while there is evidence that the top criminal elements in Cape Town do communicate with each other to broker deals and limit the damage caused by conflict, that does not mean that they enjoy trusting relationships.[51] In cases such as Moses, criminal bosses from different organisations may come together to eliminate those who are disruptive to the market. That speaks to the success of individual assassinations as a strategy and a utility.

Overall, however, the ecosystem of violence remains too dynamic and too often at the mercy of killing driven from the bottom up. While the mobilisation of young men, which sustains this conflict, is a product of the bosses' own actions, they do not always fully control it. Assassination continues to feed the system of chronic instability that characterises Cape Town's criminal underworld. Yet precisely because it is seen to have utility, assassination in Cape Town's gangland is one of the key ways in which competition between gangs can be regulated in a fairly controlled way.

It has been suggested in the context of organised crime that violence may be contrary to the objectives of some criminal groups. Violence attracts attention and disrupts the processes behind illicit commercial gain.[52] The system of gangs and their internal regulation in Cape Town is therefore arguably in a transition phase: gang bosses are increasingly reliant on more targeted forms of assassination to retain control, while seeking to limit open violence despite the fact that this at times plays an important role in gang management. In Cape Town the result is messy conflicts that flare up, then quickly dissipate as gang leaders seek to damp them down.

The outcome of these forms of regulation among the Cape gangs may well reach a tipping point soon. As we saw earlier, the city's homicide rate is now one of the highest in the world, comparable with many of the worst cases of gang control and violence in the world's murder capitals. Can it go on? In a city that is heavily dependent on tourism and eager to demonstrate that local government is in competent hands, the issue of gangs and associated violence remains a bleeding sore that will have to be addressed. This may either come externally as legitimate, elected leaders address the problem, or it may come internally as power consolidates in the underworld. The latter occurs because, as studies elsewhere have demonstrated, a fragmented underworld is likely to be more violent; when only a few mafia bosses are in control, deal making is more likely to preserve the peace, which, in turn, helps generate criminal profit.[53]

If open violence is a mechanism for mobilisation, defending turf and maintaining gang coherence, assassinations are increasingly a tool for gang management to both maintain internal discipline and ensure market expansion. As we have seen, the assassins are expendable tools in the gang bosses' repertoire, the killers almost as vulnerable as those whom they set out to kill.

The gang leaders are also highly vulnerable. Being the boss is a torturous balancing act and there is a high turnover among the city's criminal chiefs, where 'turnover' often means a dead body. Gang leadership can be determined as much by the discreet application of the gun as by decisions made in smoked-filled rooms, reminiscent of mafia movies about who should be the next *capo*.

This fragility within the leadership corps does not mean, however, that the system as a whole is a fragile one. In fact, it is highly resilient and sustained by established practices of violence embedded within a set of structural conditions. Gangs are maintained by an ecosystem where policing is often complicit in the maintenance of gang power, and where violence has long been a tool to promote fear.

The violent resources available in this ecosystem have serious implications for society as a whole. Most particularly, the use of assassination has seeped outside of gang culture, and is used by criminal interests that are external, but connected to, gangs in the city, as well as by political and other actors. As an interview with a member of the Americans gang illustrates, 'the gang boss can order a hit on any individual or group. The principle of "guns for hire" takes on a new dimension as various people can have a business relationship with the gang boss and, in return, they get a killing capacity.'[54]

It is for this reason that analysis of the gangs of Cape Town has wider national applicability. Gangs are nurseries of violence maintained through the city's drug and extortion economies. Breaking this cycle will require a coordinated national, provincial and city-wide effort, including law enforcement, and educational and developmental interventions, at a far higher level than has been implemented to date. A much more integrated and effective response, drawing on local, provincial and national government, and with greater resources, is long overdue. However, as we will see, achieving this kind of response is hampered by a core weakness – the engagement and interests of the state itself in sustaining the criminal economy.

# 6

## Quiet outsiders:
## Why the Nigerians won and Krejcir lost

I n 2014 and 2015, two South African police informers were badly tortured then killed, their bodies found in different parts of Cape Town. Neither case has been solved and neither is likely to be. To protect witnesses and the people who told me the story, I have changed their names to Jenny and Rose.[1]

The two women, like many police informers, were sex workers, connected to the underworld through their Nigerian pimps and their contacts in the hardscrabble place where they grew up, the Cape Flats, with its resident gangs. Both were pretty yet streetwise and tough: 'They could fight you and they had fought unruly clients before,' said someone who knew them both.

I am not sure that Jenny and Rose knew each other, and there is nothing to suggest they did, but there is little doubt that Rose would have heard about the murder of Jenny, who was killed first. News travels fast in the underworld, particularly when someone has paid a price.

Prostitution is a precarious business for young women. Jenny and Rose were among others who worked for two Nigerian bosses. They appear to have made the decision to work with Nigerian pimps partly because the arrangement offered a number of advantages over working on their own or for the prostitution networks controlled by the Cape Flats gangs. Like many women, they appear to have been lured into prostitution by slick-talking Nigerians who recruited them by offering promises of money and a better life. Rose is said to have been able to speak fluent Ibo, the main language of the Nigerian underworld in South Africa.

Safety is a key concern for sex workers, and this was a service the Nigerians provided Jenny and Rose – albeit at an extortionate cost. The women would receive around R2 000 per 'jump' (the term used for having sex with a client); the pimps took about 90 per cent of that for 'protection', the cost of advertising their wares on the web, for renting the rooms and consumables. So the women pocketed only about R200 a time. Jenny recognised this as exploitative, said a friend whom I interviewed, but safety was an important consideration, and, as streetwalkers, both she and Rose must have feared for their lives.

The advertising element of the fee is important, women in the sex industry explained. When there is a big conference or gathering, the Nigerian criminal networks have a way of making sure that word gets out. Meetings like the World Economic Forum on Africa, for example, said a police officer working on Cape Town's prostitution networks, bring a surge of work, and the Nigerians market their prostitutes to attract the potential trade. The women would also travel to Johannesburg and Durban, as demand for their services required, taking the bus to keep costs down for their ever profit-conscious Nigerian bosses.

They were also paid by the police as informers, giving titbits of information to their handler. In return, a dedicated and honest cop tried, as far as possible, to look out for them. That protection turned out not to be enough.

Jenny's body was found in her room in a Cape Town city-centre apartment block. The police had conducted a search for drugs and other contraband there on the night she was murdered. When her body was discovered, they found both her arms had been broken and her neck was badly damaged. A plastic bag had been placed over her head and she had been suffocated.

Rose was killed several months later; she was found dead in a children's play park in the north of the city after having been tortured – the skin on her face had been removed, her teeth torn out and her lips cut off – and then brutally beaten with a blunt object.

Although the two women may not have known each other, they appear to have had one thing in common: they had both tried to deceive their Nigerian controllers.

Jenny appears to have stolen 'something big', in the words of her police handler. It is not quite clear what, but most likely drugs or cash, or both. She had been asked by her Nigerian pimp to travel to Johannesburg to service a conference that was taking place there. She would take clients to a house in the suburbs, where quantities of drugs and possibly some cash may well have been present. It is likely that she stole some of this and headed back to Cape Town because, on arrival, she called some of her friends and went on a shopping spree before returning to her flat. Surveillance footage captured from the building's CCTV system showed a large, powerfully built man entering the building during the night. He was there for some time, then left, closing the door carefully behind him. Jenny's broken body was found later during the police raid.

Rose's death was more complicated. Her boyfriend was a gang member and hitman from the Cape Flats. (Let's call him Girl Goat – his street name is something equally strange.) Girl Goat's connections to the gangs put Rose in a dangerous place: it made her a particularly vulnerable accomplice to the theft of drugs by the gangs. The story of Rose's death goes something like this: she was to meet a client who liked to take drugs during sex, so the obvious place to get it was from her Nigerian contacts. She phoned and the deal was made to buy the drugs in the northern suburbs of the city, where the Nigerians have a strong presence. She must have either mentioned the handover to Girl Goat or colluded with him. Either way, when the Nigerian dealer turned up, Girl Goat and fellow gang members stole the drugs from him.

The Nigerians were understandably livid. What seems intriguing, however, and something that we will explore in greater detail later, is that they did not retaliate against the gang. Instead, they took it out on Rose. They gave her a beating that was meant to kill her, but also, said a police officer who was in contact with her, 'to show their displeasure'.[2]

People in the underworld and a police source say these cases will never be solved. 'Nigerians don't talk' but there is no doubt that the killers are Nigerian, a police investigating officer with extensive experience on similar cases told me. 'They melt back into their community and while we may get a hint of who they are, there is no evidence to bring the cases to court.'[3] The man who tortured and murdered Jenny seemed untroubled by the presence of the CCTV cameras. He has never been identified.

Yet the fact that it is known that Nigerians did the killing is of important symbolic value: they wanted to be identified as the killers, with word being put out that they were Nigerian hitmen. The message communicated on the street was that the bosses had been displeased. 'Never, ever, steal from the Nigerians,' said a police investigating officer. 'They will extract revenge from the weakest point in the system, the part that is least likely to give rise to a response from the local underworld.'

'For them, it is like trimming the fringes,' one gang member explained. In this case, it was Jenny and Rose who were 'trimmed', and, as the police officer suggested, no one has sought to avenge their killing. They are now largely forgotten, two more casualties in South Africa's ongoing and under-reported drugs war.

## Fugitives, fortune-seekers and competitors

The interesting question is why the Nigerians themselves killed the two women. As we have seen, there are plenty of South African hitmen who could have done the job. Why would they get blood on their own hands? Most likely, being visibly and directly associated with the killing was a strategic decision. It showed who was in charge.

Answering this question also explains how foreign organised-criminal networks in South Africa operate. If symbiosis is the deriving of mutual benefit from an otherwise abnormal relationship, then foreign and local criminal operators have found common cause with each other. Foreign criminal networks have shaped the South African underworld, as suppliers, competitors and disruptors, and will continue to do so. How that process occurs, however, is not uniform.

Some recent arrivals have provided a resource to the local criminal economy. Zimbabwean and Mozambican migrants, because they are largely undocumented and have had some military exposure or training, have been recruited as hitmen for the underworld and as recruits in armed robbery and hijacking gangs. These loose networks, while harbouring the potential for violence and playing an active role in some parts of the criminal economy (car theft is a Mozambican speciality, for example), are not of the same order, however, as the various foreign criminal organisations that made their home in South Africa from the late 1980s and early 1990s. This chapter explores some of the most important foreign crime groups, their evolution and their use of violence in South Africa.

The emergence of foreign organised-crime networks in South Africa largely coincided with the country's transition to democracy, when it began to open its economy to the world. Foreign criminal networks had been present in South Africa from the 1970s, but were limited in number. There was a surge of new entrants, however, during the transition period. This reflected not only the opportunities on hand locally, but also the fact that the global criminal economy had expanded, and a series of new players, most notably from Eastern Europe, the former Soviet Union and China, as well as those fleeing anti-mafia operations in Italy, looked for a new home.[4] The phenomenon has changed the nature of the South African underworld, which now interacts with a global criminal network, ensuring a connection to international markets. This is why local crooks, eager for foreign connections, migrate towards newly arrived foreign figures.[5]

The Italian mafia had a foothold in South Africa during the 1980s. Although there had been a small mafia presence before then, the arrival of Vito Palazzolo provided a conspicuous connection. Palazzolo laundered money from the mafia's heroin supply operations, in a case known as the 'pizza connection', where cash from drug sales was channelled through pizzerias before being deposited in a Swiss bank.[6] Palazzolo was convicted and sentenced but, during a 36-hour leave pass from prison in Switzerland to celebrate Christmas with his family, he escaped to South Africa in December 1986.

Why Palazzolo chose South Africa is unclear, but one theory is that an Israeli businessman in the gem business, in which Palazzo had dabbled, had outlined possible ventures. He moved quickly to secure his position. Within a short time of arriving in South Africa, Palazzolo was said to have met with several ministers, and no less than the president, PW Botha, and the head of organised crime of the then South African Police, General Neels Venter.

Palazzolo would survive well into the democratic dispensation, despite a probe into his actions by the Mandela government, and he expanded his business interests in the region. He was arrested in Bangkok in 2012 on charges of money laundering, after the Italian authorities requested his extradition.

Palazzolo clearly made wide connections in the Cape underworld, which may have provided long-standing linkages to South Africa for the Italian mafia. Both of the powerful Italian organised-crime groups, the Cosa Nostra and the 'Ndrangheta, now have a presence in South Africa. The country has become a place for the Cosa Nostra to hide from the authorities. In September 2014, for example, Antonino Messicati Vitale, a Cosa Nostra boss, was arrested days before he was to leave Italy. Italian police suspect that he was on his way to South Africa to visit family (including 'family' in the wider sense of criminal affiliates).[7] And, according to Italian journalists who follow the issue closely, the Calabrian mafia, or 'Ndrangheta, the most globalised of the Italian organised-crime groups, has been present in South Africa since the 1980s.[8]

The reason why individuals with mafia links chose to settle in South Africa was largely to launder criminal proceeds. South Africa has been seen as a place where law enforcement is weak and where there are opportunities for doing business across the region. Europol's 2013 threat assessment of Italian organised crime, for example, cites South Africa as one of four countries where the mafia has 'the most significant presence outside the EU' in terms of money-laundering activities.[9]

But it was other criminal networks that were beginning to emerge after Palazzolo had been resident in the country for several years that were destined to have a more violent and longer-term impact than the mafia.

When the Chinese triads arrived in South Africa, it precipitated an internal conflict within the closed world of Chinese organised crime. A comprehensive review of the Chinese triads notes that the advent of democracy in South Africa sparked new interest in the country among Chinese organised-crime figures.[10] In 1994 Cape Town police intervened at the docks to break up a turf war between Taiwanese and Hong Kong Chinese gangs. Later in the year, a Taiwanese businessman who refused to pay protection money was shot multiple times and several other murders followed.[11]

Chinese organised crime had been present in the country since at least the late 1970s, however, linked to expatriate Taiwanese communities (the South African government had good connections with Taiwan at the time.[12]) A Taiwanese group, dubbed the Table Mountain Gang, had cornered the shark-fin trade, a highly lucrative business export to China.[13] In the early 1990s, a new group of Chinese triad operators, this time with links to Hong Kong and mainland China, began to appear. They controlled the abalone-smuggling market.[14] A spate of violence ensued in the mid-1990s – a struggle for control between a resident, older Chinese criminal network, with its roots in Taiwan, and the newcomers.

Shortly before the first free election, in April 1994, two Hong Kong-based triads, the Wo Shing Wo triad and the 14K Hau triad, moved into Cape Town, eager to capture a broader market share of illicit business in South Africa. The Table Mountain Gang seems to have been a loose collection of individuals. They were to prove no match for the new arrivals.[15]

There followed a spasm of violence as the triads laid claim to the market by effectively killing off key members of the Table Mountain Gang. The latter were highly vulnerable; they had enjoyed an uninterrupted run of business. That vulnerability provided an opportunity for a new group of entrepreneurs of violence. A security company calling itself the Paragon Foundation (with links to the old white bouncer networks that we have already explored) is said to have extorted money from the Taiwanese in exchange for protection. The new triads made a deal with the money-hungry members of Paragon, who agreed to kill the people they were protecting in exchange for payment. The old generation of Taiwanese criminals effectively disintegrated under pressure from the newcomers.[16]

At the same time as the boundaries of the Chinese underworld were shifting, another major group was also setting up shop: the Nigerians. Nigerian networks had been trafficking heroin from East Asia to the developed world through their compatriot networks in Europe and North America since the 1970s. But, at the same time, instability in South Africa and the region slowed the movement of people – and thus of criminal networks – southwards. That would change in the early 1990s as democracy dawned.[17]

The slow uptick of the Nigerian criminal network in the early 1990s in South Africa also coincided with the introduction of high-quality cocaine in the country. The South African authorities had their eyes firmly on other priorities around the management of the political transition and did little to stem the flow of the contraband.[18] The influx of Nigerians also increased sharply after the return of military rule in Nigeria in 1993, as numbers fled the consequent economic decline and state corruption there.

Following 1994, Nigerian migration was also facilitated by the fact Nigerians could now apply to South Africa for political asylum, and the opportunity to obtain permanent-residence status. Obtaining South African documents at a time when Nigerians could not travel widely was an attractive option in the heyday of the new democracy.[19]

It must be emphasised, of course, that not all Nigerians who moved to South Africa became involved in the drug trade. However, harsh counter-crime measures imposed in Nigeria at the time made many so-called 'crime barons' question their long-term future at home, so there was a marked influx of criminals.

Finally, over the last few years, another foreign criminal group operating in South Africa, Israelis, long involved in the illicit diamond trade, have displayed a strong propensity for violence, although this is almost exclusively related to proxy gang wars whose origins lie in Israel. A particularly violent group, the Ramat Amidar gang, is said to have moved to

Johannesburg in the 1990s, running an extortion racket targeting Jewish families and businesses. While the links between the white bouncer networks in Johannesburg and the Israeli mafia have never been conclusively established, several of the bouncer thugs had Israeli connections. In the last few years, a spate of hits linked to various Israeli mafia groups have been reported in South Africa. But this violence is almost entirely internally contained as groups engage in violence against one another, causing little local disruption to underworld relations in South Africa.[20]

These examples show the disparate contexts of various foreign crime networks in South Africa and how each sought to influence the environment in different ways. What unites them, however, is that these groups arrived roughly at the same time, the early to mid-1990s, during South Africa's turbulent democratic transition. While individual crime kingpins, such as Palazzolo and Radovan Krejcir, are of interest, it is perhaps the broader national criminal groups, such as the Chinese, and in particular the Nigerians, that give a picture of how foreign criminal organisations have shaped the local underworld and of the alliances they have formed with South African organised crime.

As we have seen, abalone was the major business objective of the Chinese triads, and under their control illegally smuggled quantities of abalone leaving the country far outweighed legal volumes.[21] By the late 1990s abalone was a multimillion-rand industry. Low input costs, a falling rand and profit margins around $40 to $50 a kilogram meant that the estimated 300 000 kilogram of abalone recorded as entering Hong Kong between January 2002 and June 2003 would have made a whopping $15 million at the time.[22] Profit margins have grown since then as abalone has become increasingly scarce.

The growth of the trade – and the obscene profits that it generated

– attracted the triads to South Africa, where they invested in local partners. They drew in local fishing communities, paid for secret warehouses
for drying the produce, ensured sophisticated systems of transport, and
generated a whole protection economy around the trade. To manage
this supply chain as efficiently as possible, the Chinese triads needed to
cooperate with local gangs, particularly in the Cape area and along the
west coast.

In what was a symbiotic relationship, the local Cape gangs served two
critical purposes for the triads. The first is that they provided an interface
with the coastal communities where the abalone was harvested. Coloured
fishing communities, having been denied access to fishery resources in
the apartheid past, considered access to the sea in the 1990s as part of a
democratic dividend. Exploiting abalone, even illegally, was seen as a right
that had previously been denied them.[23] As a result, the legal industry was
decimated and locals were forced into greater reliance on smuggling.

The second reason for cooperation with the local gangs is that the abalone trade provided an active opportunity for barter: drugs were paid in
return for the endangered species. Security sources in South Africa have
pointed to the connections between key figures in the abalone trade and
their involvement in the shipment of drugs.[24] This barter trade obviated
the need to transfer money between Asia and South Africa.

The triads have remained a significant and active part of the underworld in South Africa, but they maintain that position with little public
visibility.

Like them, the emerging Nigerian criminal networks in South Africa
also needed local partners in crime, in this case for drug distribution, and,
as in the case of Jenny and Rose, for the burgeoning sex industry. Nigerian
drug-trafficking syndicates in the late 1990s and early 2000s based themselves, to a large degree, in Johannesburg and Durban,[25] where they built
a platform for market expansion. This coincided with the period when the

old bouncer mafia in Johannesburg was fading and Nigerians were beginning to form a critical new resource for drug trafficking.

The penetration of Nigerians in Cape Town happened later and has a particular geographical profile. They are unlikely to be found on the Cape Flats, the home turf of the local gangs, and the Nigerian dealers have also been largely pushed out from the inner city and the now redeveloping area of Sea Point. They have a strong presence, however, in the city's northern suburbs around Milnerton. The big bosses are said to live in areas that are at some distance from the places where the drugs are distributed and stored.[26]

What is remarkable is how quickly the Nigerians have assumed prominence in South Africa. Yet, as indicated, they are seldom publicly recognised as key elements in the underworld, partly because there is little coverage of their activities and because they are careful to maintain a low profile. But speak to any police officer on the street in a major South African city about drug markets, and Nigerians dealers will come up quickly in the conversation. Crime-intelligence officers and detectives say that they struggle to recruit sources within the Nigerian community, and that their South African sources are unable to tell them much about the details of the Nigerians' operations.[27] Unsurprisingly, there has been no prosecution of a Nigerian crime baron recently in South Africa.

Nigerian crime bosses do have a flashy lifestyle, with the cars and women to go with it, but pinning their illegal business on them is hard. 'Nigerians compete with each other, but they also look after each other,' is how one police detective explained their elusiveness. 'They help each other get established – a bit like Portuguese business did in the south of Johannesburg. The primary objective is to establish a broader community from which to operate. The success of the community as a whole means success for everybody in it.'[28]

The Nigerian networks seek compromise, and not conflict, with the police. This has been a key driver of lower-level corruption in the police force. There is some evidence that the police view Nigerian drug dealers as an easy source of cash, people whom they can target for bribes: 'They don't belong here and it is only drug money,' said a police sector commander, describing how his officers view the relationship.[29] But it is likely that the money that the Nigerians possess also goes higher up the system: one officer reported a case where a drug dealer paid R5 000 'without even flinching' for a police investigation docket in which he was implicated.[30]

The Nigerians who killed Jenny and Rose are part of a worldwide network of organised criminality that is arguably one of the most dynamic, and understudied, fields of global crime. Nigerian networks are having a decisive impact on the nature of the South African criminal underworld. While high-profile cases like that of Radovan Krejcir constantly make the news, Nigerian criminals seldom appear in the newspapers; reporters don't know where to find them, and even if they did, they are usually unwilling to talk.[31]

Nigerian nationals control significant portions of the global trade in cocaine and heroin integrally related to the presence of an expatriate population of Nigerian nationals in significant numbers in countries such as Brazil and Thailand, for example, close to the source markets for these drugs.

It has been noted that their networks operate like flexible organisations that rely heavily on trust among close-knit communities, drawn almost exclusively from the country's southeast.[32] Using strong ethnic ties as a trust-building measure has been widely noted in historical research on organised crime.[33]

The Nigerian model seems to rely on making sure all business dealings are 'clean', meaning that they are concealed from outside scrutiny. At the same time, however, Nigerian networks rely on locals to act as couriers, to be recruited into prostitution networks (as we have seen in the case of Jenny and Rose), and to interface with the gangs and the state. These local agents are paid for their services, but they seldom know more than they should, certainly not enough to implicate members of the network. The Nigerian criminal business model therefore relies on drawing locals to the fringes of their network, but never to its centre.

Nigerian men often have local wives or girlfriends, but these women seldom know what is going on, or they know better than to ask. In one case reported to me, for example, the wife of a Nigerian is always asked to leave the room when talk gets down to 'business', particularly when money is to be handled.[34]

A good recent example of how locals are used by the Nigerians, but excluded from the operations, was recounted to me by a police officer working on Nigerian organised crime. Anel (not her real name), a young woman from a township background who had fallen on hard times, became involved with a Nigerian man, Sam. Finding her sleeping one day on a park bench, Sam brought her food. Eventually he let her stay in his house. Over time they became romantically involved and eventually got married. Later, Anel spent some time in Nigeria and learnt to 'cook' tik. The use of tik has grown rapidly in South Africa over the last ten years, in parallel with the presence of Nigerian criminal networks. This drug has fuelled violence, as we have seen, between the Cape gangs. Sam was subsequently shot in a dispute with one of the gangs over drug turf.

Within weeks of his death, Anel was contacted by several of Sam's compatriots. Sam owed them money, they said, and Anel, being his wife, was liable for the debt. Anel had never known that Sam owed money to the network in which he worked, and doubted that it was true. But Sam's former partners seized the passports of Anel's children and they were flown to Nigeria. 'You can work off your debt,' Anel was told, and she was once again employed as a tik cook, forced to work as a captive in a remote area in Limpopo. She feels she has little choice other than to pay off the fictitious debt.[35]

And there must be many other examples like Anel – women who are drawn into the network of Nigerian drug traffickers, desperate to make a living or on the edge of destitution. There is also evidence that Nigerian criminals target women who work in call centres and have access to databases of phone numbers. A text message sent to thousands of numbers saying 'I have new shit' is likely to reach at least a few people who want to buy drugs, providing an opportunity for expanding market share.[36] But it is these women who, while drawn into the networks, are most likely to be victims of violence from the Nigerians.

As we saw in the context of the bouncer extortion groups in Johannesburg, Nigerians are skilful at capturing market share in a way that does not confront the interests of other criminal groups. Nigerian organised crime conveys a sense that it is not in competition with other groups, yet it is in fact highly competitive, seeking to deliver a service in the shape of quality drugs that are quickly delivered. Theirs is the language of cooperation and compromise, all the while creeping forward in the space in which they operate. Because of this, there is a common perception that Nigerian criminal groups are not violent, but, as the cases of Jenny and Rose indicate, the contrary is true – they just happen to be selective in where and when violence is used.

In Cape Town, Nigerian criminal groups provide a service to the gangs, supplying them with drugs, while seeking to grow market share for their own drug sales. In areas where they have crossed into the drug sales turf of the established gangs, there have been violent clashes. Three Nigerians were killed in 2015, for example, in the northern suburbs in an area where drug territory was contested. It is significant that the Nigerian criminal networks did not retaliate in an openly violent way, however. Had the dispute been between two Cape Town gangs, it is likely that things would have spiralled into an orgy of violence. The approach the Nigerians took, insiders say, was to negotiate a deal with the gangs, with an underworld truce bringing peace.[37] Violence, a Nigerian dealer told me, is 'bad for business'.[38]

There are some irregular exceptions, however. In July 2013, for example, four armed Nigerians were killed in Benoni when their car was ambushed, apparently by other Nigerians. In what appears to have been a local gang war, three Nigerians had earlier been killed in a cellphone shop in the same town.[39]

And, as the deaths of Jenny and Rose show, brutality can be applied in a highly targeted way that is designed to send a message: 'If you work with us, don't cross us.' But that violence was applied by Nigerians themselves – South Africans are seldom involved in hits when it comes to the Nigerian networks.[40]

Violence can be a risky strategy in an environment where foreign criminal networks are less established than they would be at home. Nevertheless, as we have seen in the case of the triads in South Africa, targeted violence may be needed to break into new markets where competitors are already present. However, the degree to which that violence targets locals appears to be limited.

The Chinese triad societies are regarded worldwide as being highly focused, ruthless criminal businesses. Certain triad societies are said to cooperate with one another and provide mutual protection. The reality, however, is that there have been increased conflicts among triad groups.[41] How the triads have killed in South Africa reflects such conflicts and says a lot about their modus operandi in countries outside of the Chinese mainland and Hong Kong.

There are now said to be four triad groups active in South Africa – the Sun Yee On group and the 14K-Ngai group, in addition to the two mentioned earlier. In addition to the abalone trade, they appear also to be active in extortion, loan sharking and the illegal sale and transfer of property. The Chinese groups have a presence, albeit a shadowy one, and a reputation for violence among themselves. They are unlikely to hire external actors to do their dirty business, and cases are seldom, if ever, solved.[42]

One case, involving the murder of a Chinese family in Pretoria in November 2004, shines a light onto the nature of targeted killings by Chinese organised crime. The main victim, Jia-Bin Li, had refused to sell a property to the triads, and the murder was described by a triad member in the city as 'intended to send a message to the Chinese community. ... In future they will listen.'[43] The four victims, Li and his wife and two daughters, were strangled and stuffed into a drain by a main road. A leader of one of the triads present in South Africa, Hei Dao, of the Sun Yee On triad, talked openly about the murders to the media: 'Contract killings in the Chinese community are performed by hired hitmen brought in from outside the country.'[44] The Secretary of the Beijing Police Cooperation Centre, Hai Yao, confirmed the identity of the suspected hitman: 'He is a well-known operator in triad circles. He is thought to operate from Hong Kong or mainland China.'[45] He has never been arrested.

In one particular case that proved to be an exception to the triad practice of recruiting hitmen from within their own circle, a member of a Chinese criminal group was murdered by three hitmen hired in Johannesburg and flown to Cape Town for the day to conduct the deed.[46]

But, generally, among ethnic-based organised crime groups in South Africa, violence tends to be an internal affair. It has utility only if contained and used strategically. If violence becomes too rampant, it might expose the group to uncomfortable scrutiny by domestic institutions, and their 'foreignness' makes them an easily identifiable target. An illustration of this is the degree to which Chinese, Israeli and, to some extent Italian, groups may have targeted their own communities for extortion

– presumably because their compatriots would be less likely to report cases to the police, and more likely to pay and keep quiet.

## The great disruptor

Foreign organised crime has an impact on the South African public's perception in markedly different ways, which brings us to the widely reported case of Radovan Krejcir. The errant Czech has attracted, and continues to attract, an enormous amount of media attention. That is partly because he courted the media closely, but also because he is in so many ways a stereotypical mafia-like figure – dressed in a black leather jacket, surrounded by acolytes at his favourite Johannesburg restaurant, boasting of his links to top politicians and the state.

Yet, despite assertions to the contrary, Krejcir did not belong to a mafia group. He had underworld connections in the Czech Republic and some apparent links to men of violence in Serbia, but he seemed very much on his own. That meant, unlike the Chinese and Nigerian criminal entrants to South Africa, that he had no network in which to embed himself – he had to seek it out.

Radovan Krejcir earned his criminal spurs in the chaotic days at the end of the Soviet Union and the creation of the Czech Republic, when he appeared to establish a low-level network of criminal contacts. All the evidence suggests that he did not initially fare well in the post-transition Czech economy and struggled to make ends meet. However, he soon stumbled onto a scheme that involved illegally manipulating an oil-import subsidy, from which he is said to have generated considerable profits.

With the money, Krejcir bought the support of a circle of state actors – politicians, prosecutors and police – and received protection for his activities. However, his scheme turned bad: Krejcir appears to have funded a politician who ultimately lost his gambit for power, leaving him vulnerable to attack by political opponents. While mafia figures may look for new markets globally, they are as often as not forced to flee their homeland and seek new operations elsewhere. Following a crackdown in 2005 by the Czech authorities, Krejcir fled the country for the Seychelles.

Krejcir was arrested on arrival in OR Tambo Airport in 2007, having tried to enter South Africa on a Seychelles passport under a false name. He had been 'red-flagged' by Interpol for his offences in the oil scam, so when the Czech Republic alerted the South African authorities, Krejcir was detained for a month. He was released on bail of R1 million, following which he applied for refugee status, claiming political persecution in his homeland.

Although his spell in prison was brief, it had been fortuitous in helping him gain a foothold in South Africa's underworld. He shared a cell with a Greek Cypriot, George Louca. Prisons, as studies of criminal movement have suggested, are important interfaces for criminal networking and building credibility.[47] As if to demonstrate precisely this point, Louca provided Krejcir with an array of introductions to the Johannesburg underworld, particularly around the suburb of Bedfordview, where, later, Krejcir would set up shop.[48]

Krejcir was a complete outsider who rapidly found a network in Johannesburg. But to credit the development of that network only to the serendipity of his short imprisonment belies Krejcir's demonstrated skill in taking advantage of opportunities that were offered. By all accounts, Krejcir knew what counted in the Johannesburg underworld: he promised money and paid some of it; he began to seek out police officers to befriend; and he scanned the environment for political connections.

Krejcir's strategy appeared to be a combination of bombast and claims to great wealth. He may also have been assisted by the particular nature of the Johannesburg underworld. His interlocutors, from the city's fragmented criminal networks, would have had an eye on making quick money.[49] But what was remarkable was the speed at which Krejcir managed to connect with key figures in the South African underworld. Within a few months, Krejcir had been introduced to a criminal network that included Glenn Agliotti, Lolly Jackson and Cyril Beeka, over whom Krejcir would later exert his influence.

Krejcir had arrived at a time when the old apartheid-era distinctions separating the underworld pockets were being eroded. Introductions were made across these old boundaries as criminal markets and networks extended, and new patterns of criminal governance were formed. Beeka was looking for Johannesburg connections and entered Krejcir's milieu. Krejcir got down to business: he made sure he was known and started to wheel people into his employ.

When the body of Uwe Gemballa, a German luxury-car dealer who had been in correspondence with Krejcir, was discovered in October 2010, after he had gone missing eight months earlier at OR Tambo Airport, the Czech started making the headlines. But the subsequent murders of night-club owner Jackson and Beeka placed him firmly in the public spotlight, with rumours that he had been involved. All three had been one-time associates or business partners of Krejcir, and each was said to have fallen out with him over financial or personal matters.

Associates alleged that Gemballa had been involved in money launder-ing, with Krejcir concealing cash in the cars that Gemballa imported to the country. One such exchange had gone awry when the money was sto-len from the car en route.[50] Paul O'Sullivan attributes the motive for the murder to a disagreement over money owed to Gemballa and an attempt to extract more money from him.[51] Krejcir, however, was never charged for this murder and has denied involvement.[52] Three others were convicted.

Jackson and Krejcir subsequently fell out when Jackson accused Krejcir of stealing money from him.[53] Jackson was shot multiple times in May

2010 in a house that Louca was renting.[54] The murder was first pinned on Louca, who allegedly confessed to Gauteng crime intelligence head, General Mabasa, but he changed his story just before he died, stating in a sworn affidavit that Krejcir had in fact pulled the trigger.[55]

Beeka was assassinated in March 2011, just weeks after he had been in a public brawl with Krejcir. According to a statement by Miloslav Potiska, an associate of Krecjir, the Czech had ordered Beeka's death because of a gold deal gone bad and the 'humiliation' he had suffered in the fight with Beeka.[56] According to another source, Beeka knew too much about the Jackson murder and had to be killed.[57] Krejcir had allegedly ordered the murder through two prominent Cape Town underworld figures and businessmen. This apparently suited the Cape Town mobsters, as it enabled them to expand their control over the criminal markets in the city. However, Krejcir apparently failed to pay for the hit and this created lasting resentment.[58]

The day after Beeka's death, Krejcir's home was raided by the specialist police unit, the Hawks, who discovered a hit list of assassination targets (including Beeka, and private and police detectives). Although it is unclear whether Krejcir wanted this list discovered, it spread fear through the underworld and among the police engaged in the investigation. Krejcir, through his hired hitmen, was known to have the capacity to kill. Two days later Krejcir handed himself over to face the much more mundane charges of defrauding his medical-aid scheme, a case in which his former physician had turned state witness.[59]

Over the next two years, Krejcir was believed to be linked to – and on several occasions arrested for – the murder of another five people. These were Lolly Jackson's lawyer, Ian Jordan, who was engaged in a dispute with Krejcir over Jackson's estate; Mark Andrews, who also had claims against Jackson's estate; Phumlani Ncube, who worked as a debt collector for Krejcir and may have stolen R50 000 in Krugerrands from him;

Bassam Issa, believed to be supplying drugs to Johannesburg nightclubs (the same gun was used in Issa's murder as in Ncube's); and Veselin Laganin, a Serbian criminal and a co-accused with Krejcir on an earlier armed-robbery charge.[60]

A murder with less tangible links to Krejcir was that of Kevin Trytsman, a private investigator, who also claimed to work for the National Intelligence Agency. Trytsman, who had provided information to Krejcir, was shot by his own lawyer in 2009.[61] The lawyer reportedly received a phone call afterwards from Krejcir expressing his thanks. The following year, Chris Kouremetis was shot in a botched drug deal, which intelligence sources also link to Krejcir.[62]

Krejcir also allegedly ordered assassinations to be carried out in Eastern Europe; O'Sullivan believes he is responsible for six murders in the Czech Republic.[63]

Krejcir's brutal strategies earned him few friends. There were at least three attempts on his life in South Africa. Dramatically, one involved a remotely activated array of guns hidden beneath a car aimed at Krejcir's habitual parking spot in July 2013, from which he miraculously escaped, and in November that year a bomb was detonated outside business premises he owned, killing two but failing to take out Krejcir.[64]

Even by the standards of the Johannesburg underworld, it was a bloody trail of bodies. Those who were killed were focal points in the South African criminal world, Beeka being perhaps the most prominent. Krejcir undoubtedly caused significant instability in established criminal relations – no doubt one of the reasons there were so many attempts made on his life. At the same time, his lack of trusted associates in South Africa and his high profile in the media made him vulnerable to the machinations of the local criminal underworld and the law-enforcement authorities as his police protection weakened and then gave way.

It is worth asking the question of whether mafia groups can readily shift to overseas territories. There is a fanciful notion of mafiosi who get on a plane and smoothly establish themselves in other countries. In reality, however, it may be much more difficult to get things going elsewhere, rather like opening a business in another country.[65] Certain studies of 'mafias that move' have concluded that mafia-type organisations are hard to export because they are essentially locally rooted, often with strong patterns of integration in the local criminal and political economies, and because they benefit from a symbiotic relationship with the state.[66] Similar conclusions have been reached by a comparative study of how criminal networks spread across the globe. These suggest that the 'density of criminal relations is higher locally than at the international level'[67] – fancy language for saying that local control and presence is the first step to building global criminal exchanges.

That does not mean that mafia-type figures or networks are unable to cross borders – only that it is essential that they find a way to embed themselves locally, either by generating or buying a local network of support (as did Palazzolo and Krejcir), or bringing the network with them (as in the case of the triads and Nigerians). In both cases, the way assassination is used and who does the dirty work are very different.

Palazzolo had sought to generate local ties by establishing corrupt relations within the white political establishment, whose cohesion was, by the late 1980s, beginning to fragment under pressure. Palazzolo's skill lay in his ability to bridge the transition between the old the new orders, although in the end he, too, proved vulnerable to law enforcement – although notably not while he was in South Africa.

Radovan Krejcir, a less skilful operator, openly engaged in violent activities to establish himself in the underworld. It was a position that could not last. But, by engaging in violence, Krejcir caused a lot of disruption in the perennially unstable underworld, where bosses constantly jockey for position.

Both the Chinese and Nigerian criminal networks, for the most part a faceless presence in the country, have been more successful in shaping local underworld relations to achieve their objectives. In both cases this has relied on their being adept at providing services to local crime groups, and using violence that is either only internally targeted or aimed at South Africans on the fringes of the network, who have little influence in the local underworld.

Both the triads and the Nigerians, fearing informants as well as competition from local criminals, have maintained high levels of internal integrity built on three intersecting features – ethnicity, language and trust. As in the licit world of commerce, their widening presence, particularly that of Nigerian criminal networks, has been key to shaping South African drug markets. The interface between local gangs and the supply of drugs from Nigerian sources is now, for example, a key feature of the Western Cape. Growing conflict and casualties, as an outcome of drug wars between gangs in Cape Town, are the result of the role played by Nigerian criminal drug networks.[68] Nigerian groups, as we have seen, have been careful not to be drawn into these conflicts, however.

Foreign criminals, like Radovan Krejcir, will appear periodically in the news. But although a high profile in the media may play to the criminal ego, it is not a sustainable strategy for long-term underworld survival. Sustainability requires the control and shaping of local supply and demand to suit global criminal markets. Alliances with local groups will be a prerequisite for stability, but so too will be a critical mass of foreign operators on the ground.

By pursuing such a strategy, Chinese triads and Nigerian criminal groups in South Africa have built a foundation for themselves for a long-term future.

# 7

## Freedom's mother:
## Crime, politics and assassination

Community-housing activist Thuli Ndlovu was at home in KwaNdengezi, a township in KwaZulu-Natal. It was a Sunday evening, 28 September 2014, dusk was falling and Thuli was watching television. At a table nearby sat Sphe Madlala, an 18-year-old neighbour who had recently matriculated and was trying to get a place at university. Sphe had come around to tutor Thuli's daughter in her matric studies. Thuli's infant son, named Freedom to denote what his mother aspired for him, was also in the house, being watched by Thuli's mother, who lived with them.[1]

This tranquil domestic scene belied the fact that it had been a stressful day. Thuli had just returned from a working visit to distant Cape Town and had received a call during the day to attend a meeting at the local police station. She did not attend, but a colleague, Ndamo Mzimela, went on her behalf. Mzimela was then warned by the police to leave the area 'or face assassination'.

If that weren't terrifying enough, an ANC councillor from the municipality, Mduduzi Ngcobo, had been driving around Thuli's house in his black Nissan Navara pick-up truck, a status symbol of his local political heft. Ngcobo had a reputation for operating on the edges of the law – a gangster politician whose connections with the local underworld were widely known. Thuli and Ngcobo were at opposing ends in a bitter dispute involving housing allocation in the town. So, when Thuli realised Councillor Ngcobo was in her neighbourhood, she is said to have told her grandmother, 'Today we are going to be shot!' She said the same thing in a phone call to a friend who worked with her in a shack-dwellers' association, Abahlali baseMjondolo, an advocacy organisation that promotes access to land and housing for the destitute.

Things in KwaNdengezi had been getting very hostile for a while, and it was becoming increasingly difficult to work out who could be trusted. Thuli was suspicious of the police. They seemed far too close to certain local politicians, including Ngcobo. It did not help that the ANC was also in charge of policing at provincial level.

Just how far the police seemed to be in the pocket of Councillor Ngcobo had been evident ever since the community had started to become active over the housing issue. The dispute, which went back five years, concerned two interconnected issues: the building of new houses and who they should be allocated to.

In 2010 Ngcobo announced that a government-sponsored housing project would be undertaken in the area. There was consensus that the new housing was essential but concerns were raised about where the state-funded Reconstruction and Development Programme houses would be built. It was agreed that there would be further consultations between the community and their representatives, but when these were scheduled Ngcobo failed to turn up. This failure to have a formal engagement around the proposed development led to considerable mistrust between local government and the community.

As a result, the residents formed a local chapter of Abahlali baseMjondolo, a mass movement for landless people in KwaZulu-Natal, as a means to represent their position and help them lobby as a group. But the NGO's launch was disrupted by political interests: they were denied the use of the community hall and Ngcobo had shown up with a group of armed men; he was also armed. The police did not intervene.

On another occasion, Thuli and members of her organisation had been protesting against corruption when they were threatened with a gun by an MK veteran from the area. A case of intimidation had been opened against the man at the police station but, as far as the activists could tell, no investigation ever took place. After that protest, Councillor Ngcobo, accompanied by police and the MK man, pointed out which of the protesters should be arrested. The police took four people into custody, but charges were later dropped given lack of evidence.

Once construction on the housing project got under way in 2012, the tension flared into open conflict. The houses were built in people's property, in their gardens and over ancestral graveyards. A sense of unease pervaded the community. There were allegations that live ammunition was fired by unknown men as the construction work in the area proceeded.

As allegations began to surface that the new houses were being allocated to people outside of the community and, worse, that Councillor Ngcobo was selling the houses and pocketing the money, things took an even more serious turn. The community, coordinated by their NGO, organised a series of protests in response. In October 2013, members of the community set up a roadblock, protesting against the allocation and selling of the houses. The police arrived, accompanied, again, by Ngcobo, and proceeded to break up the gathering. Thuli, then the interim chairperson of Abahlali baseMjondolo, was singled out for intimidation and was assaulted.

No wonder that Thuli feared for her life that Sunday evening in September 2014 when, almost predictably, Ngcobo appeared outside her house as darkness fell, firing his gun into the air.

While Thuli had been away in Cape Town, the community had turned up the heat. There had been a spontaneous protest against the housing allocation and the actions of Councillor Ngcobo. They had approached senior figures, including provincial politicians. They showed that they would not back down. It was clear that things were coming to a head as their protests became noticed at a higher level. The party was embarrassed and there were rumours that warnings were sent from the provincial ANC office to the local government to curb the conflict.

What is striking about Abahlali baseMjondolo's account of events during this period is that they anticipated and openly discussed the possibility that one of them would be assassinated over the conflict. It had reached a point where somebody was going to pay with their life and there was a general sense that Mzimela, Thuli's colleague who had attended the police meeting in September, would be the most likely target. For one, the police had already given him a clear warning.

But their speculation turned out to be wrong. It was Thuli, the activist mother of two, who was in mortal danger. She had become an increasingly powerful voice for change in her community, an obstacle to the housing development that was being hijacked to benefit the pockets of the municipality's best-connected members. An obstacle that would need to be eliminated.

If Thuli was to be removed for commercial reasons, then taking her out could be quantified in rands and cents. Ngcobo and a colleague, Councillor Velile Lutsheko, procured the services of a hitman, one Mlungisi Ndlovu. They negotiated a price: R15 000 for the life of the woman who was disrupting their plans – a standard fee for a hitman. The deal was done, perhaps in the local shebeen or at one of their homes. There would no doubt have been some discussion over the price and tactics, and an emphasis that final payment was dependent on a successful outcome. Ngcobo would have been adamant about that: make sure she is dead, otherwise no payment.

There had been reports that Ngcobo had been seen associating with *izinkabi*, with their links to the taxi industry, and the hitman, Ndlovu (who, ironically, had the same name as his victim), had killed before presumably. It is unlikely that Ngcobo would have employed some amateur; he would have had a good understanding of how things needed to be done.

And so, that Sunday evening, Mlungisi Ndlovu had set out to meet his contractual obligations. He must have waited near the house while darkness fell over KwaNdengezi. Meanwhile, Ngcobo in his sinister black Navara had already driven around Thuli's house to check whether she was at home. Perhaps, despite the payment to a third party and the risk he was taking, he wanted to be seen to be associated with the murder; perhaps he wanted to show who was in charge in this town.

Between six thirty and seven o'clock, he made his move. Mlungisi Ndlovu, hitman, remover of obstacles and soon to be killer of the mother of Freedom, burst in through the door of Thuli's small house. He identified her quickly; there was no doubt who he had come to kill. He fired numerous times at her, hitting her in seven different places. Thuli Ndlovu, Freedom's guardian and protector, local activist against corruption and for the rights of the poor and dispossessed of KwaNdengezi, was dead in minutes.

## Government by gangsters

The assassination of Thuli Ndlovu is rather unusual, in that the hitman and the two councillors who hired him were arrested and faced trial. All three were convicted and are serving life-imprisonment sentences. But that is the exception rather than the rule; according to one estimate, only about one in ten political assassinations results in a conviction.[2]

While recent media focus has largely been on issues of political turmoil at the national level, criminalised governance has proliferated in local-government municipalities across the country. The result is localised kleptocracy: ecosystems that feed on themselves, concentrating power in the hands of a few individuals and sometimes backed by violence, or the threat of it. This process of power abuse is summarised succinctly in these words by a journalist writing in the *Mail & Guardian*: 'Regional ANC power-brokers land jobs as mayors and municipal managers, with their backers at branch level becoming councillors. Tenders go to the right business people, who channel part of their financial rewards back into building support bases.'[3]

That conclusion neatly captures the motives of Councillor Ngcobo. His objective was not the use of violence to overthrow the political system but a means to gain access to resources by exploiting the existing system.[4] Under these circumstances, local-government officials and bureaucrats work in an environment where the threat of violence is high – both as recipients and perpetrators. People who threaten the economic interests of the powerful are targeted. Municipal managers tend to be a favourite because they control who accesses resources and tenders. But, in this case, Thuli Ndlovu, an outsider, did much the same: she was murdered for exposing corrupt political interests.

In South Africa the majority of targeted killings with a political colour have taken place in the lowest sphere of government. As already noted, the South African Local Government Association revealed in 2016 that over 450 councillors and local civil servants had been killed over the last decade, and this figure does not include those killed in a flurry of murders in the run-up to the 2016 local elections.[5] Our data, restricted as it is to hits as I have defined them, is more limited in number. What the numbers show, however, is a steady uptick in instances of politically motivated hits since the early 2000s. The number of political hits in the database peaked in 2016, coinciding with the local-government elections (*see Figure 5 in the appendix*). In the environment of local politics the reality is that killing has become a commercial arrangement, an investment for the future.

The mingling of crime, politics and murder has occurred in municipalities across the country, but KwaZulu-Natal has the highest number of recorded cases.[6] A recent study that interviewed survivors of violence and their relatives, like Thuli's family, concluded that 'contemporary-intra-party violence was perceived as being driven by selfish, individual motives, rather than universal goals such as freedom, equality and democracy'.[7]

The effects of 'gangster government' at the municipal level are very serious for society. Most obviously, the provision of services is threatened when money is channelled by civil servants for their personal economic gain, while fear of assassination stifles democratic political debate. When municipal contracts are awarded to political – and criminal – allies, the prospects for effective service delivery – in this case, social housing – are thwarted.

Many local communities have seen this increasing overlay of criminal and political interests, so much so that those interests have become hard to disentangle. It is a case of the criminalisation of politics and the politicisation of crime. The nature of local government is becoming defined by violence. Given the problematic nature of open violence (as we have seen in other contexts), there has been a shift to the murky world of assassination in the context of political violence. That way, obstacles can be removed while the motives and perpetrators are generally masked. (As indicated, the imprisonment of Thuli Ndlovu's murderers was an exception.)

While violence remains an important tool for organised crime in such contexts, openly perpetrated violence (as we have seen in other areas) is increasingly deemed unacceptable in circumstances where the media and community groups are active, and where the police may be forced by political and public pressure to act.[8] One implication is a shift to targeted assassinations given that the risks for the perpetrators are lower and killing is cheap. The result is assassination conducted by unseen hands for a fee. As a gang boss said to me, even if a report makes its way into the newspapers, it is still possible to 'create enough doubt about why people were killed'.[9]

As an indication of just how serious the problem is in South Africa, some 50 political assassinations occurred in the months before the local-government elections in August 2016. The South African Human Rights Commission expressed grave concern about this.[10] But it is wrong to make the assumption that such killing is confined to competition around the most recent local-government elections – it is a phenomenon that has stalked local government for at least a decade.

Access to the resources and patronage provided by local government is a high-stakes game.

Such patronage systems, epitomised by tender irregularities for local-government contracting, which have become widespread and widely reported in the media, are important sources of political power for local strongmen. In June 2016, the Auditor-General shockingly reported that irregular expenditure at local-government level had more than doubled since 2010/11 to R14.75 billion, with a larger number of local authorities involved.[11] The irregular and illegal disbursement of local-government resources is directly linked to conflict between different factions within ANC branches.

The main cause for the illegal scramble is that, in many poor communities, local government is the main source of revenue. Small towns and rural municipalities offer little in the way of economic opportunities and jobs. In such cases, the route to economic and political power quite literarily runs through the main entrance to the municipal buildings. Statistics show that there is a positive correlation between the provincial distribution of political assassinations and levels of poverty, as measured by the distribution of households in the low-income category. The greatest number of political killings has occurred in KwaZulu-Natal, which also has the highest proportion of low-income households (at 20 per cent).[12] In fact, in all primarily rural provinces where there is evidence of local assassinations – Mpumalanga, North West and Limpopo – the proportion of households in the lower-income category has grown over the last decade.[13] In provinces reporting fewer assassinations of local political figures – Northern Cape, Free State, Western Cape and Gauteng – the number of lower-income households has declined. (As an exception, the Eastern Cape, which has high levels of poverty, has experienced comparatively few assassinations.)

These are not perfect measures by any means, and the correlation is only a rough one. Nevertheless, it underscores the point that in the context of poverty and in declining economic conditions, resources generated through local government are critical tools of patronage for local elites, especially when other sources of income are absent. As civil-society group Corruption Watch noted in a recent report: 'Municipalities in poor areas that are not able to raise a lot of income rely heavily on the funds from national government.'[14] The same report concludes that much-needed money for service delivery is diverted to the pockets of councillors and officials. In one municipality, which was reported as reflecting the position in many others, officials had raised their salary by 50 per cent even though the municipality had received 14 unqualified audits.[15]

But the picture is more complex than this. Some poor municipalities have seen lower levels of violence. At least one reason for the high level of violence and assassination associated with KwaZulu-Natal is the culture of the gun that took root and the high levels of conflict in that province beginning in the 1980s. Heightened political conflict in this period also intensified long-standing resource conflicts in some communities – and this in the context of poor, brutal and biased policing.[16] In certain places, therefore, resorting to violence is not a new phenomenon: it is an established practice, drawing on local entrepreneurs of violence – hitmen like

Mlungisi Ndlovu, and those who connected him to the councillors who employed his services.

At local-government level, targeted violence has various interrelated dimensions and causes. The central issue, however, is the proportional-representation electoral system, which creates competition among those jostling to get onto the lucrative party list. Targeted killing is a way, quite literally, to remove people from consideration or from the list altogether, evidenced by the fact the killing intensified as the ANC list was being finalised in 2016.[17] In my own interviews, candidates and serving councillors reported their fear of being 'removed violently from the scene' by competitors.[18]

Salaries for councillors vary between R200 000 and R500 000 a year for what is essentially part-time employment and the positions often come with an enticing package of financial benefits in addition to the basic salary. The competition is the most intense in the ruling party. As a *Business Day* report put it, 'some ANC members claim that [party] leaders receive bribes of R20 000 from potential candidates to ensure that they are [as] high up on the party list [as possible] to become councillors ...'[19] That amount of money will also buy the ability to remove opponents who might stand in your way – permanently.

Secondly, senior civil servants in local government occupy an influential place by virtue of the fact that they manage tenders. The pressure on top bureaucrats can be severe and they live with the constant threat of violence. Take the example of Simo Mncwabe, the chief financial officer of the Mooi Mpofana Municipality, again in KwaZulu-Natal. The hit that killed him displayed all the characteristics of planning and preparation. The victim was dispatched during his regular school run at six in the morning, with his two young children in the car. The gunman, an experienced professional, shot Mncwabe through the windscreen of his vehicle with an assault rifle, hitting him multiple times. The pressure must have become intolerable as competing interests battled for his attention or threatened him with the consequences of not making the 'right decision'. Fearing for his life, Mncwabe had resigned the day before he was killed. Family members won't speak about where the threats emanated from, but, as gatekeeper to the municipality's finances, Mncwabe' held a position of managerial authority in which he was liable to enrage people who did not see contracts and other interests go their way.[20]

Another way that violence makes itself felt in local government relates to whistle-blowers who are hounded out and even killed. To illustrate this, take the case of Jimmy Mohlala, an ANC politician and speaker of the Mbombela Council. Mohlala had discovered a number of irregularities in the tender process around the construction of the new stadium for the Football World Cup. This included a scheme where provincial and municipal officials had conspired to defraud the community on whose land the stadium would be built. When Mohlala exposed this, naming several officials and ANC members, the party demanded that he resign. He refused to step down, reiterating that he was innocent, although he told his wife that he feared for his life.

In January 2009, two masked gunmen approached Mohlala's house in broad daylight, shooting him dead and wounding his son. It was later reported that two policemen had escorted the killer away from the scene of the crime in a flying-squad car.[21] Following his death, police are said to have 'arrested' and tortured his wife with electric shocks, in an attempt to get her to confess that she had ordered his killing.

Hit lists of people who had apparently stood in the way of lucrative World Cup tenders were later circulated in the media. An assassin who had reputedly been hired to do the work revealed that he had been commissioned by 'top-level politicians and businessmen' to kill people who they believed would expose how contracts were illegally acquired.[22]

In a similar case, in March 2009, Moss Phakoe, another whistle-blower, was assassinated. Phakoe was also an ANC councillor, in this case for Rustenberg, who had attempted to expose corruption within the municipality. Phakoe had tried to use channels in the ANC to raise his concerns, including at the highest levels of government, but was unsuccessful. According to his family, he felt increasingly isolated and threatened. He had spent some time gathering evidence of corruption into a dossier, which after his death, mysteriously disappeared and was found when police raided the home of former head of crime intelligence, Richard Mdluli.[23]

The discovery of Phakoe's corruption dossier in Mdluli's possession raises serious questions around the connections between local-government assassinations and the interests of provincial and national government politicians. Such linkages are often opaque and difficult to draw conclusions from, but linking local violence with politics at the national level is an important step in understanding the implications of how complex criminal networks have aligned themselves with the state and certain national political interests.

One of the consequences of violence targeted at local government officials is the pressure on municipalities to allocate scarce resources to private security. Given the degree of violence councillors may be exposed to, a national government notice on the use of personal security services for councillors was gazetted in January 2014, making provision for councillors to be provided with 'personal security', subject to the condition that 'a threat and risk analysis' should be conducted by the police.[24] In large municipalities the issue of VIP protection has been fiercely debated in council. In Pretoria, seven bodyguards were allocated to the mayor alone.[25] In Durban, private bodyguards had been protecting 28 city councillors at a cost of some R36 million a year to the taxpayer.[26]

And it's not just in the big cities where the taxpayer funds councillors' security. For example, the mayor and deputy mayor of the tiny Emnambithi-Ladysmith Municipality in KwaZulu-Natal were allocated no fewer than 15 bodyguards between them.[27] In Mbombela the cost of contracting private-security personnel increased from R7.3 million to R11.3 million in the space of a few years for the mayor, deputy mayor and numerous councillors.[28] Vast expenditure on bodyguards has become increasingly the norm. In the context in which many municipalities face an ongoing crisis with funding, this is an expensive addition to already constrained budgets.

Their presence also creates a thuggish arms race among councillors, some of whom view bodyguards as a perk of the job and a status symbol.[29] And, ironically, in some cases the bodyguards are recruited from the same nurseries of violence that spawn the hitmen. Indeed, there is some evidence that bodyguards are used offensively, conducting hits against opponents.[30]

The linkage between local government and violence is not confined to South Africa. It is a feature of governance in other countries, including Central America and elsewhere, in cases where organised crime and local government blur into each other – and it is dependent on a set of historical factors. A recent study conducted by the Institute for Democracy and Electoral Assistance (IDEA), reviewing how organised crime has evolved in the Baltics, draws conclusions that are remarkably pertinent to South Africa. The study concludes that relationships between crime and politics at local level are functional, as opposed to ideological: 'A nexus is formed where there is mutual benefit for both parties.'[31] That symbiotic relationship – a theme we have seen in other criminal contexts – thrives on close-knit social and economic ties. In communities where crime and politics become blurred, mutual interests build a dynamic of gangster governance. As IDEA notes in its study, the exercise of politics in resource-constrained environments has shifted from the ideological domain to 'an increased focus on individualistic extension of private interests'.[32]

Hence, the intersection of violence and poverty at local government level is closely linked to securing opportunities for accumulation, as power brokers compete for contracts and access to resources. For example, in a municipality where I conducted interviews in the Western Cape (which I won't name to protect the businessman who told me the story), a taxi and shebeen boss was said to have set himself up as the recipient of several tenders from local government. The person in question also owned a private-security company, which he deployed to threaten and intimidate his competitors. Municipal officials, I was told, feared they would be killed if they did not do as the local strongman said. The police are said to be in his pay, so they may have been unwilling to take action. He is alleged to have threatened potential contractors and staff responsible for a refuse-removal tender; when he was finally awarded the contract, its implementation was substandard.

In such cases, in impoverished communities, a combination of the threat of violence and local contacts is the path to secure tenders. Power brokers in these contexts often control several overlapping interests, often in the taxi, alcohol and private-security businesses – and they have access to, and use, violence when their interests are threatened.[33] Richard Pithouse, who has traced the history of the Abahlali baseMjondolo movement to which Thuli Ndlovu belonged, has documented how its members were subjected 'to armed violence by local party structures with the explicit sanction of Municipal and Provincial ANC leaders and the tacit but clear sanction of the police. People were imprisoned, tortured, driven from their homes and subject to open death threats.'[34] (The hit on Thuli had not been the first targeting the movement. In June 2013, for example, a charismatic Abahlali baseMjondolo leader, Nkululeko Gwala, was assassinated in Durban.[35]) Pithouse recounted on Facebook a case involving the eviction of a shack settlement, another example of the evident merging of criminal and political interests:

> ... before the eviction the members of the Land Invasion Unit were drinking and eating, for free, in the local bar owned by the local gangster. They also reported that he appeared to be directing the eviction. ... As things unfolded it turned out that the gangster co-owned the local bar with a senior officer in the local police station and could have people arrested at will. ... When challenged he would boast of his connections to Zuma. I don't know whether he really had these connections or not but he certainly thought that by making that claim would make people back off. This is not an isolated case. There are cases all over Durban where politics and gangsterism have intersected and captured pieces of the local state.[36]

There have also been cases of violence – sometimes involving killing – targeted at activities opposing certain types of industrial development that are seen to financially benefit only a few. In one widely reported example, Sikhosiphi 'Bazooka' Rhadebe (mentioned in Chapter 1), a community anti-mining activist, was gunned down outside his home near Port Edward. Rhadebe had been opposing a large-scale mining development by an Australian company, likely to cause extensive environmental damage, a project from which certain powerful individuals would have benefited. In a modus operandi that has become chillingly common, Rhadebe's assassins posed as police officers. They arrived in a car with a blue light fitted to the roof and shot him eight times. Community members opposed to the mining investment reported that they 'could no longer rely on the [police] to protect them against attacks by thugs ... instead of arresting the attackers, police chose to search the homesteads of anti-mining leaders and supporters'.[37]

Indeed, one of the most worrying trends in the collusion between politics and crime is the role played by the police. We saw earlier how in particular criminal markets, the police often have a clear conflict of interest, linked, as some are, to powerful underworld interests. This is evident in relationships that exist in the twilight zone where security and the underworld engage with each other (more of which in the next chapter). But it is also evident where there are coalitions of a political-criminal nature. Police have been known to harass civil-society activists, break up demonstrations and use arrest as a tool to intimidate innocent citizens.

The role of the police in supporting local politicians and power brokers has been documented in a number of instances. For example, in a detailed overview of violent events in 2009 at the Kennedy Road shack settlement near Durban, Kerry Chance has shown how what purported to be a crackdown on shebeens and criminal gangs had an ulterior political motive – targeting those seen to be in opposition to prevailing political interests.[38] There is a disturbingly similar pattern across a number of cases, with the police doing the bidding of political power brokers. According to veteran scholar of policing in South Africa, Bill Dixon:

> The police are more likely to police for specific domination in the interests of a dominant class, 'race' or other social groups in unequal, divided societies. This tendency will be particularly pronounced when the interests of that elite are (or thought to be) threatened by some form of insurrectionary action, and when, at the institutional level, mechanisms for the democratic governance of the police are absent or fail to function effectively.[39]

And when that 'elite' is associated with criminal elements, the police, already compromised through corruption and a history of brutality, act in the interests of criminals. This is unfortunately the case in many South

African municipalities. It is more likely to occur in small towns and rural areas where external oversight is weak, and which are away from the prying eyes of the media. A combination of corruption, political pressure and the way local governments regulate aspects of politics all influence how policing is conducted.

As the case of Richard Mdluli exemplifies, maintaining political alignment to the powers that be is often a way to fast-track promotional prospects in the police and to gain impunity. As one senior police officer stated in court, to have given evidence against Mdluli in his investigation would have been tantamount to 'career suicide', as the officer in question had been identified for rapid promotion.[40]

How local governments regulate protests in conjunction with the police is also manipulative. As Jane Duncan has noted: 'Local government ... have developed myriad ways to manipulate the procedures for regulating gatherings, including protests, to protect not only themselves from criticism, but other powerful interest groups as well.'[41]

Ongoing instability in the police service and the overlap between private, political and police interests have contributed to a general weakening of the chain of command, resulting in less attention to what occurs at station level, and a trend towards a greater politicisation and criminalisation of the police, providing ample opportunity for corruption.[42]

For example, in the Western Cape the now suspended provincial commissioner, Arno Lamoer, and other senior officers stand accused of benefiting from corruption and racketeering in their association with a business figure.[43] In KwaZulu-Natal, the provincial police chief was suspended after allegations of a corrupt relationship with a prominent businessman, which resulted in contracts going his way.[44] It's telling that, since the advent of democracy, no police commissioner since the officer appointed by President Mandela, George Fivaz, has left office without being suspended on charges of corruption or misconduct.[45]

It is not difficult to discern the overall direction of the trend. The saga of Mdluli and the fate of crime intelligence illustrates the crisis of the sordid relationship between police and politics in South Africa. Mdluli, widely regarded to have developed close relations with President Zuma by ensuring that the investigation into Zuma's 2006 rape case was subverted, stands accused of murder, kidnapping, corruption and fraud.[46] Mdluli's highly unorthodox appointment to the top post in crime intelligence was made by then Minister of Police, Nathi Mthethwa, a close ally of Zuma. A former national police commissioner, and widely respected former ANC cadre, Tim Williams, described the process as 'completely unusual' and as having been 'hijacked' by politics.[47]

Under Mdluli, crime intelligence increasingly became a political tool, collecting information on political opponents and intercepting communications.[48] An internal police report covering the extent to which Mdluli abused crime-intelligence resources for his own private purposes was quietly buried in the weak parliamentary system of intelligence oversight.[49] The report, however was leaked to the media. It stated: 'Crime Intelligence sought to influence political processes in [KwaZulu-Natal] through the deployment of a select few covert intelligence field workers from Head Office. This activity included buying influence and access.'[50]

Since Mdluli (who was suspended in 2012), crime intelligence, has been left weakened and poorly placed to provide intelligence on organised crime. Several police officers I spoke to indicated that they placed little weight on crime intelligence and regarded many of its operatives as compromised.[51]

The reality is that police intelligence gathering, with some notable exceptions, inherited a system that is more politically than criminally focused. One of the first deep-cover agents used by crime intelligence to penetrate organised criminal activities in the country described to me how the process of tackling organised crime was poorly understood and often 'strategically mishandled', despite a core group of committed officers on the ground: 'The system was built on the political collection of intelligence,' he said, 'and not one that was aimed at bringing criminals to court.'[52]

In the first years of the democratic regime, institutional weakness within the police service left the new South African state poorly placed to counter the growing threat from criminal networks. The political status of the SAPS was low at the time, as the service was still seen as carrying its apartheid baggage. By the late 1990s, prominent figures in the ANC had become concerned at the growth of criminal activity. The global focus on responding to what was perceived as a new generation of criminals in the wake of the fall of the Soviet Union had spurred new thinking in South Africa about what the response should be.

Influenced by global discussions on countering organised crime, a new high-level crime-fighting body was established, known as the Scorpions.[53] Combining police investigators, prosecutors and former intelligence personnel, and led by a charismatic lawyer close to former president Thabo Mbeki, Bulelani Ngcuka, the new division quickly developed a reputation for having teeth.[54] This, combined with a formidable set of new legislative tools passed by Parliament in the late 1990s, defined the period as the heyday of combating organised crime in the country.[55]

Despite these gains, the Scorpions ruffled too many feathers in the corridors of power and were to last only eight years, running into a set of obstacles as their investigations increasingly threatened powerful political interests.[56]

The disbanding of the Scorpions saw the establishment of a more politically pliant organised-crime unit, the Hawks. The first head of the Hawks, General Anwar Dramat, a former member of MK, was regarded as honest. But he, too, over time was regarded to have overstepped the line between politics and law enforcement by threatening investigations around the grey economic interests of those associated with the president and his family.[57] Dramat subsequently lost his job and has joined a vocal group of senior officials who have alleged high-level corruption and wrongdoing in the Zuma administration.[58]

Dramat's successor, Berning Ntlemeza, has a similar profile to Mdluli's. A former policeman under apartheid, Ntlemeza has a chequered record, described by a judge in a court ruling as 'biased and dishonest ... lack[ing] integrity and honour, and [making] false statements under oath'.[59] It tends to be police officers from the old order, eager to curry favour, and with their own skeletons in the closet, who are most vulnerable to political manipulation. The Hawks' activities under Ntlemeza have taken on a markedly political flavour, including alleged intimidation of the former finance minister, Pravin Gordhan, with whom Zuma was widely reported to be in conflict. Gordhan was subsequently fired in March 2017 in a Cabinet reshuffle.

The success rate of the Hawks in combating organised crime, however, is much less evident. There have been few prosecutions of major organised-crime figures as a result of Hawks investigations. According to statistics released by the government, there has been a decline of 60 per cent in the number of arrests and an 83 per cent reduction in the conviction rate since January 2009, when the Scorpions were disbanded.[60]

At the same time, an investigative unit in the South African Revenue Service that was tackling organised criminal interests was also disbanded amid allegations that it too was threatening the interests of the president and his family.[61]

It is hard not to come to the conclusion that the institutional structure for countering organised crime has been weakened for political purposes.

Why this has occurred has less to do with resources allocated to law enforcement, or even lack of skills (although these remain a serious concern) than political interference with law enforcement. That the police, including its most specialised unit, have become a political instrument undermines the overall ability of the state to respond to the growth of organised crime. Law enforcement has become increasingly politicised in a context in which politics itself has become criminalised. These phenomena have moved in tandem and are closely linked.

Over the last few years, a growing body of academic writing has noted with concern the degree to which politics in South Africa has shifted from ideological conflict to increasing competition around resource access.[62] The focus in particular has been on the nature of competition within the ANC itself[63] – as has been outlined above in relation to local government. At national level this is highlighted by the growth of patronage networks around Zuma and the degree to which these extend to certain provincial and local leaders. The result is a party divided against itself, illustrated most clearly, before Gordhan's departure, by the open conflict within government over the control of the Treasury and Finance Ministry, which are lucrative sources of funds for sustaining patronage politics.

If the old adage 'all politics is local' holds true, can we draw a connection between the evolution of politics at the local level, including the growing trend for targeted assassinations, such as the gunning down of Thuli Ndlovu, and developments at the provincial and national level? In a system with hierarchical political-party structures, violence at the base of the system may be spurred by developments at national level. Stated differently, if assassination has utility at local level as a form of political control, then that utility may apply further up the political system too.

Take the case of Chris Mabunda, who was nominated for the ANC's party list in Alexandra, Johannesburg, for the 2016 local elections, despite being charged for murder, involving the brutal assault and killing of two people accused of stealing from a businessman. His appointment to the party suggests a nexus between criminal, business and political interests. Mabunda was nominated despite local opposition. Internal ANC sources said that he was a 'tough guy' who was needed to campaign in the IFP-dominated hostels in the area, and considered a vital cog in what was set to be a bruising election contest in Johannesburg.[64]

The idea that violent crime is diametrically opposed to the state or elite political interests, then, is not always the case. Local forms of criminal governance can prove to be a crucial supplement to South African politics by enhancing political influence – as the case of Mabunda shows. In systems with weak or contested rule of law, political interests may seek allies from the world of crime to maintain political power.[65]

As Vincenzo Ruggiero notes in a criminological study of political violence: 'The collapse of law and order … not only characterises marginalised communities, but also permeates the very core of economic and political life. When gangsters become politicians, politicians find in gangsters new allies who can mobilise voters, and amidst immunity for all, local governments become complicit in, when not promoters of, criminal activity.'[66]

Ruggiero's research on the relationship between organised crime, politics and violence is fascinatingly pertinent to South Africa. Councillor Ngcobo, in the account that opened this chapter, epitomises those connections at the level of local politics. Ruggiero suggests that the relationships between crime and politics, while often present and part of the general rumour mill, remain largely hidden but become manifest at particular public events when the ties that can be concealed in everyday life, become clearer by the presence of certain individuals.[67] How otherwise can one interpret the presence of politicians or relatives of the president at weddings or parties thrown by well-known gang bosses?[68]

A good example was exposed by the *Mail & Guardian* in 2015. On the basis of two independent sources, several gang bosses were said to have met with the president in the Western Cape on the eve of the 2011 local-government elections to discuss political strategy in the province. The meeting was said to have been arranged by Lloyd Hill, an underworld figure from Durban and cousin of the leader of the Americans gang.[69] Another underworld figure, Mark Lifman, whom we came across in Chapter 5, notoriously attended Zuma's birthday rally in April 2014, sporting an ANC T-shirt with Zuma's face printed on it for the occasion.[70]

In such cases the potential alliance between the underworld and a political party is predicated on the requirement that the gangs deliver votes in the community and that, in turn, the gangs will be rewarded by government impunity. Sadly, this kind of alliance between political and criminal elements occurs more often than is recognised. Once established – because of the enduring benefits it creates on both sides, and the degree to which it can be sustained by violence – the arrangement may be very hard to dismantle.[71] The symbiosis becomes a vicious cycle. Imagine if Councillor Ngcobo had been able to block the police investigation into the murder, or the docket was lost: he would have continued to stand at the centre of local-government power, gloating over the death of Thuli Ndlovu. There are other Councillor Ngcobos out there, and the line between their political power and criminal interests is a fine one.

The interconnections between the underworld and politics breed an environment where what can be sourced from the underworld has utility for the upperworld. There is a mutuality in the services that are exchanged. As Vincenzo Ruggiero points out in a study of the links between crime, politics and violence, 'Organised criminals depend upon political protection for their criminal and illicit activities and, therefore, have a vital business interest in the success of certain candidates whom they believe will be favourably disposed towards them.'[72] A landmark report on organised crime in Chicago in the 1920s concludes that politicians, 'even the most upright, have a lively sense of the active part played in politics and elections by underworld characters'.[73] For both criminals and politicians, violence has an instrumental value.

It should be added that such alliances result in increased degrees of violence, as both organised criminals and politicians gain a clear appreciation of the instrumental value of violent means in pursuing their respective profits.

In such contexts, as we have seen elsewhere, targeted assassination may be a more powerful tool than regular, wanton violence. Each 'hit' has a wider demonstration value: it delivers a clear threat to the system. The hits also suggest a randomness that allows the system to absorb the violence, without necessarily needing to react.[74] Hits are used in the South African context to regulate intersecting political, economic and criminal interests. The difficulty of disentangling them is a reminder of their overlapping nature in South Africa's violent democracy.[75]

This kind of violence, secretly arranged and seemingly random, does great damage in any political system, introducing uncertainty and discouraging honest political candidates from standing. In many cases considered in the course of the preparation for this book, victims' families reported that they had received threats. Politics is often left to the gangsters – those who either have the ability to propagate violence, or have their own violent capacity with which to resist. The system of assassinations is a vicious political cycle: it empowers those whose power comes through the gun, and disempowers those who rely on their standing and capacity for delivery. Unchecked in South Africa, it will undermine the very foundations of the democratic system.

# 8

## Twilight zone:
## The police as organised crime

After arriving in South Africa in 2007, Radovan Krejcir, whom we met in Chapter 6, needed police protection. The exiled Czech mafia figure, who in later years would be wanted as one of the top criminals in South Africa by law-enforcement authorities, spent a month in prison for immigration offences. He had money, plenty of it by all accounts, but no local criminal empire to cushion him. Krejcir did not need police protection in the ordinary sense that the term implies but a more shadowy form of shielding, one that would allow him to operate in the illicit economy without being constantly harassed by the police. As he began to develop his criminal network in South Africa, Krejcir saw the police as a critical part of his offensive and defensive strategy.[1] Protection and facilitation were services that he was prepared to pay for, and powerful individuals in the police obliged.

The Czech was practised in navigating the underbelly of transitional politics and seemed almost instinctively to know where to look. He sought out the police, but not just anyone in the force. He approached the secret elements of the service, known in South Africa as the Crime

Intelligence Division. These were people who, he reasoned, could both justify and benefit from maintaining a link with him. They understood his world and, if he could prove his utility, they might protect him when the chips were down.

Once out of prison, Krejcir swiftly made contact with the Gauteng Crime Intelligence Division. Whether he offered himself as an informer is not clear, but he had done it before when he was on the run in the Seychelles, and presumably elsewhere, so he may well have deployed the same strategy. Either way, within a short space of time, senior members of provincial crime intelligence were drawn into a symbiotic system of 'dirty togetherness'[2], receiving funds from Krejcir and delivering the necessary services to him in return.

Krejcir's shortcut into these senior levels of crime intelligence came through General Joey Mabasa, the division's Gauteng head, to whom Krejcir allegedly regularly paid money. It is possible that another senior figure within crime intelligence was also receiving pay-offs. Mabasa was a long-time cop, with over 30 years' service in the SAPS. Krejcir was introduced to Mabasa by his attorney after the Czech expressed fears of being kidnapped. Even if those concerns were genuine, there is little doubt that Krejcir took advantage of the opportunity to develop a relationship with the country's secret-police establishment.

The relationship between Mabasa and Krejcir entailed a web of associations and payments. Krejcir's wife, Katerina, and Mabasa's wife, Dorcas, started a company together called Radlochro, a front for their husbands' financial relationship.[3]

There are now corroborated accounts that Krejcir regularly paid Mabasa for his services. Juan Meyer, who was involved in a money-laundering and gold-smuggling scheme with Krejcir, observed cash being handed to Mabasa at meetings at Krejcir's favourite hangout, a restaurant in Bedfordview, and at a Johannesburg hotel.[4] A former employee of Krejcir,

Miloslav Potiska, also described meetings in which Mabasa received money from Krejcir, some of which was then distributed to lower-level police henchmen:

> Every time Krejcir arranged to meet Mabasa ... one of Krejcir's asso-
> ciates ... would pick Mabasa up ... on his way to the meeting place
> at Krejcir's house. ... Mabasa and Krejcir would have their meeting
> inside the house, on the balcony in the dark and in secret ... The times
> I was there I would see Krejcir give Mabasa money but I don't know
> how much ...[5]

In return, Mabasa helped recruit police officers to Krejcir's network to act as debt collectors and intimidate his enemies. In one case, a payment made to an ANC-connected businesswomen, Brenda Madumise, alleg-edly to fast-track Krejcir's asylum application didn't produce the necessary results. (Interestingly Madumise never denied receiving the payment but gave a garbled explanation as to the purpose of the money.[6]) So, an associate of Krejcir, George Louca, later revealed to be a police informer for Mabasa, appeared at Madumise's house demanding the money back. With him was none other than Mabasa himself, who allegedly 'instructed three members of crime intelligence to help to resolve the debt'.[7]

Krejcir called the police in as muscle on several occasions. When he fell out with his partner, Meyer, the latter began to receive threatening phone calls that he believed originated from crime intelligence. Meyer was later arrested on spurious charges by policemen he believed to be on Krejcir's payroll.[8]

In 2014, after Krejcir was eventually charged, several police officers appeared in the dock with him, allegedly having murdered or assaulted people for him, and it appears that they too may have been recruited through Mabasa. Sergeant Nandi Nkosi, co-accused in the Phumlani

Ncube murder case, provided SAPS intelligence software and equipment to Krejcir that allowed him to locate and monitor his opponents.[9]

Amazingly, Mabasa and Krejcir allegedly also had discussions, in the presence of Meyer, about arranging 'safe passage' for gold through South African borders and customs.[10] The *Mail & Guardian* reported that crime intelligence was tapping the phones of the Hawks, who were involved in investigating Krejcir.[11]

Mabasa's relationship with Krejcir was publicly exposed by the 2010 murder of nightclub owner Lolly Jackson, a known business associate of Krejcir. Mabasa was on the scene of Jackson's murder before the body was examined by the police. Following the murder, private investigator Paul O'Sullivan told journalists that a source had informed him that Mabasa had been called soon after Jackson's murder (see Chapter 6). Mabasa later claimed that the call he had received was from Louca, confessing to the murder.[12] Yet Mabasa made no attempt to arrest Louca at the crime scene, and sources claim that Louca was fast-tracked through Johannesburg airport by crime-intelligence officers.[13] He left the country for Cyprus, where he remained for several years before his extradition back to South Africa. It seems Mabasa may have wanted Louca out of the way because he had witnessed Krejcir murdering Jackson.

But even before much of this came to light, speculation was rampant in the South African press about the scope of Mabasa's dealings with Krejcir. As evidence mounted, pressure grew on the SAPS to act. In October 2011 Mabasa was removed from his job and given a R3.5 million golden handshake.

'Krejcir did not want to pay Mabasa any more money,' Potiska said in his affidavit. 'I formed the opinion Mabasa was no longer any use to Krejcir as he had left the police.'[14]

Mabasa has never been formally charged or arrested for his association with Krejcir. He has never commented publicly on the allegations.

## One hand washes the other

Although several law-enforcement sources have suggested that Krejcir's influence over the police has been overplayed, it is nevertheless symptomatic of the wider challenge of 'dirty togetherness' between police and organised crime. As one investigating officer said to me, 'There are many little Krejcirs, although we sometimes don't always see them as a threat, as they are too close to us.'[15] Another officer previously involved in financial investigations made a similar point: 'What you see in the Krejcir case is hidden in other cases – but it is often the daily stuff of law enforcement.'[16]

This web of apparent interdependence between the criminal world and the police is something that should be of great concern. Ordinary citizens rightly expect the police to fight organised crime, and not join forces with it. But, what form does this symbiosis take? A review of the illicit markets that we have already considered in previous chapters provides some insight into the changing nature of police–criminal relations, and particularly how the actions of the police result in protection for criminal enterprises and, by implication, the perpetration of targeted violence.

The changing face of the police service in South Africa is a critical element in how officers engage in policing underworld activities. As we saw briefly in Chapter 4, the criminal network that was associated with the nightclub extortion business had close links to the police – indeed, many involved in the business had been or were serving police officers. The nature of the two partners – the police and the bouncer mafia – shifted concurrently. Mass recruitment in the police force meant that the face of policing in South Africa changed sharply. The SAPS increased in numbers by 65 per cent from 2002 to 2012,[17] but there were far fewer white officers. At the same time, the recruitment of white bouncers dried up as companies replaced them with cheaper black foreigners. Therefore, the connections that had allowed the white bouncer industry to flourish increasingly fell away, and so did the interactions between policemen and bouncers. That relationship became increasingly commoditised as bribe money replaced white ethnic allegiance.

One bouncer company manager sighed when he remembered the old times: 'Now', he said, 'we need to pay to keep the police sweet.'[18] In the contemporary underworld, money has become the only true currency of protection and paying off the police is now the norm in the markets for violence, including the taxi and illicit drug industries. The gangs of the Western Cape seek out members of the police to corrupt. All senior gang members are said to have police on their payroll. Many police officers grew up in the areas where the gangs operate. Despite their shared history, or perhaps because of it, the gangs manage to get a hold over them. In an interview in the strife-torn township of Manenberg, a tough-looking gang member of the Clever Kids, who run an extensive network of extortion, explained the position with disarming frankness: 'We pay them and they do what we say.'[19]

A senior police officer added some nuance: 'The gangs don't corrupt just any police officer. What is the point of corrupting a station commissioner who does not even know his own area? It is a waste of money. They target people who they know can open doors for them. That is the nature of protection.'[20] A police sergeant who grew up in a gang-dominated area described how the process works:

> The first step is for the gang to compromise you. It is not direct and they are prepared to take their time. They look for ways in which a small corrupt relationship can be established – R250 for school fees, say, or some cash for lunch. And then they exploit that. This first step is the most important: it establishes a relationship that the cop can't then walk away from without consequences.[21]

Whatever form the process takes, the result is that corruption compromises police operations. For example, corrupt officers often warn their gang contacts in advance of a planned police drugs raid.[22] The relationship has been exacerbated by the rapid dispersal of the drug economy across the Cape Peninsula and the expansion of gang territories into rural areas and small towns.[23] The same is true of other cities, with several local-government officials reporting that drug dealing and consumption have become their main challenges.[24] And with the growth of the drug-dealing networks has come the corrosive effect of corruption on policing. Corruption is now present at almost every station.

As with drug gangs, the taxi protection system is linked to money and its inevitable partner in crime – violence. 'The taxi industry,' as Dugard says, 'was born out of corruption.'[25] The Goldstone Commission, an independent judicial body that investigated acts of violence during South Africa's transition to democracy, identified widespread corruption and collusion among law-enforcement officers in the transport industry in the 1990s.[26]

Police and traffic officers bought into the taxi business as a form of long-term investment.[27] The result is an entwining of individual and police interests, which extends to the violence perpetrated in this industry. A national police instruction that taxis cannot be owned by police officers or traffic law enforcement officials continues to be violated. To get round it, police officers simply register the businesses in the names of family members.

In 1998, the police were blamed for a spate of taxi wars in Gauteng, which claimed the lives of 20 people. At the time, the Provincial Department of Transport and taxi organisations said police turned a blind eye to taxi-related crimes or were involved in the crimes themselves.[28]

In August 1999, a commission of inquiry into taxi violence in Soshanguve found that the police were complicit in the violence and revealed that senior policemen, including a station commissioner, were implicated in violent clashes. One of the commission's main findings was that the 'endemic violence had been fuelled by the fact that taxis were directly owned by members of the SAPS'.[29] Another commission of Inquiry into taxi violence in KwaZulu-Natal noted that many cases involving taxi violence were either inadequately investigated, the charges retracted or stifled because of illicit involvement by police officers.[30]

The problem continues today. In February 2016 the then Member of the Executive Council for Transport in KwaZulu-Natal, Willies Mchunu, said that strong allegations had emerged of police officers fuelling conflict within the industry.[31]

Remarkably, there is even evidence that police officers have been hired as assassins by organised-crime networks. In a case that once again involves the taxi industry, reported in August 2015, two detective constables, Thubelihle Nxumalo and Phakamani Zondi, were charged for murder of a taxi boss, one Makhosonke Mpungose, whom they kidnapped, and then murdered. Mpungose operated a taxi business in Johannesburg. A dispute arose between associations at the main Johannesburg rank and a decision was said to have been taken by a collective of owners that Mpungose should be killed. Members of the taxi association sought out the assistance of police officers and the two detectives were allegedly recruited to do the hit.[32]

Police officers have also been known to collaborate in the theft of firearms, bulletproof vests and uniforms. Our interviewees suggested on several occasions that police officers rented or loaned this equipment for use in taxi-related crime.[33] A report published back in 1998 noted this trend: 'Policemen hire out their weapons to be used in hits, if they don't actually perform the hits themselves ... they further hamper investigative work by stealing dockets ... and [by] warning suspects of impending arrests.'[34]

Western Cape gangsters and private investigators reported during interviews that corrupt police officers have been known to release gang killers from prison to carry out a hit, thus providing the perfect alibi.[35]

There are several motives for the police to engage in this sort of behaviour. One reason that is often given is that if a gangster or other criminal is killed, then, essentially, nothing has been lost. Another is that members of the police are supporting the operations of organised-criminal groups in which they have a vested interest, as was presumably the case with the assassination of Mpungose. Of greater concern – and this is reminiscent of the way police death squads in Latin America are known to operate – there is evidence that the police in South Africa target criminals for assassination who have previously been involved in the killing of police. The real danger with this vigilantism is how motives become blurred, as some criminals are targeted and others left alone depending on interests that are hard to discern.

In the complicated symbiotic relationship between the police and criminals, death may take many forms – and for multiple reasons. If a gang boss with whom I spoke is to be believed, the police are prepared to give up informers to the gangs when they have served their purpose, or stopped talking. They are essentially now expendable. One hand washes the other: the gangs have their 'rat' and the police have achieved the death of a criminal without recourse to the criminal-justice system.[36]

Establishing the truth, however, in such cases can be hard to achieve. In 2013/14 there were some 117 killings by police officers in KwaZulu-Natal alone. Although not all of these were assassination-style killings, David Bruce, an expert on police violence has noted that certain special police units responsible for combating organised crime have a reputation for violence and vigilantism. Bruce concludes:

> Those [suspects] killed were often in the process of being arrested
> or were already in custody. In a number of cases, suspects who had
> been arrested were taken out of custody, allegedly for purposes of

investigation. They were then killed in circumstances in which it was alleged they had suddenly attacked police or tried to flee. One police officer told a commission of inquiry that it was common knowledge in the unit in which he worked that 'suspects were taken out' and officers knew 'when a killing was going to occur'. The suspect would then be shot 'in self-defence by a member of the unit, while trying to escape'.[37]

But, ironically, the most widely publicised claim about a police hit squad turned out to be an elaborate set-up – a reflection of the heavily politicised nature of the police. A 2015 case of a so-called 'police hit squad' in Cato Manor, near Durban, rang the usual alarm bells around illegal police shootings. The unit designated as responsible for the fight against serious and organised crime allegedly committed scores of assassinations, both in retaliation for suspected cop killings and in relation to taxi wars. From 2008 to 2010, the Cato Manor Unit cops were found to be responsible for a huge number of suspects killed during an escape, an investigation or an arrest. The *Sunday Times* obtained testimony and documentation, including evidence from a pathologist, a ballistics expert and senior police officers, that concluded that the killings had been conducted execution-style. Photographs of the unit allegedly celebrating after the kills appeared in the national media.[38]

Investigations into the unit by the *Sunday Times* – whose journalists, ironically, won an award for their work – descended into a mud-slinging match with independent current-affairs publication, *Noseweek*. The story that emerged through what was revealed to be a sophisticated disinformation campaign relates to political interference within the SAPS involving the police officer in charge of the unit, General Johan Booysen. Booysen denied knowledge or involvement in any assassinations, but he happened to have been engaged in the investigation of a sensitive case of a businessman, Thoshan Panday, who is connected to Zuma's family. Booysen appears to have been targeted in an elaborate set-up to discredit him and remove him from the police.[39]

Such 'false news' stories demonstrate the degree to which coverage of the underworld may have wider political impacts. In the course of another research project, my colleague Simone Haysom interviewed a range of journalists and what might be termed 'information brokers' with close links to the underworld.[40] The interviews suggested the degree to which journalists in South Africa, hard-pressed to deliver headlines and with fewer resources to support longer investigations, were increasingly reliant on a limited number of sources. These information brokers include private investigators and others who occupy the grey space between the licit and illicit. Given that it has become harder for journalists to draw on sources within the police, a greater reliance is placed on the brokers. That has greatly increased possibilities that individual journalists are fed stories that may push a particular political line, or underworld interest, or a combination of both.

Part of the problem seems to be the fact that the old-style crime reporter is now almost an extinct species. Contacts within the police establishment and the underworld may take years to develop. Another challenge is that reporters are focused, in the words of one investigative journalist, 'on bringing people down and that the [information brokers] cottoned onto this, and began to use it'.[41] There may be some merit in the press targeting individuals, but this may miss the dynamics of the underworld. It also means only one part of the underworld is covered in the press (the case of Krejcir is a good example), while stories of powerful taxi bosses and their violent industry seldom make the papers.

Coverage of policing and underworld issues is representative of the degree to which the country's security provision has become increasingly politicised, with a strong taint of commercial interest too. Almost inevitably, a character who featured heavily in the Cato Manor story was the then head of the Crime Intelligence Division, Mdluli, touting an intelligence report targeting the then National Commissioner, Bheki Cele, who was an ally of Booysen in the ongoing dispute. At the time, Mdluli was under investigation for corruption, investigations that had been approved by Cele.[42]

This narrative is just one that illustrates the worrying degree to which competing factions within the police, motivated by political and commercial interests, have shaped decision making, and created a system of internal protection for wrongdoing. Fragmented and divisive police politics, essentially the politicisation of the police by external interests, has allowed the space for institutional systems of protection to become involved in underworld illicit markets.

But why would senior officers become corrupted? After all, they are well paid, they have been beneficiaries of rapid promotion within the post-apartheid police, and they are close to senior political figures. Surely, therefore, corruption would only cause embarrassment for them and their principals. On the face of it, they should be above corruption. And yet the allegations involving Mabasa are not the first of police corruption linked to the provision of protection for known criminals. Former national commissioner and Interpol chief Jackie Selebi was found guilty of the offence and spent time in prison.

In the political context in South Africa, understanding the motives for high-level corruption is important. One needs to look more closely at the role of the state, in particular the security sector, in protecting organised-criminal activity, which is an area that is understudied.[43] In that sense, the activities of the likes of Selebi and Mabasa are crucial to understanding what has gone wrong and how the interests of police and organised crime have coalesced.

The literature on how states play a role in criminal protection identifies a spectrum along which the activities of state actors fall. On one side of this spectrum are weak states, which provide protection for criminal activities at their most senior level. In Africa, the best example is Guinea-Bissau, where senior members of the military used state powers to facilitate drug trafficking by protecting the activities of drug cartels.[44] In this example, the most senior members of the governing system are the ultimate protection racket. The political process and the process of protection are fused in such environments.[45]

On the other side of the spectrum are strong states, whose governance is based on the rule of law. Here, organised crime struggles to obtain protection from the law, and when such behaviour is detected, there is a clear and unequivocal response. That does not mean that law-enforcement officials do not offer protection to criminals in such states – sometimes the temptations are too great – but, on the whole, in these countries there is a separation of political consent from law enforcement's role in implementing it. Corrupted people who are caught in these contexts are often described as 'bad apples', although it is true that in many cases the rot may run deeper. But, generally, in the context of strong and democratic states, there are self-correcting systems in place, and that system separates political decision-makers from the police, insulating them against corruption.

Somewhere in between are a number of more ambiguous cases – and it is here that South Africa finds itself. In such cases there is a fusion of political interests and law enforcement, although this may not be always clearly visible. In the most dramatic manifestations, such as in Mexico and Central America, where there are ample resources for corrupting police and politicians, secret agreements or 'understandings' shape how law enforcement is conducted. This is critical for people who control criminal networks, as 'maintaining good relations with the government matters even more to illegal businesses than it does to legitimate ones'.[46]

Although South Africa fits broadly into this middle model, it is a more complex case. In South Africa an entrenched system of patronage and influence has distorted the policing of organised crime. It is less about the payment of protection fees than about providing political support up through the system. To illustrate with the case of Mabasa, he was protected not because he was allegedly conducting illicit activities but because he fitted into a system of political patronage and support that gave him virtual impunity for his actions. His political protectors supported him, or he perceived that they did, providing some licence for him to operate so openly.

State officials become corrupted, then, not only for the money that they earn, but also because corruption, when linked to political interests, brings bureaucratic power. In the symbiotic relationship that develops, that power is deployed to protect political interests who return the favour. The result is that the skeletons become ever more closely packed in the closet.

While Krejcir's relationship with Mabasa was publicly exposed, the extent of his relationship with Mabasa's boss, Mdluli, is largely unknown. One source within law enforcement claims Mdluli protected Mabasa when the allegations about his relationship with Krecjir came out, indicating that Mdluli himself had an interest in protecting Krejcir.[47]

Mdluli – a colourful player with a story much larger than simply his Krejcir connection – is a nexus where criminal, political and economic interests intersected in the police, as we saw in the previous chapter. As long as Mdluli was in control (and his position was secured through his political links to the president), then Mabasa was safe. There is strong evidence that Mdluli buried an internal investigation into Mabasa, filing away a report that had been requested and not sharing it.[48] Mabasa was protected, despite the evidence, including affidavits that suggest he ran a protection racket for Krejcir. As we saw, he was released from the SAPS with a golden handshake.

## Policing in the twilight zone

There is another angle to the story that is crucial to the protective arrangements that the police provide to organised crime. These corrupt relationships are created in a secret space – a twilight zone of policing, a space where informants are recruited and protected. It is in this zone where actions of the secret state, through the corrupted and fragmented police agency that the SAPS is, allow for a network of cooperation between organised crime and the police. Contrary to assumptions that may be made by ordinary citizens in the upperworld, Krejcir did not avoid the police. In fact, he actively sought them out. He connected with them in that twilight zone.

Police intelligence is a process that is largely masked from public view, but my interviews with participants who are part of this process suggest that all is far from well. Maintaining a network of police informers is probably as old as policing itself. My colleague Don Pinnock recounts during his research on gangs in Cape Town in the 1970s and 1980s how police officers would turn up at the gangs' headquarters and pay them for information.[49] Yet paying for information provides a perverse incentive to the police and the informers, who sell them information from the underworld, creating a web of obligations and ties sealed with the payment of cash that is hard to account for.

When this system of paid informers becomes one of the main means of conducting policing, and when the flow of funds creates a system that begins to maintain itself, rather than one whose objective is to end or reduce crime, the process is self-defeating. One of the challenges facing post-independence systems of policing is the need to transition from a system that essentially collected information for its own sake to one that uses that information for the arrest and prosecution of criminals.

For now, though, the evidence suggests that policing in the twilight zone is dysfunctional. In just one documented case, a commission of inquiry into police service delivery in Khayelitsha found crime intelligence at station level to be poorly managed, described by one of the experts who gave evidence as resulting in 'policing by chance and luck', rather than efficient information gathering.[50] In the context of the collapse of the broader system of crime intelligence, the cash-driven relationships that develop in the twilight zone of secret policing are corrupting.

The officer whom Krejcir allegedly identified for his criminal needs, Joey Mabasa, held a position of critical importance for the police in Gauteng. But the crime intelligence function in the SAPS was at the time gripped by crisis. This was the most hidden part of the police, and the one most susceptible to corruption and political manipulation, and yet it was drifting without a clear strategy – at least it certainly did not appear to be particularly concerned with curbing crime. In a seminal study, Jonny Steinberg shows that crime intelligence, based on the same foundation of compromised political relations as was the apartheid regime's Security Branch, was well on its way to being subverted by political forces, with operatives often collecting information for opposing factions within the ruling party's own struggles.[51]

Krejcir did not corrupt the crime intelligence function in Gauteng, rather he quickly identified it as corrupted and sought out those who he believed could help him. A link to crime intelligence also led him to a network of potentially much more influential political connections. Meanwhile, the top brass of crime intelligence, Mdluli, and other senior associates, were illegally drawing money from a secret account for their private purposes, including the purchase of cars and houses that were used by family members and lovers.[52]

This was the context in which Krejcir met Mabasa. Engagement in the twilight zone of informant recruitment in any police agency is beset with challenges of accountability and the potential for corruption. But in the South African Crime Intelligence Division, where the leaders were already engaged in corrupt practices, that level of vulnerability to corruptibility was extreme. The secret world provides considerable space for abuse. There is largely no oversight over how informants are managed and the transactions are made in cash, providing ample opportunity for abuse. The case of Mdluli is perhaps the best and most recent example of this.

It's important to remember that this kind of police corruption is not a problem particular to South Africa. However, weaker forms of accountability, which typify South African institutions, are less likely to respond to abuse within the system. A classic and well-publicised case of where the informant function was subverted is that of Whitey Bulger, an underworld figure in Boston who was recruited by a handler in the Federal Bureau of Investigation (FBI) to provide intelligence on the Italian mafia, which the federal law-enforcement authorities at the time were eager to target. Bulger provided excellent information to the FBI on the mafia. In exchange, his FBI handler, John Connolly, turned a blind eye as Bulger consolidated his own criminal empire. Connolly deceived his superiors over the extent of the advantage Bulger was given.[53] In the end Connolly went to prison, but the point is there can be little doubt that where there is extensive corruption, or where there are wider connections or political influence, they may provide opportunities for the long-term growth of organised crime.

There was a case more recently in Germany, where the intelligence service (or Office for the Protection of the Constitution, as it's grandly known) had to answer some uncomfortable questions as to why key figures in the country's far-right National Democratic Party and other associated groups were paid by the government; 130 far-right-wing members, including senior party leaders, were listed as government informers, some playing a key role in inciting unlawful activities.[54] There were accusations that the intelligence service was sustaining rather than seeking to stop these activities.[55]

The issue of informants and the problems with the system were often raised as I conducted interviews with various figures. Crime intelligence is said to maintain a wide network of informants, as is the State Security Agency. As mentioned, Cyril Beeka, is now widely believed to have been an informer for the Security Branch and, later, the post-apartheid intelligence establishment. Mabasa seemed to justify his relationship with Krejcir because he was running an informant – better to be close to the underworld than without information, or so the argument goes. In such cases the question is, do the authorities run the informants or vice versa?[56] In South Africa, as elsewhere, this is an issue that is little discussed and is possibly 'least subject to internal organisational control'.[57]

Officers who run informants have an interest in protecting them, and they do. A senior officer involved in investigative work told me: 'I watch how an officer's career rises with his association to an informant. They mutually benefit each other. It is a symbiotic relationship. At some point that relationship needs to be broken.'[58] The fact that police intelligence can provide a protective embrace for them is not lost on key underworld figures. 'Many are happy to act as informers, it essentially provides them with protection,' said the officer.[59] According to a police detective in the Western Cape involved in gang investigations, some gangsters offer their services quite openly. 'It is not for money. They see it as a way of getting protection. And, to be honest, that is often what they get.'[60] That was by all accounts the case with Beeka. While he pulled together an extortion network, he was providing information to the state. As a consequence, he was never arrested.

Clearly, by running agents and informers, the state runs the risk of bolstering the underworld. A former deep-penetration agent for the police said that part of the challenge is that the culture of crime intelligence is political, and less focused on policing and dismantling criminal organisations. 'A lot of information is collected, but it is not analysed. The focus is always on information and not how it might be used,' he said.[61]

A senior detective told me that he no longer trusts crime intelligence to provide him with intelligence and that he runs his own informant network. He is prepared to wait years to develop sources within criminal organisations: 'I want the whole network, not just a few prosecutions for individual crimes at a lower level.'[62] The implication is clear: in the case of many crimes the police may well know who the perpetrators are, but they don't act on this information because it may expose their source or long-term investigations.

These factors, combined with the reality that, after Mdluli, South African crime intelligence is now widely regarded as dysfunctional, suggest that all is not well. It is almost impossible to determine clearly the degree to which the state is protecting and sustaining criminal networks under the guise of information collection. In fact, this may be something that eludes even the most privileged of insiders. But what is clear is that in a context in which corruption within the police is now regarded to be widespread, and where the goals of crime fighting are ambiguous, the likelihood of officers going rogue in the 'twilight zone' is much greater. There are several examples of this, but Mabasa is perhaps the best.

The story of Mdluli suggests the connections between the police and organised crime in South Africa are not new. They have evolved over time – and they continue to evolve, based on the often conflictual interests of policemen and their links to markets that are conducive to criminal activity, as well as the continued evolution of South Africa's political landscape. Here the taxi industry remains a strong bridge between the police and a crimogenic market beset with violence. There are strong indications that this crossover began in an earlier period.

The reality was that, as conflict in the country spiralled in the 1980s, a symbiosis developed between state-security functions and organised-criminal activities. That was both a function of need but also increasingly greed, the latter combined with a sense of disillusionment that affected those at the front end of the country's worsening political and security crisis.

The linkage between the police and the growing criminal economy was a feature of the late-apartheid period in South Africa – and it was to have a long legacy for organised crime. A parallel process was also underway in the liberation movements. Apartheid-era policing had always priori-tised the policing of politics over that of crime, including more organised forms of criminality. That left opportunity for personal accumulation. As a Soweto gangster explained: 'Even the white policemen worked with us but they were dangerous because they don't take any shit. If you don't have any money for him, he'll blow your head off.'[63]

The result of apartheid-style policing was to push legitimate political activities more closely towards criminal networks and gangs. Criminal activities had utility for political actors.[64] And, likewise, the need for the ANC to resource its liberation struggle brought it into direct contact with criminal networks.[65]

As networks of power and governance became fragmented, criminals sought connections with both the police and the liberation movements. One high-profile drug trafficker at the time, Sharif Khan, was reported to have had good links with the state and the ANC.[66] 'Politics, state security and crime,' noted one seasoned observer, 'did more than rub shoulders, they went drinking and whoring together. Policemen ceased simply to monitor criminals, but even went into business with them.'[67]

On the eve of democracy, then, the war for liberation had led to complex patterns of governance in the underworld. An emerging criminal class could buy protection from multiple actors. The arrival of democracy was to dramatically shift the underpinnings of all of these relationships, while ensuring that an interwoven network of political, criminal and security actors were present.

This is the legacy of Mdluli and Mabasa: a messy and compromised system of policing, where historical legacies have been coloured over with economic interests. Old established systems of policing, in the form of the widespread recruitment of informants from the criminal world mean that the state and these illicit markets have become entangled, complicated by the interests of both those engaged in twilight policing and those who have become corrupted. As in the case of Mdluli and Mabasa, it is now almost impossible to disentangle these two elements.

# Conclusion:
# Bozwana's end

On a Friday afternoon in October 2015, a small Citroën bearing the logo of a new brand of energy drink, Orgazma, drew to a stop on the busy Garsfontein off-ramp on the N1 near Pretoria. In the passenger seat was a prominent businessman, Wandile Bozwana; a female colleague, Mpho Baloyi, was driving. As Baloyi brought the car to a halt, a silver BMW pulled up alongside. One of the occupants of the BMW stepped out and coolly fired an automatic weapon at the Citroën, hitting Bozwana nine times. Baloyi was hit twice, but managed to drive them both to a nearby car dealership, from where police and paramedics were summoned. She survived, but Bozwana died several hours later at a Pretoria hospital.

The murder bore all the characteristics of a hit, South African-style. The police investigation showed that the hit had been well planned: the perpetrators appeared to know Bozwana's movements and they targeted him at a vulnerable spot. Nothing was taken from his person or from the car, so it was evident that their motive was only to kill him. The hitmen had been well armed with automatic weapons, and were proficient in their use. They were also later found to be in possession of cellphone-jamming devices. A hit list of Bozwana's associates subsequently emerged. As reported by the media, the hitmen showed all signs of being professional killers, although perhaps not professional enough – by April 2017 the main hitman had been named but not yet arrested; three others were behind bars and a fourth out on bail.

Bozwana's murder was extensively reported by the press because of his high profile in the North West province. He had benefited substantially from provincial-government tenders. Formerly a Bophuthatswana policeman during apartheid, Bozwana had made good across a number of service industries and later had become a prolific funder of the ANC. He was widely respected and had a following in North West. After his death, he was styled by some as one who had opposed corruption, having taken the provincial government to court, where he had accused the provincial premier, Supra Mahumapelo, of enriching himself, interfering in government procurement and awarding tenders to those close to him.

But the reality is more complex. Bozwana was in fact a sharp-elbowed operator whose business had benefited from his political connections in the award of tenders. He had been forced to resign from a job at the North West Housing Corporation after a forensic audit found irregularities. This was followed by several cases of tender fraud or substandard service delivery. In one example, Bozwana had won the contract for the disposal of medical waste in Kimberley in 2015. His company lacked experience in this line of work, and the service was badly implemented. The same trucks used to transport the medical-waste samples were also used for drinks deliveries and the waste was not disposed of according to correct standards.

With little compunction about using violence himself, Bozwana had been arrested along with four others in 2015 for torching the vehicles of a businessman, allegedly in a dispute over a government tender. The list of other cases and illegal activities connected to Bozwana goes on.

Bozwana had made powerful enemies and, at the time of his killing, he was threatening to expose through the courts a network of corrupt practices. Given how much he must have known about how 'business' worked and who was involved, his increasingly public comments must have posed a threat to certain vested interests. Much was at stake, economically and politically – and Bozwana paid with his life.[1]

Over the last few years, a growing body of writers and scholars have noted with concern the degree to which political contestation in South Africa has shifted away from ideological conflict to increasing competition around resource access associated with clientelist politics.[2] Their work has often focused in particular on the nature of competition within the ANC itself.[3] At the national level this is highlighted by the growth of patronage networks around President Zuma, and the degree to which these extend to certain provincial and local leaders. The result is a party divided against itself, illustrated most clearly by the widely reported conflict within government in 2015 and 2016 over the control of the Treasury and Finance Ministry.

Connected to this trend at the national level has been the nature of conflict over resources generated by local government, as we saw in Chapter 7. Systems of patronage, epitomised by tender irregularities, have become major sources of political power for local strongmen. As a result, there is significant factional conflict within the ANC branches. Here violence has become a purchasable tool, the hit a payable commodity, and the suppliers the criminal protection provided by the underworld. This is imparting violent entrepreneurs with real power, especially in isolated or rural communities where external oversight is weak or absent.

The assassination of Bozwana is a good example. He is thought to have been 'removed' because he threatened economic and political interests, in this case within the ANC itself. A businessman with political connections, Vusi Nyawane, was initially arrested for Bozwana's murder. In an apparent confession obtained by the *Sunday Times*, Nyawane claimed that 'Bozwana had stood in the way of lucrative state contracts [he] hoped to get' and said that he had sought out hired killers through his contacts in a local taxi association.[4] Bozwana's family subsequently suggested that Nyawane (who at the time of writing remains in custody on other charges) was the fall guy for someone else and no new details have emerged.[5] A prominent taxi hitman from KwaZulu-Natal, Senco Mncube, has been identified as the chief suspect in the killing.[6]

Speculation is rife that this case is somehow linked to senior political figures. On the FaceBook page dedicated to the murdered businessman, there has also been speculation that the takeover of the investigation by the Hawks was done just before the investigating team, who were all replaced, were about to make an arrest of a 'big fish'.[7] Whatever the outcome, it is clear that there is high-level political interest in the case – and, as suggested, swirling rumours that powerful people are being protected.

Bozwana's case is a good example of the context in which assassination has become a feared element of local politics in South Africa. A recent study that interviewed survivors of violence concluded that 'contemporary intraparty violence [in local communities] was perceived as being driven by selfish, individual motives, rather than universal goals such as freedom, equality and democracy'.[8] Another review of violence in South Africa concludes, 'This violence is not insurrectionary; rather it is a tactic used to gain access to the existing political system.'[9]

As one gang boss with knowledge of assassination tactics, and who has allegedly delivered on several 'contracts', said to me, purchasing targeted assassinations provides a clean way of eliminating people, particularly if there are doubts that it is an assassination at all – like the proverbial car accidents in Zimbabwe.[10] In any other context, the regular murder of political and government functionaries would denote a crisis. But in contemporary South Africa, a hits culture has developed, and the response from the state has been surprisingly muted. One reason is that its security agencies may not be neutral players. The costs are high. Many of those who have been killed or silenced have stood for the interests of their community over a narrow set of criminal objectives.

Take the case of Khanyisile 'Malumekazi' Ngobese-Msibi. Her story is the same as many that have been recounted in the preceding pages.

Over the last ten years of her life, Khanyisile, a teacher by background, had devoted herself to uplifting her community. She had, among other things, established a soup kitchen to feed the many destitute children in the area, most of whom had been scavenging for food from a dump site. Her popularity had led to the community nominating her to be a ward councillor in the August 2016 local-government elections. It was not to be: her position on the ANC electoral list had displaced others whose interests in accessing the resources of local government trumped the chances of a former school teacher with an interest in community upliftment.[11]

On Mandela Day, 18 July 2016, Khanyisile was gunned down in Acaciavale, KwaZulu-Natal, as she was delivering blankets to the elderly in the area. She was killed in her car, by someone with a degree of professionalism and preparation, who shot her multiple times with an assault rifle. There was little doubt it was a hit.

In the wake of Khanyisile's assassination, as well as several others in the run-up to the elections, the Minister for Police said that detectives were investigating the possibility that taxi hitmen had been paid to kill selected political candidates, including Khanyisile. The same suspects, it seems, are wanted in relation to a number of targeted killings.[12]

As this book has shown, Khanyisile's murder is a reminder of how the resources of the underworld have been drawn upon to rearrange things in the upperworld, rarely to the benefit of the average South African citizen. That is a sad reflection on the state of South African society – and the nature of how criminal interests can subvert attempts to improve people's lives.

Our tour of the South African criminal underworld has been to show how its trajectory and the evolution of its culture of organised crime have harmed the lives of ordinary South Africans – people like Khanyisile Ngobese-Msibi and those whom she served. Much too little has been done to respond to these kinds of crimes.

I suggest that, more than anything else, organised crime in South Africa is embodied by a key activity: the application of mafia-style and secretive violence to achieve economic and political objectives. This mode of violence has utility for the perpetrators by masking who they are and, in many cases, their motives. This sort of violence is largely possible because there is a constituency willing and able to reach into the underworld to source potential hitmen from the criminal protection economies that have spawned them. Those protection economies, as has been shown, are actively engaged in and adept at the use of violence to regulate their own activities.

This mafia-style violence is by no means restricted to rural areas, such as where Khanyisile or Thuli Ndlovu met their ends. It is also evident among the gangs and organised-criminal organisations in the Western Cape; it bleeds along the transport arteries where most ordinary citizens travel in taxis; it protects those who engage in extortion; it distorts state institutions, most specifically the police but more broadly those active in the 'secret state'; and it has assumed a hold on the country that only concerted action will remove. Its formation has not been overnight but is linked to longer-term trends in the country's political economy. Its tentacles reach into some of the highest offices of the government and it continues to erode the state at all levels. Only a concerted effort will remove the cancer.

One might be forgiven for thinking that the weakening of the ANC's hold on political power may slow the use of the hit as a political or economic tool in the years ahead. That is unlikely and in fact it may well increase the incidence of violence at local level. Targeted violence as a lever may have even greater utility when the risks are greater and the rewards sweeter, and it has even more dangerous consequences when the state is drawn further into the morass, with institutions and individuals in government both perpetrators and beneficiaries of the killing.

## Hitmen and their masters

Hitmen, like those who killed Bozwana and Khanyisile, are, to use the term coined by Steve Hall, 'the criminal undertakers' of the underworld. Theirs is hardly a glamorous pursuit. It is apparent from the accounts in this book that hitmen may be as vulnerable as their victims – and their masters. Theirs is a world made by violence, and violence extracts a terrible revenge.

Hitmen, for the most part, are drawn from the very bottom of the socio-economic spectrum. Some, like Simon, whom we encountered in Chapter 2, have made it – to the degree hitmen can be said to make it. He has secured a retirement plan for himself in the taxi industry and, if he can stay alive, there is every chance he will be able to settle down in a rural area and watch other people's children grow up. Others will not be so lucky. In recent years there has been a wave of inexperienced practitioners of violence entering the market. These, in some ways are more dangerous individuals, less professional, more prone to gratuitous violence, and eager to offer their services cheaply. Such assassins are in every way the foot soldiers of organised crime: many will pay the ultimate price for occupying some of the lowest rungs that the underworld can offer. A select few, most of whom we will never hear about, will graduate upwards because of their skill with a gun or a knife, and their ability to manage the fractious politics of the gang or taxi boss.

The bosses are no less an endangered species than the hitmen they employ and seek to control, perennially threatened, as they are, by the very instrument they use to exert that control. The South African underworld is likely to remain unstable for some time to come. All attempts at accumulating control by certain groups or crime bosses have been shattered by the reality that it is fairly easy for new, well-armed groups to break into the market. The role of the criminologist is to watch these trends and look for indicators of change as new individuals rise and fall. Measuring the number of hits, whom they are targeted at and the degree to which they affect the upperworld of legitimate commerce and political and social interaction is an important tool.

The power of the bosses – in rural villages and in the big cities' networks of violence – will depend on what course the state takes. South Africa is at a tipping point: if the state seeks to align itself with certain criminal groups, a few politically connected criminal figures will dominate, and this will come at a cost. Individual criminals will successfully bridge the divide between crime, politics and business. Bozwana's case is instructive in this regard: it exemplifies the merging of all three forces. What happens in the upperworld – particularly in relation to the country's unfolding politics of turmoil – will have a decisive impact on the nature of the underworld, and its ability to be sourced for violence.

The violent trajectory of the underworld, and the functions it has come to perform, is an integral part of the story of South Africa's own ongoing transition, and one shapes the other. The relationships and networks that formed around the late 1980s and early 1990s lie at the heart of organised crime in South Africa – and of the underworld itself. Understanding the nature of the system of organised crime in South Africa is important not only from a criminological perspective, but also to our understanding of the social, economic and political evolution of the country. Yet criminologists have largely steered clear of organised crime, citing methodological, ethical and other constraints. It is a gap that must now be filled.

Like all markets, the market for criminal violence in South Africa needs buyers and sellers. In this case, the buyers are criminal but seemingly legitimate actors. The sellers are, to use a term I have borrowed, 'violent entrepreneurs' – people who operate in the criminalised protection economies that are endemic to the South African underworld.[13] The increasing use of violence for political and commercial ends has not only sustained and resourced violent and criminal actors, but has also resulted in the growing commercialisation of the market for targeted killing. By examining the development of the South African underworld, this book has tracked the evolution of the criminal protection economies and their associated mafia-style organised-crime groups that were born in and have been sustained by the use of violence.

During the 1980s a confluence of two major trends provided the opportunity for a new class of violent entrepreneurs to emerge in South Africa. These were, firstly, the weakening of the state's policing as it came under a sustained onslaught from anti-apartheid forces and reallocated its resources to face this and, secondly, the exposure of the country to a series of economic activities that the state had little capacity or interest in regulating – one was a dramatic increase in the inflow of drugs, the other was the phenomenal growth, outside of any form of effective regulation, of the minibus-taxi industry. Added to this was the flow of weapons into the grey space that exists between the political and criminal spheres.

The important point is that the post-apartheid underworld was born during a period of considerable instability in South Africa (and the region). The attention of the state was focused elsewhere and, ironically, it was a period in which certain state actors benefited from having allies in the criminal underworld. By seeking out partners in the underworld, the state succeeded in strengthening them and promoted violence.

The transition to democracy in South Africa was characterised by high levels of political violence, although drawing a clear distinction between political and criminal violence was difficult in many circumstances,[14] with the state deliberately fostering violence in some cases.[15] For this reason, during the late-apartheid era the police were ill-prepared to deal with the emergence of organised crime. Their focus was on controlling political opposition and managing the policing challenges of the transition, and on interventions designed to bolster certain criminals at the expense of the liberation movements.[16] In any event, the police lacked the skills to engage in complex organised-crime investigations and the issue was not a priority at the time.[17]

The process of engaging with underworld actors for political purposes led to a criminalisation of the state. In the smoke-and-mirrors world of the secret war against the liberation movements, state actors within the police and military intelligence engaged in activities that were purely criminal, including drug trafficking, prostitution and smuggling.[18] The ANC was drawn into these crime networks.[19] On the attainment of democracy in 1994, portions of both the old state and those who were to occupy the new one had already developed underworld links.

In the immediate aftermath of apartheid, perhaps the closest thing to a mafia network was already in place in South Africa in the form of the virulent youth gangs in Cape Town. Drawn from communities who had been forcibly removed from settlements around the peninsula and relocated to housing on the Cape Flats, these gangs had formed partly in response to the extreme social disruption caused by that process. Characterised by high levels of unemployment, exclusion from mainstream society, and confined to the periphery of the urban area, the 'Coloured gangs' were both a refuge from and a response to apartheid policies.[20]

By contrast, Johannesburg had a marked white working-class culture, with concentrations of poor whites in the east, west, and particularly the south of the city. These neighbourhoods were tough places where a propensity for violence was a key defining factor of masculinity.[21] These gangs of violent entrepreneurs became the manpower drafted by the state and by the bouncer mafia. In the white working-class areas of Johannesburg many young men with few livelihood alternatives were recruited into the apartheid military or police.

In this social mix, there were also township gangs, which operated lower-level systems of violence, most often demonstrated by the regular fleecing of commuters by tsotsis – local slang for thugs or gangsters. But these groups generally lacked the broader international networks for illicit trafficking that were beginning to transform other parts of the South African underworld.

The next generation of armed gangs, recruited in part from among disaffected young township men, have engaged in vehicle hijacking and robbery, most notably around Johannesburg and, later, Durban, but, for the most part, these networks could be described as 'disorganised organised crime'.[22] They were confined by apartheid policing to the townships, were often drawn into township self-defence units in the 1980s and 1990s, and then became responsible for the growth in armed robbery.[23] Some, like Junior 13, went on to build their own criminal empires. From this milieu emerged some criminal 'bosses' mainly associated with the taxi industry, with its web of contacts and more systematic use of targeted violence.

Shockingly, criminalised elements within the state proved a key catalyst of violence by providing criminal networks with huge quantities of firearms. This fairly recent large-scale injection of firearms has been a defining factor in shaping and strengthening the networks. If drugs transformed the nature of some South African criminal groups by bolstering their revenue, the ability to access firepower was a key way for them to strengthen their control.

The capacity of guns to transform the underworld is starkly evident in the recent drastic increases in the homicide rate in Cape Town, where murder rates in 2016 reached levels equivalent to those in Central America. Unbelievable though it may seem, as described in Chapter 5, about 2 400 firearms were taken from the police armoury by its commanding officer, Colonel Chris Lodewyk Prinsloo, who sold them to the criminal networks.[24]

The impact of this flood of weapons has had disastrous consequences for the Western Cape. It strengthened the hands of several powerful individuals, placing greater control in the hands of gang bosses, raising the assassination rate and promoting gang turf wars. There was a shift from open conflict to more controlled forms of assassinations, as gang bosses recruited groups of hitmen. Assassination developed into a marketable commodity that can be bought and sold. Targeted assassinations, as opposed to open conflict, are an efficient way to manage gang conflict, including maintaining internal order within the gangs.

With the growth of the drugs market and the emergence of a powerful group of criminal actors, there was some evidence in the early 2000s that criminal control was beginning to fall into the hands of fewer gang bosses.[25] However, the availability of guns in Cape Town has strengthened the smaller gangs too, who now have more firepower than they could have dreamt of in the past.[26] This has put them in a position to sell their own services and expand their turf. Weapons mean power in this environment, and power often comes through the unexpected and unexplained hit.

In South Africa, linkages to globalised illicit markets were made through drug traffickers who had been active from the 1970s and 1980s. South African organised criminal networks were also involved in the international diamond trade and in the smuggling of abalone. These and other commodities relied on foreign criminal groups to provide gateways to international markets. Chinese triads dominated the abalone business, with strong links also to the illicit trade in drugs. Israeli and Russian organised-crime networks have also been key players in the illegal diamond trade.

Foreign groups that arrived in South Africa often engaged in overt conflict with one another as they fought for control. What is perhaps most remarkable is the degree to which these individuals integrated rapidly into the local evolving South African criminal networks.

A spate of murders of Chinese and South African-Chinese nationals occurred in Cape Town in the late 1990s. In the case of the Israeli mafia, criminal assassinations have been a regular feature of their presence in South Africa.[27] The Italian mafia was also present in South Africa, most visibly personified by Vito Palazzolo's networks, as were various Eastern European gangsters.

But the growth of Nigerian criminal groups in South Africa over the last two decades has perhaps been most notable. The Nigerian organised-crime groups engage in violence but are careful to limit its scope and its targets to ensure that they do not attract unwanted attention.

The growth in the number of taxis and the competition between the extortion-funded taxi associations paralleled shifts occurring in the drug markets. The result was a rapid development of a network of mafia-style protection economies rooted in the taxi underworld. Our database of hits shows clearly how the majority of targeted killings in South Africa have been associated with the taxi industry. The huge numbers are a testament to the violence that has marred the industry and the degree to which it has become heavily criminalised.

These groups were by no means the first criminal formations in South Africa that practised violence and criminal protection. Decades earlier, in the years before Union in 1910, violent criminal organisations in the shape of a series of Irish bandit groups emerged on the goldfields.[28] Later, systems of violent entrepreneurship evolved as an economic and social response to the conditions of migrant mine workers. One of the most famous was the so-called Russians, or Marashea. These were groups of Basotho mine workers who provided access to contraband and, where necessary, violent capacity to communities who needed it.[29] Back then, such activities took place far from the beat of newspaper reporters, and few would have described them as organised crime at the time.

Nonetheless, these early examples are important because the growth of violent underworld activity – including the provision of criminal protection – in earlier South African history was closely linked to weaknesses within state structures, and often included coalitions between state and criminal actors. Parallels can therefore be drawn to developments in the country in the late 1980s and 1990s. In both cases, a weak state allowed the growth of alternative forms of market regulation – essentially, forms of criminal governance or protection based on violence, which enjoyed a symbiotic relationship with the state.

The response to banditry at the turn of the 20th century constitutes a form of state building in its own right. In his classic study of Irish bandits on the Witwatersrand, Charles van Onselen presciently noted that the disorder they created – and the degree to which policing had become corrupt – was the rationale behind local elites investing in strengthening the Johannesburg police force.[30] It has been noted elsewhere that responses to organised crime by the state may be an important way in which state-security capacity is built.[31] Indeed, it does seem that as the South African state consolidated after the Union in 1910, forms of what we might call organised crime today went into decline. And from the 1960s, as the apartheid state strengthened, organised-criminal or mafia-like violence was not of significant concern.

The critical point here is that where forms of organised criminality remain at manageable levels, after a period of disruption, states generally respond where their interests are threatened – as in the case of the nascent

South African state in 1910. However, when criminal interests overlap with those of the state to such an extent that they weaken or distort any response, the state may itself become a criminalised entity, in whole or in significant parts.[32]

Reminiscent of the South African state in 1910, the newly democratic South African state became increasingly concerned by the growth of organised crime. In the first days of the new democracy a series of actions were taken by the SAPS to respond to organised crime. This was a period when I worked at the National Secretariat for Safety and Security in Pretoria. The growth of organised crime was clearly perceived as something that needed attention. There was a discernible shift in policy from what had been the dominant discourse of improving the legitimacy of the police, under the framework of 'community policing', to one that focused more on what was seen as an emerging challenge – organised crime.

The growth of organised crime and criminal markets were also key policy concerns for the international community throughout the 1990s. Although the focus of this policy debate was mostly the threat of organised crime to developed countries, most particularly from criminal networks emerging in the post-Soviet states, there was a general conception at the time that organised crime posed a new general global threat.[33] One of the outcomes of this was the formation of a new global convention, the UN Convention on Transnational Organized Crime, which South Africa ratified in 2001.[34] These responses reflected significant changes in global illicit supply-and-demand patterns – a process that has continued to evolve.

Reflecting these global developments, several steps were taken in South Africa, including conducting an organised-crime threat assessment, passing relevant legislation and the formation of a multidisciplinary law-enforcement unit, the Scorpions, tasked with investigating serious crimes. An important response from the last days of the old order, however, was the training and deployment of several deep-cover agents to infiltrate criminal groups. Two of these agents provided material for this book. Their story waits to be told in full, but central to it are two aspects: a general recognition that organised crime was an issue that was first identified as the tectonic plates of South African politics shifted; and, secondly, that the nascent forms of organised crime that emerged were often built on established political-criminal networks, both within the state and among those fighting to overthrow it.

But those efforts were beaten back, with the consequence that, today, the South African state is weaker in its capacity to fight this complex criminal challenge than perhaps at any point in its history. The Scorpions were to run foul of political, criminal and bureaucratic interests after investigations threatened members of the ruling ANC, and the unit was seen to usurp the role of the police and its then powerful National Police Commissioner, Jackie Selebi. Selebi was later fired after he was convicted of corruption. He had associated with known members of the underworld and had shared intelligence dossiers with them. In 2008 the Scorpions were replaced by a unit within the police, the Hawks, whose record in combating organised crime is much poorer, with growing evidence that the unit is used a tool for the interests of President Zuma.[35]

On the face of it, the unprecedentedly high number of assassinations we see today suggests that the underworld is fragmented, the leadership of criminal organisations unstable and that conflict between groups is rife. That should arguably offer opportunities for a coordinated state response to break down the potency of the criminal underworld. Sadly, though, this has not occurred – partly because different factions within the underworld have achieved linkages to the upperworld, thereby protecting themselves. Nowhere is this clearer than in the state's crime-intelligence apparatus. South Africa's system of crime intelligence has become corrupted and is in disarray, its thinking too conditioned by the past political work that its constituent elements have been focused on. The organisation's tools are too often used for political purposes, and not crime fighting. There is also a strong argument to review the state's system of informant recruitment and management. Has the secret state, even unwittingly, become part of a symbiosis of collective interests that maintains the underworld's status quo? This requires an urgent review.

The state's fight against organised crime is now largely in the hands of a few brave and dedicated police officers who seldom receive the institutional or political support that they require. It is such officers who have pursued the case, for example, of Prinsloo, the head of firearms registration who sold weapons to the underworld. Yet these officers have often conveniently been shifted within the police service when their investigations appear to have touched on areas where criminal markets overlap with political and police institutional interests.

The contemporary picture of state responses to organised crime is therefore not a positive one – and without a more strategic response the consolidation of the criminal economy will continue, strengthening those political figures who cross easily between the upper and underworlds. The costs for ordinary people will be great.

The challenge will be to target and tap into these nurseries of violence by denying them access to weapons, recruits and criminal resources. It means ensuring that the police are cleaned up and subjected to proper independent oversight, so that they cannot be used for political purposes. Longer-term forms of state regulation and governance must focus on those markets of violence where hitmen are nurtured and learn their trade. That will necessitate unbiased policing, free from political influence and with personnel who have the skills to do the job.

What is clear from our overall research study, the findings of which have informed this book, is the degree to which forms of criminal violence and regulation rise when the state is weak or when its focus is elsewhere, when new economic opportunities – both licit and illicit – are available for criminal exploitation, and when wider forms of economic development fail, allowing organised crime to draw in recruits as a resource. In such cases, the evidence suggests that, although overall levels of violence may be in decline and open conflict less common than in the past, targeted violence as a commercialised service is on the rise – available to those who can pay for it. And many do. It is discreet, affordable and powerfully effective, and consequently it is insidiously damaging to the achievement of a safe and stable democratic country. The dark hand of assassination stalks the land.

# Appendix

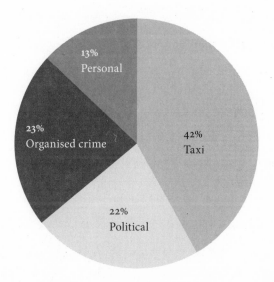

**Figure 1**: Breakdown of categories of reported hits, 2000–2016

Source: UCT hits database

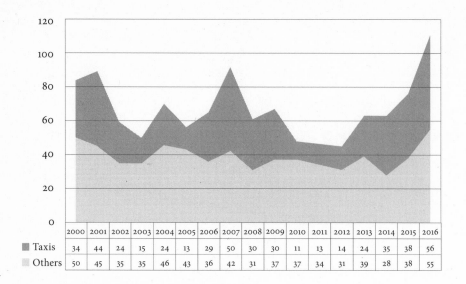

| | 2000 | 2001 | 2002 | 2003 | 2004 | 2005 | 2006 | 2007 | 2008 | 2009 | 2010 | 2011 | 2012 | 2013 | 2014 | 2015 | 2016 |
|---|---|---|---|---|---|---|---|---|---|---|---|---|---|---|---|---|---|
| ■ Taxis | 34 | 44 | 24 | 15 | 24 | 13 | 29 | 50 | 30 | 30 | 11 | 13 | 14 | 24 | 35 | 38 | 56 |
| Others | 50 | 45 | 35 | 35 | 46 | 43 | 36 | 42 | 31 | 37 | 37 | 34 | 31 | 39 | 28 | 38 | 55 |

**Figure 2:** Cases of hits recorded for the period 2000–2016

Source: UCT hits database

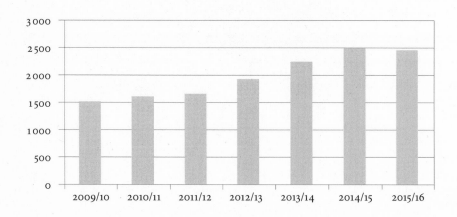

**Figure 3:** Raw murder figures for the Cape Town metropolitan area, 2009–2016

Source: Annual SAPS release of statistics

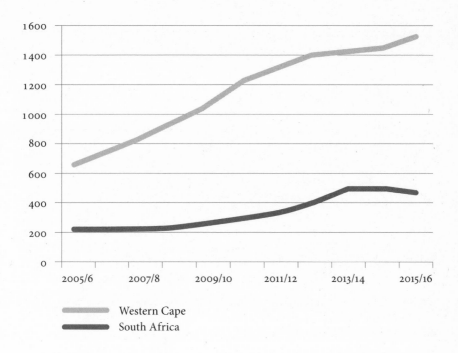

**Figure 4:** Incidents of drug-related crime in the Western Cape and South Africa compared (per 100 000 citizens)

Sources: Annual crime statistics release, SAPS, http://www.saps.gov.za/resource_centre/publications/statistics/ crimestats/2015/crime_stats.php; Statistics South Africa, provincial population projections, http://www.statssa. gov.za/?page_id=1854&PPN=P0302

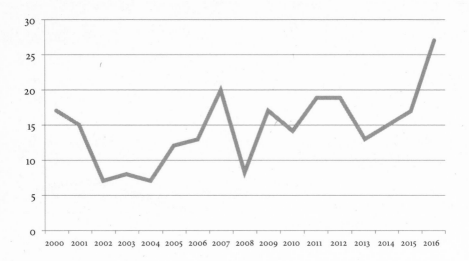

**Figure 5**: Hits with an overt connection to politics, 2000–2016

Source: UCT hits database

# Notes

## Preface

1 A similar methodology was adopted in Donal Macintyre, David Wilson, Elizabeth Yardley and Liam Brolan, 'The British hitman: 1974–2013', *The Howard Journal of Criminal Justice*, 35, 4, September 2014, p. 326. In that study search terms were applied to a database of newspaper articles. As with our research, this was followed up with interviews.

2 See, for example, Mandy Wiener's excellent, *Killing Kebble: An Underworld Exposed*, Johannesburg: Macmillan, 2011; Peter Piegl and Sean Newman, *Glenn Agliotti: A Biography*, Johannesburg: Penguin, 2013; Barry Sergeant, *The Kebble Collusion: 10 Fateful Days in a R26 Billion Fraud*, Johannesburg: Jacana, 2012; Angelique Serrao, *Krejcir*, Cape Town: Jonathan Ball, 2016.

3 Some recent examples are Jana Arsovska, *Decoding Albanian Organized Crime: Culture, Politics and Globalization*, Oakland: University of California Press, 2015; Alexander Kupatadze, *Organised Crime, Political Transitions and State Formation in Post-Soviet Eurasia*, London: Palgrave Macmillan, 2012; Stephen Ellis, *This Present Darkness: A History of Nigerian Organised Crime*, London: Hurst, 2016.

4 For an introduction to conducting interviews with organised-crime and underworld figures, see the introduction to Frederico Varese's *The Russian Mafia*, Oxford: Oxford University Press, 2001.

5 In one case I have combined three interviews into one to mask people's identity. In this case the accounts of the different people were remarkably similar and the interview, as it is reflected on these pages, is, sadly, an accurate representation of the reality of commercialised violence in South Africa.

## Introduction: Removing obstacles

1 Quoted in Andrew Kramer, 'More of Kremlin's opponents ending up dead', *The New York Times*, 20 August 2016.

2 See, for example, the characteristics of the murder contract, as identified by Jenny Mouzos and John Venditto, 'Contract killings in Australia', Australian Institute of Criminology and Public Policy Series, No 53, 2003, pp. 9–10.

3 Calhoun notes that, in this respect, contract killing by a criminal murderer is no different from the objectives of killings by executioners or soldiers. See Laurie Calhoun, 'The phenomenology of paid killing', *The International Journal of Human Rights*, 6, 1, Spring 2002, pp. 1–18.

4 Donal Macintyre, David Wilson, Elizabeth Yardley and Liam Brolan, 'The British hitman: 1974–2013', *The Howard Journal of Criminal Justice*, 35, 4, September 2014, p. 326.

5 Liam Brolan, David Wilson and Elizabeth Yardley, 'Hitmen and the spaces of contract killing: The doorstep hitman', *Journal of Investigative Psychology and Offender Profiling*, 13, 3, 2016, pp. 220–221.

6 Steve Hall, *Theorizing Crime and Deviance: A New Perspective*, London: Sage, 2012, p. 203.

7 'Answers wanted in alleged Pule assassination plot', eNCA, 12 August 2013, https://www.enca.com/south-africa/pule-linked-alleged-assassination-plot; 'SAPS: Pule not involved in assassination plot', *Mail & Guardian*, 11 August 2013, https://mg.co.za/article/2013-08-11-saps-pule-not-involved-in-assassination-plot; personal communication with former parliamentary staffer, Cape Town, January 2016.

8 Tom Lodge, 'Neo-patrimonial politics in the ANC', *African Affairs*, 113, 450, 2014, pp. 1–23.

9 Karl von Holdt, 'South Africa: The transition to violent democracy', *Review of African Political Economy*, 40, 138, 2013, p. 590.

10 A comparative study also confirms that hits are cheap, particularly in what have been labelled as 'personal' cases, where there may be a gift involved, as opposed to cash. See Samuel Cameron, 'Killing for money and the economic theory of crime', *Review of Social Economy*, 72, 1, 2014, p. 37.

11 See the arguments in two studies on the impact of global change on local forms of violence and economic interaction: Maria Luisa Maniscalco, 'A new global risk: The rise of the killer sects', *International Review of Sociology*, 7, 3, 1997, pp. 485–497; Rodolphe Durand and Jean-Philippe Vergne, *The Pirate Organisation: Lessons from the Fringes of Capitalism*, Boston, MA: Harvard Business Review Press, 2013.

12 Robert Baer, *The Perfect Kill: 21 Laws for Assassins*, London: Weidenfeld and Nicolson, 2014, p. 84.

13 Cameron argues that most people who initiate a paid killing may never have done so in the past and so seek out a 'pool of agents' where they believe a killer may be found. See Samuel Cameron, 'Killing for money and the economic theory of crime', *Review*

*of Social Economy*, 72, 1, 2014, p. 37. The word 'nursery' works better in the South African context, as it suggests a deeper historical trajectory of violence.

14 John Landesco's landmark study of organised crime in Chicago, quoted in Vincenzo Ruggiero, *Understanding Political Violence: A Criminological Analysis*, Maidenhead: Open University Press, 2006, p. 77.

15 Diego Gambetta, *Codes of the Underworld: How Criminals Communicate*, Princeton: Princeton University Press, 2009, p. 79.

16 Annemarie Jansen, *Eugene De Kock: Assassin for the State*, Cape Town: Tafelberg, 2015.

17 For a recent account, see Koos Stadler, *Recce: Small Team Missions Behind Enemy Lines*, Cape Town: Tafelberg, 2015.

18 See Stephen Ellis, *External Mission: The ANC in Exile*, Johannesburg: Jonathan Ball, 2012 (in particular Chapter 5).

19 Rupert Taylor and Mark Shaw, 'The dying days of apartheid' in David Howarth and Aletta Norval (eds), *South Africa in Transition: New Theoretical Perspectives*, London: Palgrave Macmillan, 1998, pp. 3–13.

20 Interviews conducted with hitmen suggested, for example, that past experience, including the role of gangs in targeting anti-apartheid activists on behalf of the state, had been translated into a new environment and had become commercialised.

21 Jan van Dijk, 'Mafia markers: Assessing organised crime and its impact upon society', *Trends in Organised Crime*, 10, 4, 2007, pp. 39–56.

22 Vadim Volkov, *Violent Entrepreneurs: The Use of Force in the Making of Russian Capitalism*, Ithaca: Cornell University Press, 2002.

23 Interviews with gang bosses and hitmen, Cape Town, October to November 2015. See Chapter 4.

24 Anna Jarstad and Kristine Höglund, 'Local violence and politics in KwaZulu-Natal: Perceptions of agony in a post-conflict society', *Third World Quarterly*, 36, 5, 2015, p. 982.

### Chapter 1   Junior 13: A grey ghost brings death

1 Despite his notoriety, there is surprisingly little public information available on Selokwane. The following press articles provide some insight into his life and death: Karishma Dipa, 'Multimillionaire "mastermind" gunned down', 9 November 2015, http://www.iol.co.za/news/crime-courts/multimillionaire-mastermind-gunned-down-1942666; Rapula Moatshe, 'Multimillionaire "mastermind" mourned', 10 November 2015, http://www.iol.co.za/news/crime-courts/multimillionaire-mas-termind-mourned-1943025; Nompumelelo Ngubeni, 'Family of murdered criminal mastermind speaks out', 10 November 2015, http://ewn.co.za/2015/11/10/Family-of-murdered-criminal-mastermind-speaks-out; Solly Maphumulo, 'No sympathy for suspect who offered cops tea', 21 August 2003, http://www.iol.co.za/news/south-africa/

no-sympathy-for-suspect-who-offered-cops-tea-111765. The quotes in the text come from interviews, and discussions were conducted with residents, business associates and family of Junior 13 in Mamelodi West, 6–18 July 2016 and 7 March 2017.

2  Interviews with members of the Mamelodi Taxi Association, Mamelodi, 6–10 July 2016.

3  Ibid.

4  See Anine Kriegler and Mark Shaw, *A Citizen's Guide to Crime Trends in South Africa*, Johannesburg: Jonathan Ball, 2016.

5  The phrase 'solving problems' was used in several interviews and discussions on the topic of assassinations during the research for this book.

6  Statement by the SALGA spokesperson on Twitter, 3 February 2016, https://twitter.com/tahirsema/status/702066592096636928.

7  Caryn Dolley, 'Thuli shaken by "hit" reports', *Weekend Argus*, 14 May 2016.

8  See, for example, Gareth van Onselen, 'Political assassinations are on the rise', *Rand Daily Mail*, 29 February 2016, http://www.rdm.co.za/politics/2016/02/29/political-assassinations-are-on-the-rise.

9  Deputy President Cyril Ramaphosa publicly acknowledged the role of hired assassins in killing ANC candidates. See Amanda Khoza, 'We are coming for you – Ramaphosa warns assassins killing KZN candidates', News24, 22 July 2016, http://www.news24.com/elections/news/we-are-coming-for-you-ramaphosa-warns-assassins-killing-kzn-candidates-20160722.

10  In 2013/14, there were 17 068 reported murders and, although the reporting periods do not align perfectly, there were approximately 60 hits on our database, or 0.35 per cent of all murders.

11  See, for example, the annual report of the SAPS for 2008/09: South African Police Service, 'Crime situation in South Africa', *Annual Report, South African Police Service*, 2008/2009, http://www.saps.gov.za/about/stratframework/annual_report/2008_2009/2_crime_situation_sa.pdf, p. 10.

12  Using these two numbers as a rough guide, hits constituted 0.6 per cent of all murders.

13  This was a point made by several gang-related hitmen in interviews conducted in Cape Town and surrounds, November 2015.

14  One important exception is David Bruce, 'A provincial concern? Political killings in South Africa', *South African Crime Quarterly* 45, September 2013, pp. 13–24; David Bruce, 'Political killings in South Africa: The ultimate intimidation', Institute for Security Studies, Policy Brief 64, October 2014. For a list of some political assassinations, see Gareth van Onselen, 'Political assassinations: How the ANC is killing its own', *Business Day*, 12 August 2013, http://www.bdlive.co.za/opinion/columnists/2013/08/12/political-assassinations-how-the-anc-is-killing-its-own.

15  Stephen Ellis and Mark Shaw, 'Does organised crime exist in Africa?' *African Affairs*, 114, 457, 2015, pp. 505–528.

16  For a recent South African example, see Derica Lambrechts, 'Doing research on sensitive topics in political science: Studying organised criminal groups in Cape Town',

*Politikon*, 41, 2, 2014, pp. 249–265.

17  Aryeh Neier, *The International Human Rights Movement: A History*, Princeton: Princeton University Press, 2013.

18  This most notably in relation to violence perpetrated by the state during apartheid, and in the violent political conflict in the years preceding the transition to democracy. See John Aitchison, *Numbering the Dead: The Course and Pattern of Political Violence in the Natal Midlands, 1987–1989*, Pietermaritzburg: Natal Society Foundation Trust, 2015. This work involved systems of media review and reporting from community-based activists, something I had participated in as a violence monitor for the then National Peace Secretariat. This approach was adopted by several human-rights and civil-society groups that published their data. See, for example, the reports of the Network of Independent Monitors or the South African Institute of Race Relations.

19  Liam Brolan, David Wilson and Elizabeth Yardley, 'Hitmen and the spaces of contract killing: The doorstep hitman', *Journal of Investigative Psychology and Offender Profiling*, 13, pp. 220–221.

20  This blurring of categories was raised in discussions with some key informants: telephone discussion, investigative journalist, Johannesburg, November 2015; interview, local businessman on whom an assassination had been attempted, Nyanga, Cape Town, November 2015.

21  See the case of Moses Tshake, a Free State government auditor, who died in May 2013 after a brutal and mysterious hijacking. He was involved in several anti-corruption probes at the time. See http://www.r2k.org.za/2014/01/01/2014-whistleblower-calendar/.

22  Mandla Khoza, 'Municipal official's murder "a mafia plot"', *Sowetan*, 30 March 2016, http://www.Sowetan.co.za/news/2016/03/30/municipal-official-s-murder-a-mafia-plot.

23  Sabelo Nsele, '"Hit list" man believes shots fired at house were for him', *The Witness*, 12 April 2016.

24  Nokuthula Ntuli, '"Hit list" exists – but why?', *The New Age*, 2 March 2016.

25  For a comprehensive overview, see Mary de Haas, 'Local government elections, violence and democracy in KwaZulu-Natal', *South African Crime Quarterly*, 57, 2016.

26  Jan van Dijk, 'Mafia markers: Assessing organised crime and its impact upon society', *Trends in Organised Crime*, 10, 4, 2007, pp. 39–56.

27  Companies distributing bread are said to be extorted for protection money: interview with local businessman, Cape Town, December 2015. A recent unpublished report by the Department of Basic Education resulted in the suspension of all teacher hiring in an attempt to limit corruption, see Lizeka Tandwa, 'Motshekga to freeze teacher posts after releasing damning report', News24, 17 December 2015, http://www.news24.com/SouthAfrica/News/motshekga-to-freeze-teacher-posts-after-releasing-damning-report-20151217.

28  Kimon de Greef, '"Bazooka" assassination: Anti-mining activist knew his life was in danger', *Daily Maverick*, 30 March 2016, http://www.dailymaverick.co.za/article/2016-03-30-bazooka-assassination-anti-mining-activist-knew-his-life-was-in-danger/#.VwTZkxN96Rs.

29  Angelique Serrao and Shaun Germaner, 'Plot to kill five exposed: Krejcir had put out a contract on Paul O'Sullivan', *The Star*, 20 May 2016.

30  Solly Maphumulo, 'Krejcir plot to have judge killed alleged', *The Star*, 18 February, 2016.

31  See Tania Broughton and Bernadette Wolhuter, 'Failed "hit men" charged with perjury', IOL, 23 June 2016, http://www.iol.co.za/news/crime-courts/failed-hit-men-charged-with-perjury-2037983.

32  Sandile Motha, 'Hitman makes sisters pay: One wanted sibling dead', *Sowetan*, 3 May 2015.

33  'Son jailed for hiring hitman to murder "intolerable" dad', News24, 23 March 2016, http://www.news24.com/SouthAfrica/News/son-jailed-for-hiring-hitman-to-murder-intolerable-dad-20160323.

34  Kutullo Madisha, 'Suspect sought after shooting of five taxi bosses', *The New Age*, 21 April 2016.

35  'Taxi boss cop Zungu killed in ambush', *Daily News*, 26 April 2016.

36  Kutullo Madisha, 'Shock at murder of ANC councillor', *The New Age*, 24 February 2016.

37  Pertunia Mafokwane, 'Daytime taxi murder', *Sowetan*, 5 May 2016.

38  Sandile Motha, 'Cop accused of murder, stoking taxi wars', *Sowetan*, 3 April 2016, http://www.sowetanlive.co.za/news/2016/04/03/cop-accused-of-murder-stoking-taxi-wars.

39  Stergious Skaperdas, 'The political economy of organised crime: Providing protection when the state does not', *Economics of Governance*, 2, 3, 2001, pp. 173–202.

40  Although, ironically, in the prominent case of the murder of Anni Dewani, the South African government was eager to show it was in fact a contract killing, to demonstrate that more random levels of violent crime were not excessive. See Dan Newling, *Bitter Dawn: A Search for the Truth About the Murder of Anni Dewani*, Johannesburg: Jonathan Ball, 2014.

### Chapter 2   It's just a job: The hitman's work

1  Interview, Cape Town, 10 March 2017.

2  Interview, retired hitman, Cape Town, 10 March 2017.

3  This follows the approach first suggested in a groundbreaking paper by Louis B Schlesinger, 'The contract murderer: Patterns, characteristics and dynamics', *Journal of Forensic Science*, 46, 5, 2001, pp. 1119–1123.

4  The story of one notorious American hitman, who is suspected of killing over 100 people, suggests that as he acquired skills, expertise and consequently a good reputation, he graduated upwards, taking on more difficult assignments. See Frederick Zugibe and James Costello, 'The iceman murder: One of a series of contract murders', *Journal of Forensic Science*, 38, 6, November 1992, pp. 1404–1408.

5 Interviews, police officers and members of the underworld, Cape Town and Johannesburg, November 2015. No arrests have been made in either case.

6 Paul Thulare, 'Policing and society on the East Rand – Katorus area', *African Security Review*, 5, 2, 1996, pp. 80–91.

7 Interview, former senior security official, 12 April 2016.

8 Interview, taxi boss, Cape Town, 10 March 2017.

9 Interview, KwaMashu, KwaZulu-Natal, 20 January 2016.

10 Interview, Umlazi, Durban, 16 January 2016.

11 This section draws on work conducted with Luke Lee Skywalker. See Mark Shaw and Luke Lee Skywalker, 'The hammermen: Life and death as a gang hitman in Cape Town', *The Howard Journal of Crime and Justice*, 55, 4, 2016, pp. 377–542.

12 Interview, gang boss, Cape Town, 11 August 2015.

13 Interview, gang boss, Cape Town, 5 October 2015.

14 Ibid.

15 David Wilson and Mohammed Rahman, 'Becoming a hitman', *The Howard Journal of Criminal Justice*, 54, 3, 2015, pp. 250–264.

16 Interview, gang hitman A, Cape Town, 7 August 2015.

17 Ibid.

18 Interview, hitwoman B, Cape Town, 19 August 2015.

19 Interview, taxi boss, Cape Town, 3 March 2016.

20 Interview, gang hitman C, Cape Town, 3 August 2015.

21 Interview, gang hitman E, Cape Town, 12 October 2015.

22 Interview, gang hitman C, Cape Town, 3 August 2015.

23 Interview, gang hitman D, Cape Town, 6 September 2015.

24 Interview, gang boss, Cape Town, 5 October 2015.

25 Interview, gang hitman A, Cape Town, 7 August 2015.

26 Ibid.

27 Ibid.

28 Interview, gang hitman G, Cape Town, 2 October 2015.

29 Interview, gang boss, Cape Town, 5 October 2015.

30 Interview, Khayelitsha, 6 March 2016.

31 This was confirmed in several discussions: interview, senior provincial police officer, Braamfontein, 5 February 2016; interview, a person with good knowledge of the industry who mediates between taxi associations and provides services to local government, Cape Town, 3 March 2016.

32 Interview, former senior security official, 12 April 2016.

33 Interview, gang boss, Cape Town, 5 October 2015.

34 Ibid.

35 Ibid.

36 Ibid.

37 See, for example, Gary Kynoch, 'From the Ninevites to the Hard Livings Gang: Township gangsters and urban violence in twentieth-century South Africa', *African*

*Studies*, 58, 1, 1999, pp. 55–85.

38 See Graham Denyer Willis, *The Killing Consensus: Police, Organised Crime and the Regulation of Death in Urban Brazil*, Oakland: University of California Press, 2015.

39 It is difficult to determine the extent to which this occurs, but it has been mentioned on several occasions in interviews for this book.

40 Interview, gang boss, Cape Town, 5 October 2015.

## Chapter 3   Rank and file: Life and death in South Africa's taxi industry

1 Details of this story are drawn from interviews with relatives and acquaintances of Victor Nbulelo, news reports on the trial of Khobe and reports of the Truth and Reconciliation Commission. See, for example, Karyn Maughan, 'Taxi war gunmen face justice at last', 14 April 2005, http://www.iol.co.za/news/south-africa/taxi-war-gunmen-face-justice-at-last-238734; http://www.news24.com/xArchive/Archive/Criminal-mastermind-arrested-20010227; and http://sabctrc.saha.org.za/reports/volume3/chapter5/subsection58.htm.

2 Makubetse Sekhonyane and Jackie Dugard, 'A violent legacy: The taxi industry and the government at loggerheads', *South African Crime Quarterly*, 10, December 2004, pp. 13–18.

3 The documents and minutes of the meetings give a fascinating insight into the struggles of one Cape Town-based association. These documents are valuable, as few associations kept minutes or have preserved them.

4 Janet Cherry, '"We were not afraid": The role of women in the 1980s township uprising in the Eastern Cape', in Nomboniso Gasa (ed.), *Women in South African History: They Remove Boulders and Cross Rivers*, Cape Town: HSRC Press, 2007, p. 297.

5 Quoted in Thabo Jijana, *Nobody's Business: A Memoir*, Johannesburg: Jacana, 2015, p. 130.

6 Interview, taxi boss, Cape Town, 3 March 2016.

7 Ibid.

8 Thomas Blom Hansen, 'Sounds of freedom: Music, taxis, and racial imagination in urban South Africa', *Public Culture*, 18, 1, 2006, p. 187.

9 Interviews conducted for this chapter revealed that many people, including family breadwinners, have been killed in taxi-related conflicts and accidents. In particularly painful cases, killing has often occurred within families.

10 See Jackie Dugard, 'Drive on? Taxi wars in South Africa', in Jonny Steinberg (ed.), *Crime Wave: The South African Underworld and its Foes*, Johannesburg: Witwatersrand University Press, 2001, pp. 130–132.

11 Interview, businesswoman with extensive connections in the taxi industry, Cape Town, 2 February 2016.

12 Jane Barrett, 'Organising in the informal economy: A case study of the minibus taxi industry in South Africa', Geneva: International Labour Organization, 2003, p. 7.

13 Interviews with taxi owners and operators, Johannesburg, Cape Town and Durban, November 2015 to February 2016.

14 See Meshack Khosa, 'Routes, ranks and rebels: Feuding in the taxi revolution', *Journal of Southern African Studies*, 18, 1, 1992.

15 Jackie Dugard, 'Drive on? Taxi wars in South Africa', in Jonny Steinberg (ed.), *Crime Wave: The South African Underworld and its Foes*, Johannesburg: Witwatersrand University Press, 2001, p. 103.

16 Jackie Dugard, *From Low-intensity War to Mafia War: Taxi Violence in South Africa (1987–2000)*, Johannesburg: The Centre for the Study of Violence and Transition, 2001.

17 Jeff Wicks, 'Top cop on izinkabi hitlist', *The Witness*, 25 April 2015.

18 Information on Mpungose was taken from interviews in KwaZulu-Natal conducted in January and February 2016.

19 Ibid.

20 Interviews, taxi bosses, Soweto, 6 March 2017.

21 Interview, taxi-rank overseer, Soweto, 6 March 2017.

22 Mlalazi was speaking during the Gauteng Legislative Committee of Roads and Transport's inquiry hearings on taxi permits and licensing. *The Star*, 16 March 2016.

23 Clayton Barnes, Mzwanele Mkalipi and Kashiefa Ajam, 'It's easy to hire a hitman. Just ask around at a taxi rank', *Weekend Argus*, 1 September 2007.

24 Interview, taxi boss, Cape Town, 3 March 2016.

25 Interview, 11 January 2015.

26 *Drum* magazine, July 1989, quoted in Meshack Khosa, 'Routes, ranks and rebels: Feuding in the taxi revolution', *Journal of Southern African Studies*, 18, 1, 1992, p. 232.

27 Thabo Jijana, *Nobody's Business: A Memoir*, Johannesburg: Jacana, 2015.

28 Personal communication, Jackie Dugard, November 2015.

29 Interview, taxi owner, Newcastle, 18 January 2016.

30 Interview, taxi association member, Cape Town, 2 March 2016.

31 Jackie Dugard, 'Drive on? Taxi wars in South Africa', in Jonny Steinberg (ed.), *Crime Wave: The South African Underworld and its Foes*, Johannesburg: Witwatersrand University Press, 2001, p. 142.

32 Interview, taxi consultant, Cape Town, 3 March 2016.

33 Ibid.; interview, taxi owner, Newcastle, 18 January 2016; interview, senior police officer investigating the taxi industry, Durban, 8 February 2016.

34 Interview, taxi consultant, Cape Town, 3 March 2016.

35 Interview, senior police officer investigating the taxi industry, Durban, 8 February 2016.

36 Genevieve Quintal, 'Durban community to meet over taxi bosses' advert threat', News24, 5 December 2015, http://www.news24.com/SouthAfrica/News/durban-community-to-meet-over-taxi-bosses-advert-threat-20151205.

37 Derica Lambrechts, 'The impact of organised crime on state social control: Organised criminal groups and local governance on the Cape Flats, Cape Town, South Africa', *Journal of Southern African Studies*, 38, 4, 2012, p. 795.

38 Interview, taxi boss, Cape Town, 5 March 2016; interview, community leader, Manenberg, Cape Town, 19 May 2016.

39 Interview, former senior national security official, Johannesburg, 12 April 2016.

40 Charles Goredema, 'Drugs and violent crime in Southern Africa', *SADC Law Journal*, 1, 2011, p. 185.

41 Hazel Crampton, *Dagga: A Short History*, Johannesburg: Jacana, 2015, pp. 54–57; interview, police intelligence officer, Johannesburg, November 2015.

42 Interview with taxi owner and ex-prisoner, Johannesburg, 20 December 2014 and 10 February 2016.

43 'Masiphumelele protester dies in hospital', 4 May 2016, http://www.iol.co.za/news/crime-courts/masiphumelele-protester-dies-in-hospital-2017519; 'Taxi drivers versus Masiphumelele', 9 May 2016, http://www.groundup.org.za/article/taxi-drivers-versus-masiphumelele/; 'Masiphumelele residents boycott taxis after scuffle', 10 May 2016, http://ewn.co.za/2016/05/10/Masiphumelele-residents-boycott-taxis-after-scuffle.

44 Committee of Inquiry into the Underlying Causes of Instability in the Minibus Taxi Industry in the Cape Town Metropolitan Area, Report to the Premier of the Western Cape, Cape Town, 31 August 2005, p. 53.

45 Interview, taxi consultant and mediator, Cape Town, 4 February 2016.

46 Interview, police investigating officer, Durban, 9 February 2016.

47 Interview with taxi operator, Johannesburg, 19 January 2016.

48 Interview, former taxi boss, Khayelitsha, 6 March 2016.

49 Interview, senior police officer, Durban, 8 February 2016.

50 James Cockayne, *Hidden Power: The Strategic Logic of Organised Crime*, London: Hurst, 2016, p. 128.

51 Speech by Ismail Vadi, MEC of Transport for Gauteng, to the Gauteng Taxi Summit, 14 May 2013.

52 See, for example, Diego Gambetta, *The Sicilian Mafia: The Business of Private Protection*, Cambridge, Mass.: Harvard University Press, 1993.

### Chapter 4   Cyril Beeka: Clubs, drugs and the ultimate hit

1 The Gavrić account is taken from Craig McKune, Sally Evans and Sam Sole, 'Serb assassin's shadowy associates', *Mail & Guardian*, 13 January 2012, http://mg.co.za/article/2012-01-13-serb-assassins-shadowy-associates.

2 Interview, gang leader, Mitchells Plain, Cape Town, 14 December 2014.

3 Cyril Beeka's murder was widely covered in the South African press. The details were drawn from interviews and personal communication with a private investigator with knowledge of the case, from police officers and a Serbian colleague. Information was also taken from the following articles: Shanaaz Eggington, 'The many faces of Cyril Beeka', Times Live, 26 March 2011, http://www.timeslive.co.za/local/2011/03/26/the-many-faces-of-cyril-beeka; Caryn Dolley, 'Still no arrest 4 years after Beeka killed',

*Cape Times*, 21 March 2015, http://www.iol.co.za/news/crime-courts/still-no-arrest-4-years-after-beeka-killed-1.1835353; 'Cyril Beeka buried in Cape Town', *Mail & Guardian*, 2 April 2011, http://mg.co.za/article/ 2011-04-02-cyril-beeka-buried-in-cape-town; 'Terry Bell Writes: A tale of two funerals', http//terrybellwrites.com/2011/04/08/a-tale-of-two-funerals/; 'The Rottweiler from Kuilsrivier', *City Press*, 26 March 2011, http://news24.com/Archives/City-Press/the-Rottweiler-from-Kuilsrivier-20150429.

4 Interview, gang leader, Woodstock, Cape Town, 26 November 2014.

5 Fiona ni Ghiollanaraithe, 'Mo Shaik's underworld links', Independent Online, 22 December 2007, http://www.iol.co.za/news/politics/mo-shaiks-underworld-links-383661.

6 Interviews conducted with former police officers from the then South African Police 'Gang Unit', Cape Town, 12 November 2014.

7 See Irvin Kinnes, 'From urban street gangs to criminal empires: The changing face of gangs in the Western Cape'. Institute for Security Studies Monograph No. 48, 2000. The homicide rate for Cape Town is discussed in greater detail in Chapter 5.

8 Interviews, Long Street venue owners, Cape Town, November 2014.

9 In this, Cape Town was in line with the growth of the night-time entertainment economy in cities across the globe. For an interesting discussion of the trend in the UK, see Dick Hobbs, Philip Hadfield, Stuart Lister and Simon Winlow, *Bouncers: Violence and Governance in the Night-time Economy*, Oxford: Oxford University Press, 2003, pp. 25–28.

10 Interview, investigative journalist, Cape Town, 19 August 2015.

11 Interview, bar owner, Long Street, Cape Town, 20 August 2015.

12 Interview, bouncer still active on Long Street, Cape Town, 31 August 2015.

13 Interviews, bouncer and former bouncer, Cape Town, 1 September 2015.

14 Interview, bouncer working in a Cape Town nightclub during the Beeka era, Rylands, 3 December 2014.

15 Interviews conducted with several participants in the enforcement economy, including a gang member, Cape Town, November 2014 and July 2015.

16 Interview, Cape Town, February 2015.

17 This agreement was mentioned in a number of interviews, Cape Town, September 2015. Whether proceeds were paid on a sustained basis is unclear.

18 Shanaaz Eggington, 'The many faces of Cyril Beeka', Times Live, 26 March 2011, http://www.timeslive.co.za/local/2011/03/26/the-many-faces-of-cyril-beeka.

19 Ibid.

20 Interview, gang leader, Woodstock, Cape Town, 26 November 2014.

21 Interview, former analyst for the Scorpions, Cape Town, 19 August 2015.

22 Interview, former owner of a bar in Long Street, Cape Town, 3 September 2016.

23 This was mentioned in several interviews with gang-affiliated individuals conducted in November 2014.

24 See Craig McKune and Sally Evans, 'Battle for the control of the doors and the "drugs"', *Mail & Guardian*, 3 February 2012, https://mg.co.za/

article/2012-02-03-battle-for-control-of-the-doors-and-drugs; also, Kimon de Greef, 'Murder on Long Street: Congolese bouncers and the private security industry', GroundUp, 6 July 2015, http://www.groundup.org.za/media/features/murderlong-street/murderlongstreet_0018.html.

25 The term 'Congolese' in this context often includes other African national groups outside of South Africa. The same applies to the term 'Nigerian' in the Johannesburg context.

26 Interview, Congolese bouncer, Cape Town, 1 September 2015.

27 Interviews, current and former bouncers, Cape Town, July 2015.

28 Interview, former bouncer and 'security specialist' who worked with Cyril Beeka, 15 December 2015.

29 Dale Granger, 'My interview with Yuri the Russian', Independent Online, 2 June 2007, http://www.iol.co.za/news/south-africa/my-interview-with-yuri-the-russian-355799.

30 Craig McKune and Sally Evans, 'Battle for control of the doors and drugs', Mail & Guardian, 3 February 2012, http:www.mg.co.za/article/2012-02-03-battle-for-control-of-the-doors-and-drugs.

31 See report in Die Burger, http://152.111.1.87/argief/berigte/dieburger/2007/09/25/PQ/2/avlifman.html; Sporting Post, Brandon Morgenrood, www.sportingpost.co.za/profile/brandon-morgenrood/.

32 This information was provided by a former bouncer who knew of Beeka's operations, Cape Town, 4 November 2014.

33 Interview, Cape Town, 28 November 2014; interview, senior city official, Cape Town, 2 November 2015; interview, former senior enforcement official for SARS, Johannesburg, 15 December 2015; interview, senior police detective, Cape Town, 26 May 2016.

34 Caryn Dolley, 'Security bosses acquitted on 313 charges', 24 October 2015, Independent Online, http://www.iol.co.za/news/crime-courts/security-bosses-acquitted-on-313-charges-1935148.

35 Caryn Dolley, 'Lifman fights SARS auction of luxury assets', Independent Online, 23 January 2016, http://www.iol.co.za/news/crime-courts/lifman-fights-sars-auction-of-luxury-assets-1975003.

36 Selene Brophey, 'V & A Waterfront unseated as the most visited attraction in SA', Traveller24, 13 July 2017, http://traveller24.news24.com/Explore/SAHolidayGuide/va-waterfront-unseated-as-most-visited-attraction-in-sa-20160713.

37 A more detailed discussion can be found in Mark Shaw and Simone Haysom, 'Organised crime in late apartheid and the transition to a new criminal order: The rise and fall of the Johannesburg "bouncer mafia"', Journal of Southern African Studies, 42, 4, pp. 577–594.

38 Interviews, former bouncers, Johannesburg, November and December 2014.

39 Interviews, current and former club owners in Johannesburg, November and December 2014.

40 The Johannesburg-based white criminal networks with a propensity for violence are also seen in the debt-collection industry, the competitive breakdown tow-truck

business and in parts of the private-security sector, including unscrupulous private investigators.

41 For brief profiles of these companies, see Mark Shaw and Simone Haysom, 'Organised crime in late apartheid and the transition to a new criminal order: The rise and fall of the Johannesburg "bouncer mafia"', *Journal of Southern African Studies*, 42, 4, p. 584.

42 Interview with a bouncer who participated in the night's events, Johannesburg, 29 January 2015.

43 See Gill Gifford, 'Bouncer killing exposes nightclub mafia', Independent Online, 7 January 2003, http://www.iol.co.za/news/south-africa/bouncer-killing-exposes-nightclub-mafia-99573.

44 Interview, former partner in Elite, Johannesburg, 29 January 2015.

45 Ibid.

46 For an excellent account of Kebble's murder, see Mandy Wiener, *Killing Kebble: An Underworld Exposed*, Johannesburg: Macmillan, 2012.

47 In the course of over 20 detailed interviews with the Johannesburg mafia, no member ever mentioned the possibility of commandeering black gangs as allies in violence. This was partly justified (for them) in racist terms, but is also explicable because the black gangs had few linkages to the mainstream drug control and distribution business in white areas.

48 Interview, former partner in Elite, Johannesburg, 29 January 2015; see also Mark Shaw and Simone Haysom, 'Organised crime in late apartheid and the transition to a new criminal order: The rise and fall of the Johannesburg "bouncer mafia"', *Journal of Southern African Studies*, 42, 4, p. 591.

49 Interview, former bouncer and current owner of a security company, Johannesburg, 17 January 2015.

50 Interviews, bouncers and a gang member, Cape Town, November 2014 and September 2015.

51 Interview, ex-gang member and now community leader, Cape Town, 4 November 2014.

52 Interviews and personal communication with Nigerian and Congolese bouncers, Johannesburg and Cape Town, November and December 2014.

53 Several reported in discussions that they also feared the level and brazenness of the hits that were allegedly associated with Krejcir and so kept their distance.

54 Diego Gambetta, *The Sicilian Mafia: The Business of Private Protection*. Cambridge, Mass.: Harvard University Press, 1996; Federico Varese, *The Russian Mafia: Private Protection in a New Market Economy*, Oxford: Oxford University Press, 2001; Vadim Volkov, *Violent Entrepreneurs: The Use of Force in the Making of Russian Capitalism*, Ithaca: Cornell University Press, 2002.

55 Stergios Skaperdas, 'The political economy of organised crime: Providing protection when the state does not', *Economics of Governance*, 2, 3, 2001, pp. 173–202.

56 See, for example, Will Reno, 'Understanding criminality in West African conflicts', in James Cockayne and Adam Lupel (eds), *Peace Operations and Organised Crime: Enemies or Allies?*, London: Routledge, 2011, p. 75.

57  Jan van Dijk and Toine Spapens, 'Transnational organised crime networks', in Phil Reichel and Jay Albanese (eds), *Transnational Organised Crime: An Overview of Six Continents*, Los Angeles: Sage, 2014, pp. 7–27.

58  Federico Varese, *Mafias on the Move: How Organised Crime Conquers New Territories*, Princeton: Princeton University Press, 2011, p. 191.

59  Mark Shaw and Tuesday Reitano, *The Political Economy of Trafficking and Trade in the Sahara: Instability and Opportunities*, Washington DC: World Bank, 2015.

60  Federico Varese, *Mafias on the Move: How Organised Crime Conquers New Territories*, Princeton: Princeton University Press, 2011, p. 191.

61  Vadim Volkov, *Violent Entrepreneurs: The Use of Force in the Making of Russian Capitalism*, Ithaca: Cornell University Press, 2002.

62  See, for example, the arguments in Alexander Kupatadze, *Organised Crime, Political Transitions and State Formation in Post-Soviet Eurasia*, London: Palgrave Macmillan, 2012. In the case of South Africa, see South African Institute of International Affairs, 'Crime and policing in transitions: Comparative perspectives', summary of conference proceedings, Johannesburg, 2001.

63  Ashley Neese Bybee, 'The twenty-first century expansion of the transnational drug trade in Africa', *Journal of International Affairs*, 66, 1, 2012, p. 69.

64  Caryn Dolley, 'Did Beeka link cost hitman his life?' Independent Online, 16 October 2013, http://www.iol.co.za/news/crime-courts/did-beeka-link-cost-hitman-his-life-1592942.

65  Charles van Onselen, *Showdown at the Red Lion: The Life and Times of Jack McLoughlin, 1859–1910*, Johannesburg: Jonathan Ball, 2015, p. 296.

### Chapter 5   Living by the sword: Gang bosses and their prey

1  The information in the account above is taken from interviews with people who know about the death of Nathaniel Moses, from discussions with police officers with insight into the case and from a leaked police-intelligence report on the Mobsters that was quoted in the press. See the following press stories for coverage of the case: Caryn Dolley, 'Cape "gang leader targeted tourists"', Independent Online, 17 April 2016, http://www.iol.co.za/news/crime-courts/cape-gang-leader-targeted-tourists-2010674; Caryn Dolley, 'Top cop "on MEC, gangs" hitlist', Independent Online, 16 April 2016, http://www.iol.co.za/news/crime-courts/top-cop-on-mec-gangs-hitlist-2010455; Caryn Dolley, 'Sex workers "groomed for satanic rituals"', Independent Online, 20 March 2016, http://www.iol.co.za/news/crime-courts/sex-workers-groomed-for-satanic-rituals-1999937.

2  Interview, senior police officer, Cape Town, 12 February 2016.

3  Interview, senior police crime-intelligence officer, Cape Town, 13 February 2016.

4  Interviews, civil society and gang members, Manenberg, April 2016.

5  Telephone discussion, Cape Town, 18 March 2016.

6 Stefan Jensen, 'The security and development nexus in Cape Town: War on gangs, counterinsurgency and citizenship', *Security Dialogue*, 41, 1, 2010, p. 81. See also Don Pinnock, *The Brotherhood: Street Gangs and State Control in Cape Town*, Cape Town: David Philip, 1984.

7 Andre Standing, 'The threat of gangs and anti-gangs policy', Policy Discussion Paper 116, Institute for Security Studies, August 2005, p. 2.

8 Don Pinnock, *Gang Town*, Cape Town: Tafelberg, 2016, pp. 19–27.

9 A survey conducted by the University of Cape Town and Vibrand, for example, indicated that businesses, particularly on the Cape Flats and in surrounding areas, paid protection money to gangs. Interviews with police and gang members also suggest that extortion is much more widespread than often acknowledged. See also Don Pinnock, *Gang Town*, Cape Town: Tafelberg, 2016, p. 198.

10 Interview, gang boss, Manenberg, 24 April 2016.

11 Don Pinnock, *Gang Town*, Cape Town: Tafelberg, 2016, p. 119.

12 Interview, Hard Livings gang member, Cape Town, 27 April 2016.

13 SAPS police station boundaries do not match those of the city, so metro-wide homicide levels have been calculated from station-level figures. For a fuller discussion on the calculations, see Anine Kriegler and Mark Shaw, *A Citizen's Guide to Crime Trends in South Africa*, Johannesburg: Jonathan Ball, 2016, pp. 102–103.

14 'Cape Town is now among the ten most violent cities in the world', 26 January 2016, BusinessTech, http://businesstech.co.za/news/general/110133/cape-town-is-now-among-the-10-most-violent-cities-in-the-world/.

15 Although this, of course, does not mean that gangs were responsible for all homicides in these areas, the chances are high that they did account for a significant proportion. The increase also aligns with higher levels of gang conflict across the city. Depressingly, some formerly black areas also showed increases, although this does not apply consistently across these areas. I am grateful to Anine Kriegler for the disaggregation of the data.

16 Quoted in Carlo Petersen, 'Gang violence is a "national crisis"', *The Sunday Independent*, 16 December 2015.

17 See Sonja Pasche and Bronwyn Myers, 'Substance misuse trends in South Africa', *Human Psychopharmacology*, 27, 3, 2012, pp. 338–341.

18 Irvin Kinnes, *From Urban Street Gangs to Criminal Empires: The Changing Face of Gangs in the Western Cape*, Monograph No. 48, Institute for Security Studies, 2000; Andre Standing, *Organised Crime: A Study from the Cape Flats*, Institute for Security Studies, 2006.

19 This is calculated from annual police crime figures for the city. There were 4 890 drug-related crimes in 2000/1 and 27 838 in 2014/15. Although this is a measure of police activities, it is does reflect the reality that drugs are more widespread and likely to be encountered by the police in their daily work. Interview, General Arno Lamoer, former provincial commissioner, Western Cape, Cape Town, 4 November 2014. See also http://www.mrc.ac.za/adarg/sacendu/Sacenduphase35.pdf.

20 South African Community Epidemiology Network on Drug Use, 'Update: Alcohol and drug abuse trends: January–June 2014' (Phase 36), Cape Town: Medical Research Council, 2014, p. 1.

21 Simon Howell, Nadine Harker-Burnhams, Lorraine Townsend and Mark Shaw, 'The wrong type of decline: Fluctuations in price and value of illegal substances in Cape Town', *South African Crime Quarterly*, 54, 1, 2016, pp. 43–54.

22 Jonny Steinberg, *The Number*, Johannesburg: Jonathan Ball, 2004; Luke Lee Skywalker, 'Politics of the Number: An account of predominant South African prison gang influences', MPhil. dissertation, University of Cape Town, 2014.

23 Interview, senior member of the Clever Kids, Manenberg, 9 May 2016.

24 Stefan Jensen, 'The security and development nexus in Cape Town: War on gangs, counterinsurgency and citizenship', *Security Dialogue*, 41, 1, 2010.

25 Marianne Thamm, 'When hell is not hot enough: A top cop who supplied weapons to country's gangsters and right-wingers', *Daily Maverick*, 4 July 2016, http://www.dailymaverick.co.za/article/2016-07-04-when-hell-is-not-hot-enough-a-top-cop-who-supplied-weapons-to-countrys-gangsters-and-right-wingers/#.V5UZKDeeKxI.

26 These are outlined in Prinsloo's plea document, '*In die Streekhof vir die Streekafdeling van die Wes-Kaap [Gehou te Belville], Die Staat en Christiaan Lodewyk Prinsloo: Pleitooreenkoms Ingevolge Artikel 105A van Wet 51 van 1977 (soos gewysig)*'.

27 M Prinsloo, R Matzopoulos, R Laubscher, J Myers and D Bradshaw, 'Validating homicide rates in the Western Cape Province, South Africa: Findings from the 2009 Injury Mortality Survey', *South African Medical Journal*, 106, 2, February 2016, p. 95.

28 The story began to become clearer when seized firearms examined at the Western Cape ballistics unit were all noted as having been altered in an identical way, so that they could not be linked to the SAPS's own database.

29 Interview with Hard Livings senior gang member, Cape Town, 23 July 2016.

30 Interview, gang boss, Cape Town, 24 July 2016.

31 Interview, senior police intelligence officer, Cape Town, 22 July 2016.

32 Interview, senior member of the Ghetto Kids gang, Cape Town, 23 July 2016.

33 Interview, senior police intelligence officer, Cape Town, 22 July 2016.

34 Interview, senior member of the Americans gang, Cape Town, 24 July 2016.

35 Lorna Martin quoted in Tanya Farber, 'Fatal shootings have soared countrywide in recent years', *The Times*, 26 January 2016.

36 Interview, church leader, Manenberg, 27 April 2016. This fact was also pointed out in interviews with gang members, although it is suggested that gang bosses take precautions, including taking out insurance on the lives of some members, to make sure that money can still be made in times of conflict. Interview, ex-gang member, Cape Town, 5 March 2016.

37 Interview, Manenberg, 26 April 2016.

38 This is well illustrated in a network diagram of key players in the Cape Town drug

economy – see Khalil Goga, 'The drug trade and governance in Cape Town', Institute for Security Studies, Paper 263, September 2014, p. 14.

39  These individuals are household names in the communities in which they live and they have appeared regularly in the press. See for example the following reports: Michael Booysen – http://www.iol.co.za/news/south-africa/committed-cops-put -an-end-to-gangs-reign-110062; Donkie Booysen – http://www.iol.co.za/news/ crime-courts/cops-stole-my-money -claims-gang-boss-1630891; Colin Booysen – http:// www.iol.co.za/news/crime-courts/alleged-gang-boss-shot-in -arm-leg-1513702; Rashied and Rashaad Staggie – https://www.dailymaverick.co.za/article/2013-09-23-rashied-staggie-release-leader-of-the-pack-is-back-on-the-streets/#.WRx_VhOGNE4; Ernie Solomons – http://www.iol.co.za/news/crime-courts/ex-gang-boss-property-mogul-probed-2059427; Ralph Stanfield – http://www.iol.co.za/news/south-africa/western-cape/ look-alleged -gang-kingpin-dishes-out-money-to-community-8703134; Igshaan Davids – http://www.iol.co.za/news/crime-courts/alleged-cape-gang-boss-in-court-1889811.

40  Interview, recruiter for the No Fears gang, Cape Town, 24 May 2016.

41  Interview with female ex-member of a gang, who broke away with the assistance of her local church in Kensington, Cape Town, 18 March 2016.

42  For a list of gang 'high-flyers', see Pearlie Joubert, 'Cape gangs: Targeting the untouchables', *Mail & Guardian*, 28 August 2007, http://mg.co.za/ article/2007-08-28-cape-gangs-targeting-the-untouchables.

43  Interview, pastor, Hanover Park, 5 September 2015.

44  Personal communication with an individual connected to several gang leaders, 3 July 2016.

45  Interview, gang member, Manenberg, 24 April 2016.

46  Interview, ex-gang member, Cape Town, 5 March 2016.

47  Personal communication, Luke Lee Skywalker, Cape Town, 3 July 2016.

48  Luke Lee Skywalker, notes and interviews on recent developments in Manenberg, 1 July 2016.

49  Interview, ex-gang member, Cape Town, 5 March 2016.

50  Personal communication, Cape Town, 4 July 2016.

51  For example, two leaders from opposing gangs are said to have been seen meeting in a Cape Town coffee shop during the April 2016 Manenberg violence.

52  A summary of these arguments is contained in Mark Shaw and Walter Kemp, *Spotting the Spoilers: A Guide to Analyzing Organised Crime in Fragile States*, New York: International Peace Institute, 2012. See also H Richard Friman, 'Drug markets and the selective use of violence', *Crime, Law and Social Change*, 52, p. 287.

53  Mark Shaw and Walter Kemp, *Spotting the Spoilers: A Guide to Analyzing Organised Crime in Fragile States*, New York: International Peace Institute, 2012.

54  Interview, Americans gang member, Manenberg, 6 May 2016.

### Chapter 6   Quiet outsiders: Why the Nigerians won and Krejcir lost

1  The story of Jenny and Rose is drawn from two interviews and discussions with various people who may have known more about the cases, Cape Town, May 2016. One of the murders was covered in the media; see Gadeeja Abbas, 'Her face was just like a horror movie', Independent Online, 14 October 2015, http://www.iol.co.za/news/crime-courts/her-face-was-just-like-a-horror-movie-1929953.

2  Interview, police investigating officer, Cape Town, 15 March 2016.

3  Personal communication, senior crime-intelligence officer, 17 March 2016.

4  This has been detailed in several studies. See, for example, Moisés Naím, *Illicit*, New York: Doubleday, 2005.

5  Interview, private investigator, Johannesburg, 2016.

6  Judge Giovanni Falcone, the famous Italian anti-mafia prosecutor, had requested Palazzolo's extradition from Switzerland in April 1984, regarding him as a key figure in the mafia's money-laundering enterprise. Falcone was killed in 1992 in a bomb explosion orchestrated by the mafia.

7  Giulio Rubino and Cecilia Anesi, 'Married to the mob: The diamond boer and the honeytrap', *Mail & Guardian*, 17 April 2015, https://mg.co.za/article/2015-04-16-married-to-the-mob-the-diamond-boer-and-honey-trap#VTDZCYM-U-o.twitter.

8  Gianni Ballarini, 'La mafia in Africa: 'ndrangheta, affari neri', *Nigrizia*, Verona, 16 June 2009, www.nigrizia.it/notizia/la-mafia-in-africa-ndrangheta-affari-neri.

9  Europol, *Threat Assessment: Italian Organised Crime*, The Hague, June 2013, p. 3

10  Martin Booth, *The Dragon Syndicates: The Global Phenomenon of the Triads*, London: Doubleday, 1999, p. 356.

11  Within a short space of time, a Chinese businessman was found shot, his body dumped near Cape Town Airport. In 1995 an unidentified Chinese man was found floating in a river in the Free State, with a crossbow bolt lodged in his head. Before the year was out, two more Chinese nationals had been killed and several wounded.

12  Janet Wilhelm, 'The Chinese communities in South Africa', in Sakhela Buhlungu (ed.), *State of the Nation: South Africa 2005–2006*, Pretoria: HSRC Press, 2006, p. 352.

13  The story of the Table Mountain Gang appears to largely be lost. Few people are willing to speak about their past activities.

14  Only one of five species of abalone is of commercial value. It is known in South Africa as *perlemoen*. Abalone was originally listed under the Convention for the International Trade in Endangered Species, but was removed by the South African government in 2010. Local sale is prohibited and export permits are required for any abalone leaving the country.

15  Personal communication, individual with close links to the triads, Cape Town, January 2016.

16  Interview, senior police officer responsible for investigating the case, Cape Town, 20 May 2016.

17  Mark Shaw, 'West African criminal networks in South and Southern Africa', *African*

*Affairs*, 101, 404, pp. 291–316.

18 CJD Venter, 'Drug abuse and drug trafficking in South Africa', in Robert Rotberg and Greg Mills (eds), *War and Peace in Southern Africa*, Washington DC: Brookings Institution Press, 1998, p. 194.

19 This section draws on interviews conducted with Nigerians in Johannesburg in the course of 2001. See Mark Shaw, 'Crime as business, business as crime: West African criminal networks in southern Africa', South African Institute of International Affairs, 2003.

20 For example, in November 2013, Shimmy Anu's body was found in an open field near Johannesburg. Anu was said to be a 'high-ranking member' of the so-called Musli brothers crime family, a right-hand man to one of the brothers, Shay Musli. It was said that a relative of his was to give evidence against the Musli family and that he was killed to 'send a message'. The Musli organisation is said to have been based in Romania and among the Israeli community in South Africa. In August 2014, two charred corpses with links to an Israeli crime group were found near Hartbeespoort Dam. The two deceased were apparently two cousins, Dotan and Carmi Shukrun, who had fled to South Africa to escape conflict in the Israeli underworld and evade the increased focus on them by the Israeli police. The two were said to be associates of Shimmy Anu. In October 2015, the SAPS arrested Shay Musli, head of one of Israel's wealthiest and most powerful crime families, after being alerted by Israeli counterparts. He was extradited to Israel. The most prominent assassination in South Africa linked to Israeli organised crime was that of Hazel Crane, murdered in November 2003. Crane was a Johannesburg socialite and underworld figure.

21 See Peter Gastrow, 'Triad societies and Chinese organised crime in South Africa', Institute for Security Studies, Paper 48, 2001.

22 Jonny Steinberg, 'The illicit abalone trade in South Africa', in Nils Gilman, Jesse Goldhammer and Steven Weber, *Deviant Globalization: Black Market Economy in the 21st Century*, New York: Continuum, 2011, p. 159.

23 Ibid., pp. 161–163.

24 Ibid. See also Peter Gastrow, 'Triad societies and Chinese organised crime in South Africa', Institute for Security Studies, Paper 48, 2001; personal communication, former senior security official, November 2014.

25 Ted Leggett, *Rainbow Vice: The Drugs and Sex Industries in the New South Africa*, Johannesburg: David Philip, 2001.

26 Interview, former participant in the drug economy with links to Nigerian networks, 5 June 2016.

27 This was mentioned by several officers in interviews for this book; interviews, Johannesburg, Cape Town and Durban, 2014 and 2015.

28 Interview, police investigating officer, Durban, 3 May 2016.

29 Interview, police sector commander, Johannesburg, 3 November 2015.

30 This was a sting operation carried out by the police and the man was arrested. Interview, police investigating officer, Cape Town, 26 May 2016.

31 To help write this section, I asked a research assistant of mine, who is a Nigerian national, to search for articles on Nigerian criminals and drug lords in South Africa. Despite the scale of the problem, there is little reporting on it. Compare this with the hundreds of news articles covering the Krejcir case.

32 Stephen Ellis, 'West Africa's international drug trade', *African Affairs*, 108, 431, pp. 171–196.

33 For a useful summary, see Klaus von Lampe, *Organised Crime: Analyzing Illegal Activities, Criminal Structures and Extra-Legal Governance*, Los Angeles: Sage, 2016, pp. 117–119.

34 Personal communication with a friend of the woman, Cape Town, 27 May 2016.

35 Interview, police investigating officer, Cape Town, 16 May 2016.

36 Interview, police investigating officer, Cape Town, 26 May 2016.

37 Discussions with gang members, northern suburbs, Cape Town, May 2016.

38 Interview, senior Nigerian drug dealer, 18 March 2002. See Mark Shaw, 'West African criminal networks in South and Southern Africa', *African Affairs*, 101, 404, July 2002.

39 See 'Four killed in Benoni shooting', Independent Online, 5 July 2013, http://www.iol.co.za/news/crime-courts/four-killed-in-benoni-shooting-1542972; '4 Nigerian men gunned down in Gauteng', News24, 5 July 2013, http://www.news24.com/SouthAfrica/News/4-Nigerian-men-gunned-down-in-Gauteng-20130705.

40 Interview, gang leader, Cape Town, 6 February 2016.

41 T Wing Lo, 'Beyond social capital: Triad organised crime in Hong Kong and China', *British Journal of Criminology*, 50, 5, pp. 851–872.

42 Interview, senior police officer, Cape Town, 20 May 2016; personal communication, individual with close links to the triads, Cape Town, January 2016.

43 Bruce Venter, 'Chinese mafia linked to bodies in drain pipe', Independent Online, 24 November 2004, http://www.iol.co.za/news/south-africa/chinese-mafia-linked-to-bodies-in-drain-pipe-227776.

44 'Drainpipe: One suspect free', News24, 5 April 2005, http://www.news24.com/South-Africa/News/Drainpipe-One-suspect-free-20050405.

45 Ibid.

46 Interview, senior SAPS officer responsible for investigating the case, Cape Town, 20 May 2016.

47 See Jan van Dijk and Toine Spapens, 'Transnational organised crime networks across the globe', in Jay Albanese and Philip Reichel (eds), *Transnational Organised Crime: An Overview from Six Continents*, Los Angeles: Sage, 2014, p. 18.

48 Interview, Julian Rademeyer, investigative journalist, Johannesburg, 6 November 2015.

49 See Annette Hübschle, *Organised Crime in Southern Africa: First Annual Review*, Institute for Security Studies, 2010; interview with former senior law-enforcement officer involved in the investigation of Krejcir, Johannesburg, 4 November 2015; interviews, members of the Johannesburg underworld, Johannesburg, 2014 and 2015.

50 Sam Sole, 'Gembulla: Focus falls on Krejcir and Co', amaBunghane, 8 October 2010,

http://amabhungane.co.za/article/2010-10-08-gembella-focus-falls-on-krejcir-and-co.

51  Interview, Paul O'Sullivan, Johannesburg, 4 November 2016.

52  Sally Evans, 'Uwe Gemballa's widow seeks answers', *Mail & Guardian*, 22 February 2012, https://mg.co.za/article/2013-02-22-00-uwe-gemballas-widow-seeks-answers.

53  Alekos Panayi, affidavit, 1 December 2009; interview, Paul O'Sullivan, Johannesburg, 4 November 2016.

54  For a story of Jackson's life, see Sean Newman, Peter Piegl and Karyn Maughn, *Lolly Jackson: When Fantasy Meets Reality*, Johannesburg: Jacana, 2012.

55  Angelique Serrao, 'Claims that Krejcir killed Lolly Jackson – report', News24, 5 April 2015, http://news24.com/SouthAfrica/News/Claims-that-Krejcir-killed-Lolly-Jackson-report-20150405.

56  Alekos Panayi, affidavit, 1 December 2009.

57  Former law-enforcement official involved in the investigation of Krejcir, Johannesburg, 4 November 2015.

58  Alekos Panayi, affidavit, 1 December 2009. This has never been used in court; interview, Paul O'Sullivan, Johannesburg, 4 November 2016.

59  See 'Krejcir granted R500 000 bail', *Mail & Guardian*, 8 April 2011, http://mg.co.za/article/2011-04-08-krejcir-granted-bail; 'Krejcir denies Beeka murder claim', News24, 12 April 2011, http://www.news24.com/SouthAfrica/News/Krejcir-denies-Beeka-murder-claim-20110412-4.

60  In the case of Jordan and Andrews, see Sally Evans, 'Gangland killing: A Krejcir link?', *Mail & Guardian*, 30 September 2011, http://mg.co.za/article/2011-09-30-gangland-killing-a-krejcir-link; for Laganin, see S Naik, 'Serbian slain because he had a loose mouth', Independent Online, http://www.iol.co.za/news/crime-courts/serbian-slain-because-he-had-a-loose-mouth-1604692. Krejcir has been charged with the murders of Issa and Ncube.

61  Interview by Simone Haysom with a former law-enforcement official, January 2017.

62  Sam Sole et al, 'The murders: Five bodies and counting', *Mail & Guardian*, 25 March 2011, http://mg.co.za/article/2011-03-25-the-murders-five-bodies-and-counting.

63  Interview, Paul O'Sullivan, Johannesburg, 4 November 2016.

64  Alex Eliseev, 'Krejcir assassination attempt: The stuff of movies, Bond movies', *Daily Maverick*, 25 July 2013, http://www.dailymaverick.co.za/article/2013-07-25-krejcir-assassination-attempt-the-stuff-of-movies-bond-movies.

65  Federico Varese, *Mafias on the Move: How Organised Crime Conquers New Territories*, Princeton: Princeton University Press, 2011.

66  Peter Reuter, *The Organization of Illicit Markets: An Economic Analysis*, Ann Arbor: University of Michigan Press, 1985; Diego Gambetta, *The Sicilian Mafia: The Business of Private Protection*, Boston: Harvard University Press, 1993.

67  Jan van Dijk and Toine Spapens, 'Transnational organised crime networks across the globe', in Jay Albanese and Philip Reichel (eds), *Transnational Organised Crime: An Overview from Six Continents*, Los Angeles: Sage, 2014, p. 19.

68  It was evident from interviews that many gangs acquire their drugs from Nigerian dealers.

## Chapter 7 Freedom's mother: Crime, politics and assassination

1 The story of the death of Thuli Ndlovu was taken from a detailed account of the events that was released by her organisation, Abahlali baseMjondolo. See '30 September 2014 – Abahlali baseMjondolo statement on the assassination of Thuli Ndlovu', http://abahlali.org/node/14311/. Several press reports on the incident and trial were also referred to. See Sihle Manda, 'Speaker refuses to suspend councillors', Independent Online, 2 July 2015, http://www.iol.co.za/news/crime-courts/speaker-refuses-to-suspend-councillors-1879390; 'ANC councillors in dock for murder of activist', GroundUp, 20 March 2015, http://groundup.org.za/article/anc-councillors-dock-murder-activist_2775/; 'ANC councillors face Durban High Court in Thuli Ndlovu murder trial', eNCA, 26 January 2016, https://www.enca.com/south-africa/anc-councillors-face-durban-high-court-thuli-ndlovu-murder-trial; Amanda Khoza, '3 men, including 2 KZN councillors, get life for hit on community activist', News24, 20 May 2016, http://m.news24.com/news24/SouthAfrica/News/3-men-including-2-kzn-councillors-get-life-for-hit-on-community-activist-20160520?isapp=true; 'Leaders by day and gangsters by night', GroundUp, 24 May 2016, http://www.groundup.org.za/article/leaders-day-and-gangsters-night/.

2 David Bruce, 'Political killings in South Africa: The ultimate intimidation', Policy Brief 64, Institute for Security Studies, October 2014, p. 4.

3 Niren Tolsi, 'KwaZulu purge is all about No 1', Mail & Guardian, 10–16 June 2016.

4 Gary Kynoch, 'Apartheid's afterlives: Violence, policing and the South African state', Journal of Southern African Studies, 42, 1, p. 71.

5 Statement by the SALGA spokesperson on Twitter, 23 February 2016, https://twitter.com/tahirsema/status/702066592096636928. By mid-2016, the number was probably closer to 500.

6 David Bruce, 'Political killings in South Africa: The ultimate intimidation', Policy Brief 64, Institute for Security Studies, October 2014.

7 Anna Jarstad and Kristine Höglund, 'Local violence and politics in KwaZulu-Natal: Perceptions of agony in a post-conflict society', Third World Quarterly, 36, 5, pp. 981–982.

8 Catalina Uribe Burcher, 'The link between politics and organised crime in the Andean region', International Institute for Democracy and Electoral Assistance, 22 January 2013, http://www.idea.int/americas/the-link-between-politics-and-organised-crime-in-the-andean-region.cfm.

9 Interview, gang boss, Cape Town, October 2015.

10 'SAHRC concerned about political killings ahead of local government polls', http://www.sahrc.org.za/index.php/sahrc-media/news-2/item/384-media-statement-sahrc-concerned-about-political-killings-ahead-of-local-government-polls.

11 Auditor-General South Africa, media release, 'Auditor-General reports an overall, encouraging five-year improvement in local government audit results', 1 June 2016.

12 Statistics South Africa, 'Income dynamics and poverty status of households in South

Africa', Report No. 03-10-10, Pretoria, 2015, p. 18.

13 David Bruce, 'Political killings in South Africa: The ultimate intimidation', Policy Brief 64, Institute for Security Studies, October 2014.

14 Corruption Watch, 'Local government in South Africa – Part 5, Finances', 19 March 2014, http://www.corruptionwatch.org.za/local-government-in-south-africa-part-5-finances/.

15 Ibid.

16 Gary Kynoch, 'Crime, conflict and politics in transition-era South Africa', *African Affairs*, 104, 416, pp. 493–514.

17 See, for example, Matuma Letsoala et al, 'Killings signal the start of the battle for power', *Mail & Guardian*, 27 May–2 June 2016.

18 Interviews and discussions conducted in Cape Town, Durban and Johannesburg, October 2015 to February 2016.

19 Natasha Marrian, 'Why winning a municipal council seat is such a high-stakes battle', *Business Day*, 3 June 2016; see also Setumo Stone, 'Dying to be a councillor', *City Press*, 12 June 2016.

20 The murder is recounted in 'Municipal finance chief gunned down', Independent Online, 2 June 2016, http://www.iol.co.za/dailynews/news/munipal-finance-chief-gunned-down-2029477; 'Threatened municipal CFO shot dead', News24, 2 June 2016, http://www.news24.com/SouthAfrica/News/threatened-cfo-shot-dead-20160601.

21 Sydney Masinga, 'Two cops among those arrested for speaker's murder', *Mail & Guardian*, 8 October 2010, http://mg.co.za/article/2010-10-08-two-cops-among-those-arrested-for-speakers-murder.

22 Comprehensive coverage of the circumstances of the Jimmy Mohlala murder can be found at: 'My husband would still be alive today if it hadn't been for FIFA World Cup corruption', http://www.dailymail.co.uk/news/article-3121989/Widow-murdered-20...alive-today-hadn-t-exposed-multimillion-dollar-stadium-fraud.html.

23 Corruption Watch, 'Five years on Phakoe case is still wide open', 3 July 2014, http://www.corruptionwatch.org.za/five-years-on-phakoe-case-is-still-wide-open/.

24 Department of Cooperative Governance and Traditional Affairs, Province of KwaZulu-Natal, Municipal Administration and Governance Circular No. 5 of 2014, 'Personal security/Services for Councillors in Terms of Government Gazette Notice No. R 64, dated 29 January 2014', 17 April 2014.

25 'The mayors and their mini-armies', *City Press*, 28 January 2012.

26 Lee Rondganger, 'Tempers flare over councillor bodyguards', *Daily News*, 25 November 2015.

27 Municipal Manager's Office: Mayoral Office, 'Personal security/services for councillors: Department of Co-operative Governance and Traditional Affairs – Circular 5 of 2014: 17 April 2014', EXCO, 15 May 2014.

28 'The mayors and their mini-armies', *City Press*, 28 January 2012.

29 Personal communication, local-government opposition politician, Durban, 23 March 2016.

30 Personal communication, former senior government security official, January 2016; see also 'The mayors and their mini-armies', *City Press*, 28 January 2012.

31 IDEA, *Illicit Networks and Politics in the Baltic States*, Stockholm: International IDEA, 2013, p. 25.

32 Ibid., p. 26.

33 Interview, businessman, Khayelitsha, Cape Town, 23 November 2015.

34 Richard Pithouse, 'An Urban commons? Notes from South Africa', *Community Development Journal,* 49, January 2014, p. i39.

35 Ibid.

36 See https://web.facebook.com/permalink.php?story_fbid=1525078127796984&id=100008844340124.

37 Tony Carnie, 'Anti-mining activist gunned down', *The Mercury*, 24 March 2016.

38 Kerry Chance, 'The work of violence: A timeline of armed attacks at Kennedy Road', School of Development Studies Research Report No. 83, University of KwaZulu-Natal, July 2010.

39 Bill Dixon, 'A violent legacy: Policing insurrection in South Africa from Sharpeville to Marikana', *British Journal of Criminology*, 55, 2015, p. 1144.

40 Mpho Raborife, 'Investigating Mdluli would have been career suicide, senior cop tells court', News24, 7 June 2016, 'http://www.news24.com/SouthAfrica/News/investigating-mdluli-would-have-been-career-suicide-senior-cop-tells-court-20160607.

41 Jane Duncan, *The Rise of the Securocrats: The Case of South Africa*, Johannesburg: Jacana, 2014, p. 167.

42 Ibid., p. 168.

43 For a summary of the charges, see 'Lamoer's corruption trial moved to High Court', SA Breaking News, 12 June 2015, http://www.sabreakingnews.co.za/2015/06/12/lamoers-corruption-trial-moved-to-high-court/.

44 See, Matthew Savides, 'KwaZulu-Natal police chief Ngobeni confirms her suspension', *Business Day*, 19 May 2016, http://www.bdlive.co.za/national/2016/05/19/kwazulu-natal-police-chief-ngobeni-confirms-her-suspension.

45 Fivaz served from 1995 to 2000; Jackie Selebi from 2000 to 2009 (suspended in 2008); Bheki Cele from 2009 to 2012 (suspended in 2011); and Riah Phiyega from 2012 to 2015 (suspended in 2015).

46 Interview, former senior crime-intelligence official, Pretoria, 5 November 2016. See also 'Friends in high places rescue Mdluli', *Mail & Guardian*, 30 March 2012, http://mg.co.za/article/2012-03-30-friends-in-high-places-rescue-mdluli.

47 As quoted in 'The Police Commissioner's dirty secrets', *Noseweek*, April 2012.

48 Jonny Steinberg, 'Policing, state power and the transition from apartheid to democracy: A New perspective', *African Affairs*, 113, 451, pp. 173–191.

49 'Friends in high places rescue Mdluli', *Mail & Guardian*, 30 March 2012, http://mg.co.za/article/2012-03-30-friends-in-high-places-rescue-mdluli.

50 SAPS, 'Crime Intelligence Division, Report to the Inspector General of Intelligence on the Matter of the Alleged Maladminstration and Crimes Committed in Respect

of the Secret Services Account (SSA) of the Crime Intelligence Division of the South African Police Service', 4 November 2011.

51 Interview, senior police detective, Cape Town, 20 May 2016; interview, former senior officer in crime intelligence, Pretoria, 5 November 2015; interview, senior detective commander, Cape Town, 15 April 2016.

52 Interview, former police undercover operative, Midrand, 12 December 2015.

53 There was at the time, for example, extensive communication between drafters of the legislation creating the Scorpions and UN officials working on organised-crime issues. South Africa also signed the UN Convention against Transnational Organized Crime in December 2000, ratifying it in February 2004, when the Scorpions were at the height of their powers.

54 For the background to the formation of the Scorpions, see Mark Shaw, 'Democracy's blues: The politics of police reform in South Africa, 1990–2000', in Menachem Amir and Stanley Einstein (eds), *Policing, Security and Democracy: Theory and Practice*, Office of International Criminal Justice, 2001.

55 See Mandy Wiener, *Killing Kebble: An Underworld Exposed*, Johannesburg: Pan Macmillan, 2012.

56 Commission of Inquiry into Allegations of Spying against the National Director of Public Prosecutions, Mr BT Ngcuka (the Hefer Commission), 19 September 2003–7 January 2004; see Andrew Kanyegirire, 'Investigating the investigators: A summary of the Khampepe Commission of Inquiry', *South African Crime Quarterly*, 24, June 2008.

57 'Hawks boss Dramat quits after reaching settlement', *Mail & Guardian*, 22 April 2015, http://mg.co.za/article/2015-04-22-hawks-boss-dramat-quits-after-reaching-settlement.

58 Ahmed Areff, 'McBride, Dramat, Pillay claim there is a political conspir-acy', News24, 17 May 2016, http://www.news24.com/SouthAfrica/News/mcbride-dramat-pillay-claim-there-is-political-conspiracy-20160517.

59 Stephen Grootes, 'Op-Ed: Ntlemeza's appointment as head of the Hawks is absurd', *Daily Maverick*, 14 September 2015, http://www.dailymaverick.co.za/article/2015-09-14-op-ed-ntlemezas-appointment-as-head-of-the-hawks-is-absurd/.

60 'Fewer arrests since Hawks launched', *Business Day*, 12 November 2015, http://www.bdlive.co.za/national/2015/11/12/fewer-arrests-since-hawks-launched.

61 Simone Haysom, 'Sars, Krejcir and the destruction of state capacity', *Mail & Guardian*, 1 April 2016, http://mg.co.za/article/2016-04-01-00-sars-krejcir-and-the-destruction-of-state-capacity.

62 See Tom Lodge, 'Neo-patrimonial politics in the ANC', *African Affairs* 113, 450, pp. 1–23. The most widely quoted account in South Africa is by RW Johnson, *How Long Will South Africa Survive? The Looming Crisis*, Johannesburg: Jonathan Ball, 2015.

63 Susan Booysen, *Dominance and Decline: The ANC in the Time of Zuma*, Johannesburg: Wits University Press, 2015.

64 Govan Whittles and Matuma Letsoalo, 'Safety MEC punts murder accused', *Mail & Guardian*, 10–16 June 2016.

65 Global Initiative against Transnational Organized Crime, 'Development responses to organised crime: An analysis and programme framework', Geneva: Global Initiative against Transnational Organized Crime, 2016, pp. 5–7.

66 Vincenzo Ruggiero, *Understanding Political Violence: A Criminological Analysis*, Maidenhead: Open University Press, 2006, p. 75.

67 Ibid., p. 74.

68 Interview, police intelligence officer, Cape Town, 19 May 2016.

69 'Zuma "conspired with Cape gangsters"', *Mail & Guardian*, 20–26 November 2016.

70 Marianne Thamm, 'Band of brothers: ANC Integrity Commission's Fransman report contains some disturbing nuggets', *Daily Maverick*, 8 August 2016, http://www.dailymaverick.co.za/article/2016-08-08-band-of-brothers-anc-integrity-commissions-fransman-report-contains-some-disturbing-nuggets/#.V6mDVRSeKxI.

71 Take the case of the intertwining of gangs and politics in Jamaica. An excellent recent overview is Ioan Grillo, *Gangster Warlords: Drug Dollars, Killing Fields and the New Politics of Latin America*, London: Bloomsbury, 2016, pp. 109–181.

72 Vincenzo Ruggiero, *Understanding Political Violence: A Criminological Analysis*, Maidenhead: Open University Press, 2006, pp. 76–77.

73 From John Landesco's classic work on organised crime in Chicago, quoted in Vincenzo Ruggiero, *Understanding Political Violence: A Criminological Analysis*, Maidenhead: Open University Press, 2006, p. 77.

74 This is well illustrated by interviews conducted with gang bosses on the Cape Flats, who are highly conscious of the requirement not to engage in random violence but to use selected and targeted killing as a means to communicate where the overall power resides.

75 Stergious Skaperdas, 'The political economy of organised crime: Providing protection when the state does not', *Economics of Governance*, 2, 3, 2001, pp. 173–202.

### Chapter 8 Twilight zone: The police as organised crime

1 Interview, investigative journalist, Johannesburg, 8 November 2015; interview, former law-enforcement intelligence analyst, Cape Town, 3 September 2014.

2 This is a term used by Graham Denyer Willis to denote the symbiosis between police and organised crime. See Graham Denyer Willis, *The Killing Consensus: Police, Organised Crime and the Regulation of Life and Death in Urban Brazil*, Oakland: University of California Press, 2015, p. 108.

3 Sally Evans, 'Top cop's gun killed Lolly', *Mail & Guardian*, 10 June 2011, http://mg.co.za/article/2011-06-10-top-cops-gun-killed-lolly.

4 Juan Meyer, sworn statement, 11 July 2010.

5 Miloslav Potiska, affidavit, 27 February 2015.

6 See AmaBhungane, 'Was advocate tainted by Krejcir graft?', *Mail & Guardian*, 28 November 2014, https://mg.co.za/article/2014-11-28-was-advocate-tainted-by-krejcir-graft.

7 Ibid.

8 Juan Meyer, sworn statement, 11 July 2010.

9 SAPA, 'Cop accused of giving Krejcir police tracking software back in court', *The Times*, 17 January 2014, http://www.timeslive.co.za/local/2014/01/17/cop-accused-of-giving-krejcir-police-tracking-software-back-in-court-2014.

10 Juan Meyer, sworn statement, 11 July 2010.

11 Sally Evans, 'Top cop's gun killed Lolly', *Mail & Guardian*, 10 June 2011, http://mg.co.za/article/2011-06-10-top-cops-gun-killed-lolly.

12 Interview, Paul O'Sullivan, Johannesburg, 8 November 2011.

13 Interview, state official involved in the investigation of corrupt officials linked to Krejcir, Johannesburg, 3 November 2015.

14 Miloslav Potiska, affidavit, 27 February 2015.

15 Interview, police investigating officer, Johannesburg, 6 November 2014.

16 Interview, former senior law-enforcement official, Midrand, 12 December 2015.

17 David Bruce, 'New blood: Implications of en masse recruitment for the South African Police Service', *South African Crime Quarterly*, 43, March 2013, pp. 17–28.

18 Interview, former bouncer company manager, Johannesburg, 2 November 2015.

19 Discussion with several members of the Clever Kids in Manenberg, Cape Town, 19 May 2016.

20 Interview, senior SAPS officer, Cape Town, 24 May 2016.

21 Interview, SAPS sergeant responsible for foot patrols in a sector of Cape Town, Cape Town, 11 May 2016.

22 Ibid.

23 Interview, SAPS officer involved in investigations in central Cape Town, Cape Town, 11 May 2016; personal communication with person close to Nigerian drug-dealing networks, Cape Town, 10 March 2017.

24 The author attended meetings of local-government security officials of the South African Cities Network in 2016. Growing drug use was tabled as an issue of common concern.

25 Jackie Dugard, *From Low Intensity War to Mafia War: Taxi Violence in South Africa (1987–2000)*, Centre for Violence and Reconciliation, 4, 2001, p. 20.

26 See Goldstone Commission, 'Sixth interim report: Violence in the taxi industry in the King William's Town area', 26 July 1994; 'Seventh interim report: Violence in the taxi industry in the Queenstown area', 24 August 1994.

27 Personal communication with serving police officers, May 2016.

28 'Drivers blame cops for taxi violence', *Mail & Guardian*, 15 May 1998, http://mg.co.za/article/1998-05-15-drivers-blame-cops-for-taxi-violence.

29 Gauteng Provincial Government, Commission of Inquiry into the causes and extent of taxi violence in Gauteng, September 1999; see also Selby Bokaba, 'Police implicated in taxi violence', Independent Online, 12 December 1999, http://www.iol.co.za/news/south-africa/police-implicated-in-taxi-violence-22829.

30 See Cheryl Goodenough, 'The Taxi Commission of Inquiry: Cleaning up the taxi

industry in KwaZulu-Natal', *Perspectives on KwaZulu-Natal*, 1, 1, March 2001.

31 'Mchunu vows to crackdown on KZN police fuelling taxi violence', eNCA, 7 February 2016, https://www.enca.com/south-africa/mchunu-vows-crackdown-kzn -police-fuelling-taxi-violence.

32 'Cops in the dock for alleged murder', 3 August 2015, http://www.news24.com/ SouthAfrica/News/Cops-in-the-dock-for-alleged-murder-20150803; 'Cops deny taxi hitmen charges', *Daily News*, 4 August 2015, http://www.iol.co.za/dailynews/news/ cops-deny-taxi-hitmen-charges-1894968.

33 Interview, private detective, Johannesburg, 6 November 2015.

34 Chris Barron, 'Taxi bosses are making a killing', *Sunday Times*, 14 June 1998.

35 Interview, gang boss, Cape Town, 3 March 2015; interview, private investigator, Johannesburg, 2 September 2015.

36 Interview, gang boss, Cape Town, 5 October 2015.

37 David Bruce, 'Why does KZN lead in police killings?', *Mail & Guardian*, 8 May 2015, http://mg.co.za/article/2015-05-07-why-does-kzn-lead-in-police-killings.

38 There are numerous news articles on the issue and subsequent events. See 'Shoot to kill: Inside a South African police death squad', *Sunday Times*, 11 December 2011, http://www.timeslive.co.za/local/2011/12/11/ Shoot-to-kill-inside-a-South-African-police-death-squad.

39 Three stories from *Noseweek* provide a useful overview here. See 'KZN death squad controversy', *Noseweek*, 1 April 2012, http://www.noseweek.co.za/article/2714/ KZN-death-squad-controversy; 'Update: Cato Manor', *Noseweek*, 1 September 2013, http://noseweek.co.za/article/3044/UPDATE-Cato-Manor; 'No police "death squad"', *Noseweek*, 1 March 2014, http://www.noseweek.co.za/article/3154/ No-Police-death-squad.

40 Interviews were conducted with specific reference to media reporting on the Johannesburg underworld, November 2016 to February 2017.

41 Interview, investigative journalist, Johannesburg, 14 February 2017.

42 Interview, former senior SAPS officer, Pretoria, 2 November 2015.

43 This is the consensus, for example, among experts who attended three seminars hosted by the Global Initiative against Transnational Organised Crime on organised crime in Africa. For an argument around the evolution of organised crime and the role of state actors, see Louise Shelley, *Dirty Entanglements: Corruption, Crime and Terrorism*, Cambridge: Cambridge University Press, 2014.

44 See Mark Shaw, 'Drug trafficking in Guinea-Bissau, 1998–2014: The evolution of an elite protection network', *Journal of Modern African Studies*, 53, 3, 2015, pp. 339–364.

45 For our purposes here, we can leave aside more complex cases where states engage in supporting organised crime for political or strategic purposes. These are generally based on factors other than just personal enrichment, although this may also be one factor.

46 Tom Wainright, *Narconomics: How to Run a Drug Cartel*, London: Ebury Press, 2016, p. 112.

47 Interview, Paul O'Sullivan, Johannesburg, 8 November 2011; interview, state official

involved in the investigation into corrupt officials linked to Krejcir, Johannesburg, 3 November 2015.

48  Interview, former senior member of crime intelligence, Pretoria, 5 April 2015.

49  Don Pinnock, *Gang Town*, Cape Town: Tafelberg, 2016, p. 46.

50  'Towards a safer Khayelitsha', report of the Commission of Inquiry into Allegations of Police Inefficiency and a Breakdown in Relations between SAPS and the Community of Khayelitsha, 2014, p. 315.

51  Jonny Steinberg, 'Policing, state power and the transition from apartheid: A new perspective', *African Affairs*, 113, 451, 2014, pp. 173–191.

52  See Jacques Pauw, 'Mdluli Inc in top gear: BMWs, Mercs and Jeeps – the high expensive lives of Crime Intelligence head's family', *City Press*, 22 April 2012.

53  Gerard O'Neill and Dick Lehr, *Black Mass: Whitey Bulger, the FBI and a Devil's Deal*, New York: PublicAffairs, Perseus, HarperCollins, 2000.

54  'Infiltrating the far-right: German intelligence has 130 informants in extremist party', Der Spiegel, 12 December 2011, http://www.spiegel.de/international/germany/infiltrating-the-far-right-german-intelligence-has-130-informants-in-extremist-party-a-803136.html.

55  'Incendiary informants: Did German intelligence fuel far-right extremism?' Der Spiegel, 6 November 2012, http://www.spiegel.de/international/germany/german-police-document-says-informants-fuelled-far-right-extremism-a-865461.html.

56  Klaus von Lampe, *Organized Crime: Analyzing Illegal Activities, Criminal Structures, and Extra-Legal Governance*, Los Angeles: Sage, 2016, p. 386.

57  Peter Gill, *Policing Politics: Security Intelligence and the Liberal Democratic State*, London: Frank Cass, 1994, p. 154.

58  Interview, senior SAPS officer, Cape Town, 27 May 2016.

59  Ibid.

60  Interview, police detective, Cape Town, 3 June 2016.

61  Interview, former senior law-enforcement official at SARS, Cape Town, 17 December 2015.

62  Interview, senior SAPS officer, Cape Town, 27 May 2016.

63  Gary Kynoch, 'From the Ninevites to the Hard Livings gang: Township gangsters and urban violence in twentieth-century South Africa', *African Studies*, 58, 1, 1999, p. 77.

64  Tom Lodge, 'Neo-patrimonial politics in the ANC', *African Affairs*, 113, 450, p. 9.

65  Stephen Ellis, *External Mission: The ANC in Exile*, Johannesburg: Jonathan Ball, 2012, pp. 203–204.

66  Ibid., pp. 269–270.

67  Ibid., p. 259.

## Conclusion: Bozwana's end

1 There was extensive media coverage of the death of Bozwana. See, for example, Barry Bateman, 'Pretoria hit victim confirmed as controversial NW businessman', Eyewitness News, 3 September 2015, http://ewn.co.za/2015/10/03/Failed-Pretoria-hit-victim-confirmed-as-controversial-NW-businessman; the police sources mentioned are quoted in Barry Bateman, 'First on EWN: Probe into Wandile Bozwana's murder "at an advanced stage"', Eyewitness News, 10 September 2015, http://ewn.co.za/2015/10/10/First-on-EWN-Probe-into-Wandile-Bozwanas-murder-at-an-advanced-stage; Karabo Ngoepe, 'Bring on the hit – murdered businessman Bozwana's colleague', News24, 24 November 2015, http://www.news24.com/SouthAfrica/News/bring-on-the-hit-murdered-businessman-bozwanas-colleague-20151124; Baldwin Ndaba, 'Bozwana's murder plot thickens', Independent Online, 22 November 2015, http://beta.iol.co.za/news/crime-courts/bozwanas-murder-the-plot-thickens-1925791; Poloko Tau, 'Who killed prominent businessman Wandile Bozwana', City Press, 4 October 2015, http://www.news24.com/SouthAfrica/News/Who-killed-prominent-businessman-Wandile-Bozwana-20151004. A review of media reporting and interviews suggests that there are at least six cases where tenders were not delivered on, were overpriced or where there are allegations of impropriety against Bozwana. He had taken the North West provincial government to court in the case of a lost tender for the provision of office space that was awarded to another company. See Olebogeng Molatlhwa, 'R664 m tender probed', The Sowetan, 1 October 2010, http://www.sowetanlive.co.za/news/2010/10/01/r664m-tender-probed.

2 See Tom Lodge, 'Neo-patrimonial politics in the ANC', African Affairs, 113, 450, 2014, pp. 1–23. The most widely quoted account in South Africa is RW Johnson, How Long Will South Africa Survive? The Looming Crisis, Johannesburg: Jonathan Ball, 2015.

3 Susan Booysen, Dominance and Decline: The ANC in the Time of Zuma, Johannesburg: Wits University Press, 2015.

4 Mzilikazi wa Afrika and Stephan Hofstatter, 'Hit "mastermind" surrenders after months on the run', Sunday Times, 10 January 2016.

5 Karabo Ngoepe, 'Alleged mastermind taking fall for someone else – Bozwana family', News24, 13 January 2016, http://www.news24.com/SouthAfrica/News/alleged-mastermind-taking-fall-for-someone-else-bozwana-family-20160113.

6 Shenaaz Jamal and Bongani Mthethwa, 'Year-long investigation puts police on trail of alleged Bozwana shooter', Times Live, 8 March 2017, http://www.timeslive.co.za/local/2017/03/08/Year-long-investigation-puts-police-on-trail-of-alleged-Bozwana-shooter1?platform=hootsuite.

7 See https://www.facebook.com/wandilebozwana/, comment on 10 January 2016 by China Dodovu.

8 Anna Jarstad and Kristine Höglund, 'Local violence and politics in KwaZulu-Natal: Perceptions of agony in a post-conflict society', Third World Quarterly, 36, 5, 2015, pp. 981–982.

9 Gary Kynoch, 'Apartheid's afterlives: Violence, policing and the South African state', *Journal of Southern African Studies*, 42, 1, 2016, p. 71.

10 Interview, Cape Town, October 2015. The comparison with 'car accidents' in Zimbabwe, a method of assassination said to be commonly used by the Central Intelligence Organisation there, came up in more than one interview.

11 'ANCWL member shot and killed in KZN', 19 July, 2016, http://www.news101. co.za/2016/07/19/ancwl-member-shot-killed-kzn/; 'ANC saddened by the death of a ward candidate', *Ladysmith Gazette*, 20 July 2016, http://ladysmithgazette. co.za/65883/anc-saddened-by-the-death-of-a-ward-candidate/.

12 Siyabonga Mkhwanazi, 'Are taxi hitmen behind political killings?', Independent Online, http://www.iol.co.za/news/crime-courts/are-taxi-hitmen-behind-political -killings-2050578.

13 See the classic study by Vadim Volkov, *Violent Entrepreneurs: The Use of Force in the Making of Russian Capitalism*, Ithaca: Cornell University Press, 2002.

14 Gary Kynoch, 'Reassessing transition violence: Voices from South Africa's township wars, 1990–4', *African Affairs*, 112, 447, pp. 493–514. See also Mark Shaw, *Crime and Policing in Post-Apartheid South Africa: Reforming Under Fire*, London: Hurst, 2001, pp. 15–21.

15 See, for example, Nicholas Haysom, 'Vigilantism and the policing of African town-ships: Manufacturing violent stability', in Desiree Hansson and Dirk van Zyl Smit (eds), *Towards Justice? Crime and State Control in South Africa*, Cape Town: Oxford University Press, 1990, pp. 63–84; Judith Hudson, 'Riding the tiger: Urban warfare on the East Rand', in William Gutteridge and JE Spence (eds), *Violence in Southern Africa*, London: Frank Cass, pp. 108–123.

16 See, in particular, Truth and Reconciliation Commission, *Truth and Reconciliation Commission of South Africa Report*, 1998, Vol 2, Chapter 7, pp. 577–710.

17 This is a key argument in Anthony Altbeker, *A Country at War with Itself: South Africa's Crisis of Crime*, Cape Town: Jonathan Ball, 2009, and Thomas Mandrup, *National Security, Crime, and the South African Security Institutions*, Copenhagen: Institute for Strategy, Royal Danish Defence College, 2010. Also, interview, former SAPS undercover operator, Pretoria, 12 December 2015.

18 A good overview of this phenomenon is to be found in Stephen Ellis, 'The new frontiers of crime in South Africa', in Jean-François Bayart, Stephen Ellis and Béatrice Hibou, *The Criminalization of the State in Africa*, Oxford: James Currey, 1999, pp. 49–68.

19 Stephen Ellis, *External Mission: The ANC in Exile*, Johannesburg: Jonathan Ball, 2012, pp. 253–263; Tom Lodge, 'Neo-patrimonial politics in the ANC', *African Affairs*, 113, 450, pp. 1–23.

20 See Jonny Steinberg, *The Number*, Cape Town: Jonathan Ball, 2004; and, more recently, Don Pinnock, *Gang Town*, Cape Town: Tafelberg, 2016.

21 Philip Harrison and Tanya Zack, 'Between the ordinary and the extraordinary: Socio-spatial transformations in the "Old South" of Johannesburg', *South African Geographic Journal*, 96, 2, 2014, pp. 180–197.

22  See Jennifer Irish-Qhobosheane, 'Gentlemen or villains, thugs or heroes? The social economy of organised crime in South Africa', Johannesburg: South African Institute of International Affairs, 2007.

23  I am grateful on this point to the insights of a senior police crime-intelligence officer. Interview, Cape Town, 22 July 2016. A useful overview is also provided in Joan Wardrop, 'Soweto, syndicates and "doing business"', in Robert Rotberg and Greg Mills (eds), *War and Peace in Southern Africa: Crime, Drugs, Armies, Trade*, Washington DC: Brookings Institution Press, 1998, pp. 45–63.

24  For an introduction, see Marianne Thamm, 'When hell is not hot enough: A top cop who supplied weapons to country's gangsters and right-wingers', *Daily Maverick*, 4 July 2016, http://www.dailymaverick.co.za/article/2016-07-04-when-hell-is-not-hot-enough-a-top-cop-who-supplied-weapons-to-countrys-gangsters-and-right-wingers/#.V5UZKDeeKxI.

25  This was, for example, the argument made by Irvin Kinnes, 'From Urban Street Gangs to Criminal Empires: The Changing Face of Gangs in the Western Cape', Pretoria: Institute for Security Studies Monograph 48, June 2000.

26  Interview, senior police crime-intelligence officer, Cape Town, 22 July 2016.

27  By far the most notorious was the widely reported killing of a Johannesburg socialite, Hazel Crane, in November 2003, who had been engaged in a range of criminal activities and had links to the Israeli mafia, and was friendly with Winnie Mandela.

28  See Charles van Onselen, *Masked Raiders: Irish Banditry in Southern Africa*, Johannesburg: Zebra Press, 2010.

29  Gary Kynoch, 'Marashea on the mines: Economic, social and criminal networks on the South African gold fields, 1947–1999', *Journal of Southern African Studies*, 26, 1, pp. 79–103.

30  Charles van Onselen, *Showdown at the Red Lion: The Life and Times of Jack McLoughlin, 1859–1910*, Johannesburg: Jonathan Ball, 2015, p. 296.

31  See, for example, Lisa McGirr, *The War on Alcohol: Prohibition and the Rise of the American State*, New York: Norton, 2016.

32  Richard Synder and Angelica Duran-Martinez, 'Does illegality breed violence? Drug trafficking and state-sponsored protection rackets', *Crime, Law and Social Change*, 52, 2009, pp. 253–273; Tom Wainwright, *Narconomics: How to Run a Drug Cartel*, London: Ebury Press, 2016, pp. 29–51.

33  The argument was made at the time in a widely read article: Phil Williams, 'Transnational organised crime: Strategic alliances', *Washington Quarterly*, 18, 1, 1995, pp. 57–72.

34  See Dimitri Vlassis, 'The UN Convention against Transnational Organized Crime' in Matts Berdal and Mónica Serrano (eds), *Transnational Organised Crime and International Security: Business as Usual?* London: Lynne Rienner, 2002, pp. 83–94.

35  For an overview of the genesis of this development, see Ray Hartley, 'Jacob Zuma: Gangster-in-chief', *Rand Daily Mail*, 20 June 2016, http://www.rdm.co.za/politics/2016/06/20/jacob-zuma-gangster-in-chief.

# Index

# Acknowledgements

This book has been a long time in the making. I am grateful to many people who have assisted me over the years. Work in the late 1990s at the newly founded Institute for Security Studies fleshed out my thinking and allowed a focus on police reform at a time when community policing was the top policy dogma and fighting organised crime was seen as less important. I am particularly grateful to my colleagues of those years, notably Jakkie Cilliers, Antoinette Louw, Marianne Camerer and, more recently, Anton du Plessis. Later, at the Secretariat for Safety and Security, I must acknowledge Azhar Cachalia (now a judge at the High Court) and Johan Burger (now himself at the ISS) for many discussions on South African security issues. Greg Mills at the South African Institute of International Affairs provided a fellowship, and although it is now almost two decades ago, this period generated a series of ideas that shaped the book.

At the UN Office on Drugs and Crime, and later in a consultancy, I had the opportunity to work in many other countries on organised crime and criminal-justice reform issues. There are too many people to thank, but

Eduardo Vetere, Dimitri Vlassis, Antonio Mazzatelli, Jan van Dijk, Samuel Gonzalez Ruiz, Rob Boone and Brian Taylor were colleagues who helped shape my thinking on organised crime. That work serves as a reminder always that South Africa is not unique, and that organised crime has real impacts for ordinary people, whom highfalutin academic debate often does little to acknowledge. Stefano Polacco read an earlier manuscript in full and provided an important set of suggestions. I am very grateful.

The Centre of Criminology at the University of Cape Town has been a fascinating and stimulating place to work over the past two years. I am particularly grateful to Elrena van der Spuy, Clifford Shearing, Julie Berg, Andrew Faull and Simon Howell, who read earlier parts of the book or articles that contributed to its formation. I hope that I have delivered on the trust that Professor PJ Schwikkard placed in me. The group of post-graduate students with whom I have worked have had a decisive impact on the book, particularly in helping to gather data and shaping my own ideas in discussions. Without these students and several other collaborators, this book would simply not have been possible. Irvin Kinnes, Stef Snel, Sarah Henkeman and Fairuz Mullagee were the original 'gang' that introduced me to Cape Town crime. Theresa Hume and Pelumi Batanda, with poise and efficiency, solved the problems of the office so I didn't have to. Mafaro Kasipo reminded me of why policing matters.

As if to prove this last point about the police, numerous junior and senior police and law-enforcement officials gave of their time, expertise and information – as well as their frustrations. I will not name them here, but they know who they are. They are a credit to the organisations they serve and to the country. Understanding the story of organised crime in South Africa's transition and in the evolving democracy would not have been possible without the work of a small and courageous group of investigative journalists. Many of their names are cited in the notes and references. Two in particular have been more helpful to me than they know: Julian

Rademeyer and Sam Sole. Martin Welz at *Noseweek* brought out some battered documents from nowhere and did much to assist.

I am deeply grateful to Kim Thomas, who took several months from her studies to trawl through literally thousands of news reports on hits and assassinations in South Africa to create a database that is partly presented here. She uncomplainingly re-sorted the data as my ideas changed and now has the dubious distinction of being able to quickly identify a hit from hearing only a minimal amount of information. When the numbers became overwhelming, Carina Bruwer stepped in to assist. Simone Haysom joined me on an exploration of the Johannesburg 'bouncer mafia' and, later on, of the doings of Radovan Krejcir, efficiently locating people who were not always eager to talk, setting up interviews and bringing her own considerable intellectual contribution to the topic. Anine Kriegler and I worked for months on the country's crime statistics, producing a book, but also changing my thinking on levels of violence, where they are occurring and their linkage to organised crime. A big thank you.

Luke Lee Skywalker played a decisive role in opening a window for me onto the gangs of Cape Town. Whatever I asked was never too much. This book would simply not have been the same without him. Matthew Skade introduced me to the world of Congolese bouncers in Cape Town and then guided me into the domain of the taxi boss: hard to do when suspicions of the intentions of outsiders are high. Valentina Pancieri steered me through the world of the Nigerians. I am very thankful to them.

Jenni Irish-Qhobosheane, an old colleague and friend, came, as always, to the rescue. Neo Moshe provided unparalleled assistance in the field. Aimee-Noel Mbiyozo played a key role in reviewing dozens of cases of murders and their background, so that they could be used as the introductory case studies to each chapter. The book would have been much weaker without their efforts. Aimee-Noel also read the full manuscript in draft and provided useful suggestions for improvements.

At the Global Initiative against Transnational Organized Crime in Geneva, and elsewhere, I have been immensely privileged to work with a long-standing 'partner in crime', Tuesday Reitano. Despite moving cities and homes, she willingly edited the manuscript, provided suggestions, and improved it beyond measure. Tuesday, a very sincere thank you. Peter Gastrow, another colleague and friend from the Global Initiative has long been a sounding board: he performed his usual role of reviewing the manuscript and providing suggestions.

Jeremy Boraine at Jonathan Ball Publishers deserves acknowledgement for taking on what seemed like an impossible project – and then patiently listening when its focus began to change without running away or screaming out loud (as any normal publisher should have). I owe an enormous debt to my editor, Mark Ronan, who patiently transformed the text despite my attempts to reverse the process. Sincerely, thanks.

One of the first people I discussed this project with was Stephen Ellis. I am sad that he cannot read the final product. He is much missed and the book is dedicated to his memory.

At home, three people, my wife Brigitte, and children, Hannah and Nicklas, know more about the topic of assassination than they should. For all that, they have engaged good-humouredly with their husband and father – despite, and sometimes because of, his strange interests. I have spent far too much time at weekends and in the evenings on this project – certainly more than I intended. I am deeply grateful to them for reminding me what is important. This work would not have been possible without them, and so it is these three, very much happy and engaged citizens of the upper part of the world, to whom this book is dedicated.

This work is partly based on research supported by the South African Research Chairs Initiative of the Department of Science and Technology and the National Research Foundation of South Africa. Any opinion, finding and conclusion expressed in this material is that of the author, and the

National Research Foundation does not accept any liability in this regard.

The book draws and expands on material from several articles: Mark Shaw and Kim Thomas, 'The commercialisation of assassination in South Africa, 2000–2015', *African Affairs*, September 2016, https://doi.org/10.1093/afraf/adw050, pp. 1–24; Mark Shaw, 'A take of two cities: Mafia control, the night time entertainment economy and drug retail markets in Johannesburg and Cape Town, 1985–2015', *Police Practice and Research*, 17, 4, 2016, pp. 353–363; Mark Shaw and Simone Haysom, 'Organised crime in late apartheid and the transition to the new criminal order: The rise and fall of the Johannesburg "bouncer mafia"', *Journal of Southern African Studies*, 42, 4, pp. 577–594; and Mark Shaw and Luke Lee Skywalker, 'The hammermen: Life and death as a gang hitman in Cape Town', the *Howard Journal of Crime and Justice*, 55, 4, December 2016, pp. 377–542.

*Geneva, March 2017*